DATE			

AMERICAN
PSYCHOLOGY SINCE
WORLD WAR II

AMERICAN PSYCHOLOGY SINCE WORLD WAR II

A PROFILE OF THE DISCIPLINE

Albert R. Gilgen

GREENWOOD PRESS
WESTPORT, CONNECTICUT • LONDON, ENGLAND

COPYRIGHT ACKNOWLEDGMENT

The author gratefully acknowledges that portions of the text are
reproduced with permission from the ANNUAL REVIEW OF PSYCHOLOGY,
Volumes 1 through 31, © 1950-1980 by Annual Reviews Inc.

Library of Congress Cataloging in Publication Data

Gilgen, Albert R., 1930-
  American psychology since World War II.

  Bibliography: p.
  Includes index.
    1. Psychology—United States—20th century.   I. Title.
  [DNLM: 1. Psychology—History—United States. BF 105
  G473a]
  BF105.G54   150'.973   81-23740
  ISBN 0-313-23027-7 (lib. bdg.)   AACR2

Library of Congress Catalog Card Number: 81-23740
ISBN: 0-313-23027-7

First published in 1982

Greenwood Press
A division of Congressional Information Service, Inc.
88 Post Road West, Westport, Connecticut 06881
Printed in the United States of America

10 9 8 7 6 5 4 3 2 1

To my family

CONTENTS

TABLES AND ILLUSTRATIONS

PREFACE

The post-World War II era of American psychology represents a period of tremendous growth and diversity. The membership of the American Psychological Association, for example, grew from about 4,000 in 1945 to over 40,000 by the middle seventies. At the same time seventeen divisions, each specializing in a particular aspect of psychology, were added to the nineteen divisions in existence in the late forties.

While it may be somewhat premature to write a detailed history of psychology during the 1945-1975 period, many of the major developments and influences can be identified. World War II, Freud, Piaget, technological advances particularly in electronics, societal growth, and government support of research, for instance, are obviously significant influences. Within the discipline, the work of Hull, Skinner, Rogers, and Harlow are of unquestioned importance. And it is clear that psychology, while still considered a behavioral science by most psychologists, has during the last decade or two become more cognitive in orientation. It is also apparent that tremendous progress has been made in physiological and developmental psychology and that clinical psychology has grown dramatically.

This book presents a profile of post-World War II American psychology by focusing on such major influences and developments. In order to set the 1945-1975 period in a broader context, chapter 1 discusses the nature and scope of the discipline and presents a brief history of psychological thought prior to World War II.

My interest in the history of American psychology extends back to 1965 when I first taught a course in the history and systems of psychology. From the beginning I was disturbed by two things: the discipline was, it seemed to me, unnecessarily fragmented conceptually; and the unique characteristics of the post-World War II period were not dealt with at any length by books on the history of psychology.

I became intrigued in the late 1960s by Thomas Kuhn's analysis of the history of science (*The Structure of Scientific Revolutions*, 1962) and wondered whether or not psychology would ever become unified enough to achieve what Kuhn refers to as a paradigmatic stage. My research during the last decade has convinced me that a psychology unified conceptually around a comprehensive model of man and other complex life forms is possible and that much of the compartmentalization of psychological knowledge is unnecessary. At the same time it seems clear that integration will not just happen; it will have to be brought about by psychologists becoming more familiar with the formal structure of psychology as a field of inquiry. More historical and epistemological analyses of the discipline are needed.

The decision to write a book on the post-World War II period was made in 1974 after presenting a paper entitled "Converging Trends in Psychology" at the annual meeting of the American Psychological Association. In order to augment the literature search, two extensive surveys involving large samples of the membership of the American Psychological Association were planned and carried out. The first concerned important people in psychology; the second, significant events and influences. The results were published in 1980 and 1981. Selected information from these studies is included in Appendices A and B.

Three additional studies were conducted: to determine those individuals referred to most in the *Annual Review of Psychology* from 1950 through 1974; and to identify the psychologists receiving the most funds from the National Science Foundation and the National Institute of Mental Health, respectively, throughout the post-war period. All three resulted in published papers.

Because of the tremendous growth of the discipline and the literature of psychology, an extraordinary amount of selectivity had to be exercised in writing this book. In the process some areas such as social psychology and physiological psychology probably have not received the coverage they deserve. I seriously considered writing a separate chapter on physiological psychology but decided against it when I discovered that most of the important advances referred to in textbooks on the subject have been made by neuroscientists other than physiological psychologists. Instead, many of the physiological studies having some bearing on psychology are mentioned in chapter 7 on psychological processes. Social phychological developments are discussed in several chapters.

References that were particularly useful in identifying important people, trends, and influences were textbooks on the history and systems of psychology, the *Annual Review of Psychology* (1950-1981) series, a sampling of textbooks in introductory psychology, *The American Psychologist* (journal), the *APA Monitor* (newspaper), and relevant citation studies including those appearing frequently in *Current Contents*. Also taken into account were the works comprising *The Harvard List of Books* (1971), the articles included in the *Scientific American* and Bobbs-Merrill offprint and reprint series, and important awards and professional memberships.

Formal permission was granted by Annual Reviews, Inc., to include the many quotations from *Annual Review of Psychology* which appear in the book. Permission was obtained from the American Psychological Association to include Table 1 (Table 2.2 in the book) from an article by Robert C. Tryon entitled "Psychology in Flux: The Academic-Professional Bipolarity" which appeared in *American Psychologist*, March 1963, p. 137. The American Psychological Association also gave permission to adapt for the appendix section two tables included in articles by the author which were published by the Journal Supplement Abstract Service. Appendix A is a modified and shortened version of Table 4 from an article entitled "Important People in Post-World War II American Psychology: A Survey Study," February 1981, Ms. 2171. Appendix B is a modified and shortened version of Table 3 from an article entitled "Important Events and Influences in Post-World War II American Psychology: A Survey Study," November 1980, Ms. 2144.

While the discipline remains fragmented conceptually, work on the book has strengthened my belief that psychological inquiry will eventually take place within the framework of a unifying methodological and theoretical paradigm. The paradigm will, in my opinion, include four major dimensions, namely physiological processes, behavior, cognitive or mentalistic processes, and development. Progress in brain research, the cognitive revolution, and the emergence of a life-span developmental perspective are, I think, the most hopeful signs that some integration will be possible in a decade or two.

I wish to thank my colleagues, in particular, Gordon M. Harrington, Andrew R. Gilpin, Julia E. Wallace, Linda L. Walsh, and Frank Barrios whose perspectives helped me decide what was important in their various areas of expertise. The many discussions I had with Professor Harrington were particularly helpful.

My special thanks go to Carol, my wife, whose careful reading of the manuscript in its several forms increased considerably the readability of the material. It was her support throughout the project which made the book possible.

AMERICAN PSYCHOLOGY SINCE WORLD WAR II

1

NATURE AND BACKGROUND OF PSYCHOLOGY

Psychology, Psychological: The Meaning of the Concepts

Probably every literate person in Western society has heard of psychology and has some opinion as to the concerns of psychologists. Most American college students and increasingly more high school students take at least one course in psychology. The term "psychological" is used with abandon by journalists, comedians, novelists, biographers, historians, and indeed people in general. There is a psychology of almost everything. Some observers believe this is the age of psychological man; others, that ours is a psychological society.[1] One of President Carter's advisers even proposed that the president was elected to be " 'the national psychologist, to put the country on the couch and provide reassurance and therapy' after the trauma of Vietnam and Watergate."[2]

For the layman the concepts psychology and psychological generally refer to issues or processes having to do with mind, personality, emotions, self-understanding, and mental well-being or mental illness. Most students take courses in psychology in order to better understand themselves and other people. Some people view psychology with considerable suspicion either because they believe that psychologists are incessantly analyzing everyone they come in contact with or because they see psychology, along with other social-behavioral sciences, as representing a threat to traditional values and religion. There is clearly a mystique surrounding the discipline insofar as much of the general public is concerned.

Psychologists, however, tend to define psychology in terms of what psychologists do. Contemporary psychology texts, therefore, generally indicate that psychology is the systematic study of behavior or the scientific study of behavioral and mentalistic processes. And instead of emphasizing self-understanding or information that might be useful in dealing with human problems, psychology courses and books concentrate on research methods and findings that frequently seem to have little relevance to the human condition. Students, as a consequence, are often disappointed with the psychology taught by psychologists.

Adding to the public confusion surrounding what it is that psychologists do or should do is the fact there are a number of disciplines other than psychology concerned with psychological processes and problems. Foremost among these is psychiatry, a medical specialty. Of course, social workers and counselors of various types are also concerned with providing help to individuals beset by psychological as well as other difficulties. The public tends to classify all professionals involved with the mental and emotional well-being of people as "shrinks."

The definition of "psychological" that I prefer, because it acknowledges those processes and problems psychologists actually study, is the following: "Psychological" refers to any process or state involved in orienting human beings and other complex organisms adaptively to their environments. These processes or states include sensing, perceiving, thinking, imagining, dreaming, feeling, learning, emoting, and behaving. Psychology, then, is the discipline concerned with the systematic study of these processes.

Psychology as an Organized Discipline

The most prominent and prestigious psychological organization in the country, the American Psychological Association (APA), now has over 50,000 members. Founded in 1892, the organization publishes twenty journals and is made up of over thirty divisions having to do with general psychology, teaching of psychology, experimental psychology, evaluation and measurement, physiological and comparative psychology, developmental psychology, personality and social psychology, social issues, psychology and the arts, clinical psychology, consulting psychology, industrial and organizational psychology, educational psychology, school psychology, counseling psychology, psychologists in public service, military psychology, adult development and aging, engineering psychology, rehabilitation psychology, consumer psychology, philosophical psychology, experimental analyses of behavior, history of psychology, community psychology, psychopharmacology, psychotherapy, psychological hypnosis, state psychological affairs, humanistic psychology, mental retardation, population psychology, and the psychology of women.

The APA's stated objective is "to advance psychology as a science and profession and as a means of promoting human welfare by the encouragement of psychology in all its branches in the broadest and most liberal manner. It attempts to further these objectives by holding annual meetings, publishing psychological journals, and working toward improved standards for psychological training and service."[3] As we shall see later, organizations like the APA are absolutely essential to the emergence of scholarly and scientific disciplines, primarily to enhance communication and set standards but also to give some visibility to each discipline, and sometimes to serve as lobby groups.

Not all psychologists in this country belong to APA nor are all American psychological journals APA publications. By the mid-1970s, in fact, there were close to six hundred psychological and psychiatric journals published in the world.[4] Because of the tremendous outpouring of printed material, it is impossible for psychologists to stay abreast of even a small fraction of the work being done in the field. This, of course, contributes to the fragmentation of the discipline. Computer-based information pools alleviate the problem to some degree, as do the *Psychological Abstracts* and the *Citation Index*, but even so the task of information retrieval is cumbersome and time-consuming.

While a listing of the concerns of the APA divisions illustrates the nature and scope of contemporary American psychology, it tells us little about the structure of the discipline. Basically the field consists of academic-research psychology, and applied (professional) psychology. The former has to do with the major psychological principles and procedures; the latter, with the primary applications of psychological principles and procedures. While some psychologists can be placed comfortably in either the academic-research or applied category, the careers of many people in the field include some teaching, some research, and some work on applied problems.

Academic-Research Psychology

Psychologists whose main work is to add to and/or pass on psychological knowledge are for convenience classified as academic-research psychologists. Although some psychologists so engaged are employed by business or private research institutes, most work for colleges and universities.

Psychological research concerns a wide variety of phenomena and problems. In general, however, it has to do with psychological processes, the person as a whole, people in groups, intervention techniques, applied problems, and the inquiry process itself.

Psychological processes or states include sensation, perception, cognition, memory, learning, feeling, emotion, and motivation, which all together orient living entities to their surroundings and make directed and purposeful activity possible. Each process or state has both a conscious and an unconscious aspect as well as physiological correlates.

Research on the person as a whole tends to be concerned with personality, human differences, and development. The central questions are: What types of people are there? What factors are involved in the development of human similarities and differences?

Studies of individuals in group settings are conducted mostly by social psychologists. Research on small groups usually takes place in specially-designed experimental situations, while large-group investigations generally occur in more or less natural settings characterized by little or no experimental control. Systematic research on groups was facilitated, following World War II, by the development and refinement of inferential statistics which makes it possible to do quantitative research in situations wherein important variables cannot be controlled directly.

Research dealing with intervention techniques has to do with developing and refining ways to control and change behavior. The techniques of primary concern to psychologists are conditioning, the various psychotherapies, hypnosis, biofeedback, and educational procedures and strategies. Psychologists are also interested in changes induced by drugs (chemotherapy), shock therapies, and psychosurgery. Since these procedures can only be employed under the supervision of medical doctors, however, basic research by psychologists has been limited.

Research on applied problems is conducted by either academic-research or applied (professional) psychologists, and much of it has to do with intervention strategies. Applied research takes place outside the laboratory in such settings as mental hospitals, industries, schools, the military, and community settings. A great deal of the work is focused either on specific "real-world" problems, such as the influence of TV violence on children, child abuse, and ways to get the public to accept gasoline rationing, or on developing tests and training programs for business, schools, and the military.

The psychological inquiry process itself has been a key issue ever since psychology emerged as a separate discipline of study about a century ago. The major methodological controversies have centered around the questions: What should psychologists study? How should they conceptualize their research concerns? How much effort should be devoted relatively to data gathering and theory building? What are the most fruitful research strategies? Because there have been and still are important differences of opinion concerning the what and how of psychological inquiry, a number of orientations emerged within academic-research psychology. These are discussed later.

Psychological research involves animals as well as people. While academic-research psychologists study a wide variety of species, animal research has, however, centered on the behavior of specially-bred strains of rats. Human studies, on the other hand, have predominately employed college freshmen and sophomores as subjects.

In spite of the fact that much psychological research is done with animals, most psychologists are not interested in animal behavior per se. The rat, monkey, pigeon, and other animals, are generally studied because they may provide clues to human behavior in situations wherein it would be unethical, inconvenient, or too costly to use people. A particular species is also studied sometimes because a process, for example, hearing or the ability to detect certain odors, is highly developed in that animal.

In summary, academic-research psychology has to do with research and teaching. The research may concern a wide variety of phenomena and problems and may take place in laboratories or other settings using either human or animal subjects. The teaching of psychology occurs mostly in colleges or universities. Only about one-third of all high schools offer courses in the field.

Applied (Professional) Psychology

A psychologist is classified as applied or professional if his/her primary concern is the application of psychological principles or procedures to societal problems. Sometimes such applications involve very little research; at other times an extensive investigative component may be an integral part of the project.

The major applied areas of contemporary American psychology are:
a. clinical psychology
b. educational psychology (including school psychology)
c. industrial psychology
d. counseling psychology
e. human engineering psychology

Other applied fields include architectural psychology, community psychology, consumer psychology, correctional psychology, forensic psychology, military psychology, pastoral psychology, pediatric psychology, and rehabilitation psychology. As stated earlier, one of the reasons it is difficult to find a unifying model for the discipline is because there is a psychology of almost everything.

Applied psychology overlaps with academic-research psychology in two ways. First, some applied psychologists teach at colleges and universities; and second, much research is, as we have indicated before, conducted in natural settings by academic-research as well as applied psychologists.

Problem-centered applied studies are frequently stimulated by the availability of government funds earmarked to investigate specific social problems. The most dramatic catalyst for applied work, however, is usually war or the threat of war. During World War I, for example, psychologists were hired by the government to develop and administer group intelligence tests. During World War II, they developed personality inventories, designed training programs, conducted group research, worked in mental hospitals and did a variety of other tasks. The Korean War stimulated research on sensory deprivation (the study of human behavior in relatively unchanging environments), and the space race gave a boost to engineering psychology.

Major Orientations within Contemporary American Psychology

Because there continues to be much disagreement among psychologists as to the purpose of psychology and the characteristics of truly productive psychological inquiry, the discipline is characterized by a number of major orientations. They include (a) behavioral, (b) functional, (c) mentalistic, (d) psychoanalytic, (e) humanist, (f) existential, and (g) phenomenological orientations.

Behaviorism considers psychology the study of behavior because behavior is observable and usually measurable. Behaviorists tend to have faith in experimental research, animal studies, and situations that allow for the direct demonstration of relationships between manipulations of the environment and changes in behavior.

Functionalism emphasizes research designed to determine the functions of psychological processes or behavior. It is usually assumed that the capabilities of each species evolved because they help that species survive in some way. Since the members of a species are characterized by individual differences along every measurable psychological dimension, the functional orientation also brings with it an interest in testing human differences. Most applied areas of psychology are functional to some degree. Many psychologists are best described as functional behaviorists.

Mentalism sees psychology as the study of mind and such mentalistic processes as sensation, perception, cognition, thinking, willing, and attending. The study of behavior is not viewed as an end in itself but rather as a means toward unraveling the mysteries of mind, conscious experiences, and unconscious processes. A mentalist may also have a strong functional orientation.

Psychoanalysis refers to the interrelated personality theory, research techniques, and psychotherapy developed by Sigmund Freud between about 1895 and 1939; the psychoanalytic perspective, however, reflects not only Freud's thinking but that of his most important disciples and followers. In general, this orientation sees adult personality as the product of interactions occurring during infancy and childhood between environmental events and a series of genetically-determined factors. Heavy emphasis is placed on unconscious motivational processes.

Humanism is seen by many as a reaction against both behaviorism and any attempts to study man by dividing human functioning into discrete and measurable states and processes. The humanist views each person as an integrated whole incapable of being understood via reductionist research strategies and usually assumes that a person has the built-in capability to maximize him/herself if placed in an appropriate environment.

Existentialism, while difficult to condense into a simple definition, places primary emphasis on the experiences of each person as viewed by the person himself. An existentially-oriented psychologist is interested in anxiety and love as they are experienced rather than as they might be reflected in questionnaire responses. Existentialists (as well as humanists and phenomenologists) also point out the dangers involved in classifying people or dealing with individuals from the perspective of abstract personality theories. The existential influence has been manifest mostly within clinical psychology.

Phenomenology is perhaps even more difficult to define than existentialism. Phenomenologists are interested in the study of conscious experience. They assume, however, that ordinary waking experiences are highly structured by concepts, symbols, and language, which prevent us from experiencing much that is basic to consciousness without specific research procedures. The phenomenologist believes that awareness of the role played by conceptualization in organizing conscious experience is particularly crucial when studying people with different psycholinguistic frameworks or infants who have yet to develop adult ways of organizing experience.

These are general orientations rather than the professional value systems of individual psychologists. There may be a few pure behaviorists, or mentalists, or psychoanalytic types, but most psychologists are a blend of two or more orientations. The functional outlook, for example, is compatible with either behavioral or cognitive leanings; and certain elements of humanism, existentialism, and phenomenology are either redundant or compatible. The dominant orientation within academic-research psychology is probably best described as functional behaviorism somewhat tempered by cognitive, humanistic, and existential perspectives. Because of the wide range of applied psychology, it is more difficult to identify a major orientation. Certainly behavioral and functional outlooks remain strong; but in areas such as clinical and counseling psychology, humanistic and existential thinking has had an important impact. The psychoanalytic influence, while still considerable, was most pronounced during the 1935-1960 period, particularly in the areas of personality, development, and abnormal and clinical psychology.

The following represent some of the specific assumptions that generated much of the theory, research, and controversy during the post-World War II period:

1. Behavior is determined mostly by environmental factors; the relationships between behavior and its determinants are lawful (behaviorism, determinism).

2. Not all of the determinants of, or motivations underlying, a response are manifested in consciousness—that is, people are not aware of all the factors determining the course of their actions (unconscious organizing tendencies, unconscious or tacit inference, Gestalt psychology, projective techniques, directive state theories).

3. Every action or behavior serves some function, for example, it is purposive or goal directed (functionalism).

4. Behavior that reduces a bodily or psychological tension tends to be

repeated; this is the basis of most learning (dynamic psychology, tension reduction theories).

5. Behavior and mentalistic processes such as perception and cognition are functions of context, for example, framework, pattern, state, or general situation, as well as so-called specific stimuli (Gestalt psychology, holistic theory, tension reduction theories, adaptation-level theory).

6. The primary focus of research psychology should be behavior and its modification; psychologists should concentrate on the learning processes and conditioning (behaviorism).

7. Whenever feasible, behavior or psychological phenomena should be submitted to experimental examination; experiments enable the investigator to study variables one at a time (behaviorism, experimental science).

8. Insofar as possible, only concepts that can be defined in terms of specific, publicly observable operations should be used by research psychologists to describe research or build theories (operationism).

9. When it is impossible to control all variables having an important bearing on a phenomenon being investigated, groups of individuals should be studied and the data obtained analyzed statistically (group research, statistics, use of probability theory).

10. Research on animals is important because animals can be manipulated almost at will; certain studies cannot be done ethically using human subjects; animals' gestation periods and life spans tend to be short, allowing for comparisons that would take too long if humans were used as subjects (behaviorism, functionalism, physiological psychology).

11. And methods for measuring human behavioral and psychological (intellectual, perceptual, personality) differences should be perfected; the general study of individual differences among animals as well as among people is a central task of psychology (mostly within the functional tradition).

Roots of the Discipline

The basic psychological question is, perhaps, this: What is it that controls and guides human activities and, as a consequence, makes behavior possible? This query was probably first formulated several million years ago when man emerged as a separate species, although it is possible that the question was not posed until approximately three thousand years ago when, according to psychologist Julian Jaynes, man first became conscious of being conscious.[5] Whatever the case, there are probably some preconditions that are necessary for psychological speculation to occur. These include a sense of self; an awareness of consciousness generated by noticing that there are periods of wakefulness and sleep, death, and unusual states like dreams; the realization that it is only while awake that man is capable of directed activity; and some cognizance of the fact that there are a variety of conscious experiences, for example, sensations, percepts, images, dreams, and feelings, some of which seem only indirectly concerned with the present state of the body or world. Psychological speculation, in other words, became possible when people noticed, not just that some events happen without any apparent external cause, but that behavior itself is to some degree controlled from within.

Even though human beings have long wondered what it was that controlled and guided behavior, we have only been able to generate a few basic answers. These involve either God in general; some type of spirit or special deity who inhabits human bodies; a soul that, while separate from the body, goes along with it; a mind or some sort of reasoning entity; mind and feelings together; the environment; or various combinations of God, soul, mind, feeling, and the environment. Throughout the long history of theological, philosophical, and even scientific speculation, the control of human behavior has usually been ascribed to an *agent*, (God, soul, or mind). However, attributing control to an agent, although intuitively satisfying, has little explanatory potential. Only during the last fifty years or so has progress been made in accounting for the fact that man's behavior is independent to a degree of present environmental conditions without invoking a causative agent.

The major landmarks in the long history of psychological thought prior to the emergence of psychology as an independent discipline of study in the 1870s include:

1. At some unknown time in man's prehistory people begin to speculate about this question: What controls human behavior? Psychological inquiry commences.

2. Between about 600 and 100 B.C. a few Greek thinkers become enamored with reasoning and turn it into a formal art. They speculate over the nature of the universe, man and knowledge. Man's behavior is explained in terms of various combinations of soul, mind, sensation, and emotion. Centers for study (Plato's Academy) and research (Aristotle's Lyceum) are founded and serve as prototypes for later academic enterprises. Philosophy is born along with many of its basic "isms," for example, rationalism, empiricism, monism, dualism, materialism, idealism.

3. Psychological inquiry makes very little progress during the Roman (100 B.C.-A.D. 376) and medieval (A.D. 400-1500) periods. The church provides the official answer to the question of what controls human behavior, and speculation is discouraged. Faith, rather than reason, is the key word. A few events of note do, of course, take place, for example, St. Augustine's (A.D. 354-430) agonizing scrutiny of his life, and St. Thomas's efforts (1225-1274) to show that reason and faith do not have to be incompatible. Overall, though, psychological inquiry, at least from the perspective of contemporary academic-research psychology, stagnates for the remarkable period of about 1,600 years.

4. As the control of the Roman church wanes, perspectives broaden through trade and exploration, the growth of cities, and the fact that more people have access to books because of the printing press. Speculation concerning the nature of the world, man, and knowledge gradually re-

turns to Europe. The Renaissance (1450-1600), characterized by great interest in the Greek and Roman classics and the budding of science, is followed in the seventeenth century by the period of Enlightenment. Modern science and a revitalized philosophy emerge. Particularly important for psychology is Francis Bacon's (1561-1626) insistence that careful observation, induction, and experimentation, in the context of limited deduction, are the fundamentals of the scientific method.

5. Philosophical speculation on the nature of soul, mind, and psychological processes (for example, sensation, perception, cognition, memory, feeling, and will) flourish from the seventeenth through the nineteenth centuries. Of particular significance for psychology is René Descartes's (1596-1650) contention that the mind (soul) and body, while interacting, are separate. This sanctions the scientific study of the body. Before the seventeenth century, human physiological research was considered taboo because it was believed that the soul is an integral part or aspect of the body as a whole. Tampering with the flesh meant tampering with the soul. Also of direct relevance to the eventual emergence of a separate discipline of psychology is the speculation of philosophers like Thomas Hobbes (1588-1679), John Locke (1632-1704), Gottfried Leibniz (1646-1716), George Berkeley (1685-1753), David Hume (1711-1776), Immanuel Kant (1724-1804), James Mill (1773-1836), and John Stuart Mill (1806-1873). All are concerned with the nature and origin of mind, the relationships between the mind and body, and the most fruitful ways to study mind scientifically. Of particular importance is the controversy over whether or not mind can be analyzed into its fundamental elements by means of laboratory experimentation. As it turned out, those who viewed mind as a complex of associated sensations and ideas constructed from experience and analyzable through experimentation into components (empiricists) are most instrumental in bringing about academic-research psychology as a separate discipline of study.

6. The successes of physicists and chemists, particularly during the first half of the nineteenth century, give credence to laboratory experimentation. By the 1860s, attempts are made to study mind in the laboratory.

7. Finally, progress in human physiology and anatomy, particularly relative to the sensory systems and the central nervous system, makes an experimental psychology increasingly more viable. By the middle of the nineteenth century considerable knowledge is amassed about the visual and auditory systems; much less is known about the functioning of the brain. It is understandable, therefore, that the focus of the experimental psychology that emerges in the 1870s is on sensory and perceptual processes.

Factors that have facilitated psychological inquiry throughout the centuries include (a) curiosity about the nature of man; (b) interest in understanding thought, reason, and observation for their own sakes; (c) pleasure in systematic speculation and argumentation; (d) a standard of living and social order which gives some people the leisure to engage in systematic study; (e) free thought, tolerance of different viewpoints; (f) a sensitivity to the methods and pitfalls inherent in the inquiry process; (g) the scientific method; and (h) progress in the natural sciences.

Inhibitory factors, on the other hand, include (a) assuming that some agent directs and controls human behavior, particularly if that agent is believed to be supernatural; (b) dichotomous thinking, which usually creates fruitless controversies; (c) entrenched authorities who claim to have the answers to the basic psychological questions and who restrain free thought; (d) enamorment with authority; (e) special taboos such as "you can not study the body because the soul, which is sacred, is an integral part of it," or "mind and soul are spiritual entities and incapable of analysis," or "consciousness and mind are myths and not fruitful concerns of science," or "theory building is premature so concentrate on gathering data," and; (f) overspecialization. Although Descartes in the seventeenth century stimulated physiological research by proposing that the body, while interacting with the mind (soul), is a separate material entity capable of being investigated scientifically, the resulting separation contributed to the increasing fragmentation of research on human functioning, particularly during the nineteenth and twentieth centuries. Also contributing to fragmentation, since the middle of the nineteenth century, has been the emergence of many new disciplines of study, including psychology, and the increasing specialization within these disciplines during the last seventy-five years or so.

The Emergence of Psychology as a Separate Discipline

Psychological thinking extends back to the beginning of man; formal thought about psychological matters can be traced to ancient Greece; and the term "psychology" was apparently coined in the sixteenth century. Some scientific research was being done on psychological processes by the 1860s, but there was no separate discipline of psychology anywhere until the late 1870s. People with degrees in psychology have been around for only about one hundred years.

The first psychological laboratories were established in the 1870s by Wilhelm Wundt in Leipzig, Germany, and William James at Harvard University. James's facility was, however, rather minimal so Wundt is usually given credit for setting up the first psychological research facility of any consequence and thus founding the discipline. During the 1880s and 1890s, laboratories were established at other European and American universities; by 1904 there were forty-nine in the United States. The establishment of facilities uniquely equipped to do psychological research was one of the prime requisites for the emergence of a new discipline. A precondition, in turn, for the creation of psychological laboratories was the development, during the 1860s, of laboratory techniques for the study of psychological processes such as sensation, perception, feeling, thought, and memory.

Other factors were also involved in the formation of psychology as an independent field of study. Some analysts, for example, contend that psychology was first established as a separate discipline in Germany because the German university, being organized into specific academic departments, made it possible for new fields to be formally recognized. In France, where there was no clear departmentalization of the academic enterprise, or in England, where scholars were usually self-supported gentlemen with no university connections at all, a new and separate discipline of study was more difficult to establish. It is further argued that because graduate education in the United States was modeled after the German system, psychology was also able to emerge here as a separate discipline of study.

Once there is formal recognition of a new discipline by the academic community, a variety of events have to take place if the enterprise is to flourish: textbooks must be written, journals established, a professional organization formed, courses developed, students attracted to the programs, people with degrees in the field graduated, jobs created for those trained in the discipline, and so forth. All these things happened insofar as psychology is concerned, and by 1917 seventy-four American universities and colleges had psychological laboratories. Twenty-one American journals publishing psychological articles were extant, and the American Psychological Association, founded in 1892, was twenty-five years old.[6]

As psychology became accepted in the United States, especially after the turn of the century, the applied dimension of the discipline gained in importance. Clinical psychology, in particular, grew as the test movement gained momentum just prior to World War I (1904-1914).[7] Other applied specialties such as industrial psychology and legal psychology were also created, thereby extending the impact of psychology on society.

American Psychology from 1913 to 1945

In 1913 psychologist John Watson declared that psychology should be formally considered the study of behavior rather than mind or consciousness, because behavior is observable and open to manipulation and scientific scrutiny, while mind and consciousness are private states or processes not directly amenable to public examination.[8] Furthermore, Watson pointed out, animal research is inhibited when psychology is focused on mind and consciousness.

American psychologists were ready for Watson's proclamation, and behaviorism became an important dimension of mainstream experimental psychology. The precursors of this development included Darwin's theory of evolution, which made animal research credible; Pavlov's research on conditioning, which provided a basic model for the learning processes; and the studies of animal intelligence conducted by American psychologist Edward Thorndike.

As mentioned before, World War I served as a catalyst for American psychology, particularly applied psychology. Military recruits of varying educational and ethnic backgrounds had to be quickly screened, and psychologists were employed to develop group intelligence tests. Because of the apparent success of this venture, psychology was given an important boost. The discipline developed vigorously during the affluent 1920s and continued to grow modestly even during the Great Depression of the 1930s.

The 1910-1930 period is sometimes referred to as the era of "schools." A school is a general orientation concerning the nature of psychology and psychological research adhered to by a prominent, or at least professionally visible, group of psychologists. Behaviorism, discussed previously, was a school, as was structuralism which was initiated by Wundt in Germany and later transported to the United States by Edward B. Titchener. Structuralists emphasized the laboratory study of mind and consciousness using special introspective techniques. Two other schools also characterized pre-World War II American psychology. Functionalism, based heavily on Darwinian assumptions, focused on studying the functions of mind and behavior while Gestalt psychology, imported from Germany in the 1920s, emphasized the configurational or relativistic nature of perception, motivation, and learning.

By the middle 1930s, the school-like nature of these orientations had diminished. Structuralism became virtually extinct by the 1920s. A functional-behaviorism, tempered to some degree by Gestalt relativism but strongly oriented toward experimental research, statistical analyses, animal studies, and clearly defined concepts, evolved as the mainstream of American academic-research psychology during the decade prior to World War II. There was considerable optimism that psychology could become a productive scientific discipline.

This optimism was generated by the increasing sophistication of experimental-design procedures and statistical techniques and also by the belief that a behavioral orientation in combination with operationism could divest psychology of the ambiguous concepts plaguing the discipline for so long. Operationism, which derived from a philosophical movement called logical positivism, stressed the use in science of only those concepts definable in terms of specific, observable operations.

During the 1920s and 1930s conditioning and learning became the primary research areas. While Watson's influence predominated during the 1920s, four theorists vied for eminence during the 1930s: (a) Clark

Hull, who developed a complex, mathematical, learning theory based on the idea that learning involves building bonds between stimuli and responses through repeated need satisfaction; (b) Edward Tolman, who emphasized the cognitive aspects of learning; (c) Edwin Guthrie, who conceived of learning as a process by which a certain number of salient stimulus elements become associated with a response upon each successful completion of a task; and (d) B. F. Skinner, who focused on identifying the relationships between changes in the environment and changes in behavior. Hull's theory predominated during the 1930-1960 period. Thereafter Skinner's atheoretical descriptive approach emerged as the most influential perspective.

While research on conditioning and learning took the center stage of American academic-research psychology during the 1920s and 1930s, work was also going on in all other areas. Considerable progress was, in fact, being made in physiological psychology and psychometrics (test construction). In addition, by the mid-1930s, Freudian thought was beginning to have a significant influence on the discipline, thus contributing to an increasing interest in personality theory and research. Moreover, applied psychology gradually grew in importance.

One of the most significant events to take place during the 1930s and early 1940s was the flight from Nazi oppression of thousands of intellectuals and professionals, many of them Jews. From 22,000 to 26,000 of the immigrants who came to this country between 1933 and 1944 had been in professional occupations and from 15,000 to 17,000 assumed professional roles once they settled in the United States.[9] Included among the emigrés were almost all of the European psychoanalysts, the majority of whom took up residence in the large eastern cities.[10]

2

OVERVIEW OF THE POST-WORLD WAR II PERIOD

Main Developments in American Psychology[1]

When World War II ended in 1945, much of Europe and Asia lay in ruins. In contrast, the United States, while having contributed manpower and material goods toward the war effort, remained virtually unscathed. As a consequence, this country emerged as the most powerful nation in the world both militarily and economically. Because of the destruction of urban Europe and the flight here of many European intellectuals, artists, and other professionals, the United States was also transformed into the cultural and educational center of the Western world. Major American universities assumed leadership in all mainstream areas of psychology. The most important post-World War II trends insofar as the entire discipline is concerned were rapid growth and increasing diversity.

Significant developments within academic-research psychology include the rise to prominence of Skinnerian behaviorism by the early 1960s along with the concomitant ebbing of Clark Hull's influence; the return during the 1960s and 1970s of a cognitive perspective (the cognitive revolution); and the gradual emergence throughout the entire period of a more comprehensive developmental psychology. Also of considerable importance was the growth of experimental social psychology and burgeoning interest in environmental psychology and behavior genetics. Methodologically, the discipline remained experimentally oriented.

The growth of applied (professional) psychology was particularly dramatic. The major development in this sector was the expansion of clinical psychology along with its transformation from a field preoccupied by psychodiagnostics to one concerned primarily with psychotherapy. Other developments of note were the genesis of engineering psychology and the increasing influence of school psychology and industrial psychology. Of consequence, too, was the fact that the more rapid expansion of applied psychology relative to academic-research psychology resulted in a gradual shift of power within the American Psychological Association from academic-research psychologists to their colleagues in applied fields.

The most significant professional factors impacting on the discipline were psychoanalysis (1940s-1950s), Piaget's theory of cognitive development (1960s-1970s), humanism-existentialism-phenomenology (1960s-1970s), developments in psychiatry and medical research (1950s-1970s), advances in the neurosciences (1950s-1970s), refinements in applied statistics, and, to a lesser extent, ethological theory and research (the study of animal behavior in natural settings). Conceptually, the discipline of psychology continues to be fragmented and compartmentalized.

While there were many important researchers within American psychology during the post-World War II period, the most creative, in my opinion, have been: B. F. Skinner (operant conditioning), Carl Rogers (evaluation of psychotherapy), David Wechsler (intelligence tests), Harry Harlow (mothering and peer influence on infant monkeys), Kurt Lewin (group dynamics, action research), Clark Hull (motivational factors in maze learning), Donald Hebb, a Canadian psychologist (effects of early experience on development, sensory deprivation), Neal Miller (conflict resolution, biofeedback), Albert Bandura (social learning theory), Robert Cattell (factor analytic studies), Georg von Bekesy (sensory processes), Leon Festinger (cognitive dissonance), David McClelland (personality measurement), S. S. Stevens (psychophysical processes), Kenneth Spence (discrimination learning), Roger Brown (language development), Nathan Azrin (behavior modification), Herbert Simon, an economist (computer simulation of thought processes), Solomon Asch (social influence on perception), James Olds (pleasure centers of the brain), Stanley Milgram (obedience in laboratory situations), Egon Brunswik (representative experimental designs), James Gibson (ecological studies of visual perception), Charles Osgood (measurement of connotative meaning), T. G. R. Bower (infant perception), David Premack (monkey language), Stanley Schachter (cognitive factors in emotion), Roger Barker (real-world studies of behavior), Hadley Cantril (measuring rising expectations), Milton Rokeach (studies of values), Eckhard Hess (imprinting), Harry Helson (influence of context on judgment), Herman Witkin (field dependence-independence), Robert Fantz (infant perception), Wilson Tanner and John Swets (decision and detection theory), Irvin Rock (perceptual adaptation), and Donald Blough (animal psychophysics). Appendices A and B list the most important events, influences, and people relative to post-World War II American psychology according to different groups of contemporary psychologists.

Major Societal Influences on the Discipline

The societal events that most profoundly influenced American psychology during the 1945-1975 period include the war itself, population growth, the expansion of higher education, the increasing involvement of the federal government in education and research, technological developments, and accelerated social restructuring. Also contributing to the expansion of the field was the gradual emergence of a more positive view toward the social sciences.

World War II Because of the need for psychological services, the war contributed directly to the growth of the discipline, particularly clinical psychology. The conflict also (*a*) stimulated advances in electronic technology such as the computer, television, sophisticated audio equipment, and micro-electrode hardware, which, in turn, advanced psychological research; (*b*) brought about interdisciplinary studies that introduced psychologists to new theories and research procedures; (*c*) led to the emergence of a new field, human engineering psychology, and the advancement of experimental social psychology; (*d*) generated studies in military psychology; (*e*) fostered significant research on prejudice, anti-Semitism, authoritarianism, stress, and perception; and, finally, (*f*) provided many opportunities for test development, refinement, modification, and standardization.[2]

Population Growth Between 1945 and 1975 the population of the United States increased from about 140 to 220 million. This led to an increasing demand for more psychologists in both academic and applied settings. The growth of the discipline permitted more diversity in terms of theoretical perspectives, research interests, and applied strategies. This is evidenced by the many different journals which appeared during the period as well as the addition of more than a dozen new APA divisions.

Expansion of Higher Education During the three decades following World War II, enrollments in four-year institutions increased from two million to almost seven million. At the same time the number of students enrolled in two-year institutions increased from about two hundred thousand to over two million. This extraordinary growth of higher education was a consequence of population growth and federal and state support. Psychology, along with the other social-behavioral sciences, grew at an astounding rate, especially during the 1950s and 1960s. While the number of doctorates in chemistry, for example, doubled between 1950 and 1970, the number of doctorates in psychology increased about five-fold from 360 in 1950 to 1,888 in 1970.[3]

Increasing Involvement of the Federal Government in Education and Research Since 1945 the federal government has played an ever more important role in the affairs of the professions and academic disciplines as well as in the lives of the citizenry as a whole. Federal monies have supported educational and research programs, and federal laws and guidelines have influenced everything from animal-care standards and ways of doing research using human subjects to recruiting procedures. As a consequence there is now serious concern that the government is intruding too much into higher education. In 1950, for example, the federal government spent 219 million dollars on "education and manpower"; in 1970 the amount had increased to over 7 billion dollars.[4] At the same time federal support for university and college research increased from about 200 million dollars to almost 3 billion dollars.[5]

Technological Developments Accelerated by the Cold War The competition between the United States and the Communist countries, particularly the Soviet Union, has led to a continual heavy investment of tax dollars in research and development associated with real or imagined defense needs. Whenever the Soviets appeared to be a step ahead technologically, the federal investment in research increased. The *Sputnik* incident, in 1957, when the Russians launched the first orbiting space capsule, and thus started the space race, is probably the most dramatic example of this phenomenon. Progress in electronics has been profound, marked by tremendous advances in computer, television, sound reproduction, and guidance system technologies. The impact of high-speed electronic computers on most disciplines has, in fact, been revolutionary. TV, and electronic recording, monitoring, and control devices have also provided powerful new research tools.

Accelerated Social Restructuring Population growth, government laws and programs, television coverage of events, and many other factors accelerated social processes already underway. Blacks, homosexuals, mental patients, children, American Indians, Hispanics, and other minority groups as well as women all came forth to claim their civil rights. Every major institution, including schools and work settings, was affected. As these changes took place, the social-behavioral sciences were required to reexamine basic assumptions concerning racial and sexual differences, psychological testing, homosexuality, and so forth. The credibility of psychological research was also affirmed by the courts when judges began looking to the findings of relevant psychological studies in making legal decisions. The *Brown* vs *Board of Education* case (1954), which concluded that separate schools for blacks and whites are by definition unequal, was apparently the first time the U.S. Supreme Court referred specifically to psychological data in constructing an opinion.

Insofar as the Korean War (1950-1953) is concerned, the so-called brainwashing of captured American military and civilian personnel by the Chinese Communists during the conflict which involved isolating prisoners environmentally and socially apparently served as a catalyst for research on sensory deprivation. Sensory-deprivation studies concern human behavior under conditions of minimal environmental change. For example, individuals are placed in a dark, soundproof room with temperature held constant and asked to report their experiences.

It is not clear if the Vietnam War (1963-1972) had any discernible influence on the discipline. The general campus unrest and student disillusionment with traditional courses, theories, and procedures associated with the war, however, probably helped to create a more receptive atmosphere for humanistic and Eastern perspectives and for the study of drug-induced experiences.

Growth of the Discipline

The American Psychological Association (APA), founded in 1892, had one hundred and sixty-nine members by 1904, and three hundred and seven by 1917. Mostly they were academic-research psychologists. Applied psychology started to expand during World War I when the military employed psychologists to develop group-administered intelligence tests to screen military conscripts. By 1935, the membership of the APA had climbed to almost two thousand; and by 1945 to over four thousand. Most psychologists were still engaged primarily in teaching and research.

As mentioned before, one of the most important developments in American psychology during the last thirty-five years has been its impressive growth as a discipline. In comparison with 1945, there are today vastly more psychologists, psychological journals and books, people receiving advanced degrees in psychology, individuals being counseled by psychologists, college and university departments of psychology, and funds from state and federal government supporting research and instruction. Some of this expansion was, of course, due to the increase in population, but as can be seen from Table 1, the growth rate of American psychology as measured by membership in APA was much more rapid than population growth.

Table 1
The Growth Rate of American Psychology as Reflected by Several Indices

	MID-1940s	MID-1970s	% CHANGE
Population	140,000,000	220,000,000	+ 57
APA Membership	4,200	40,000	+ 850
APA Divisions	19	36	+ 89
APA Journals	7	17	+ 142
Psychological Abstracts entries	3,600	25,000	+ 594

While the discipline as a whole experienced manifold growth during the three decades following World War II, the most significant increases took place within applied professional psychology, particularly within clinical psychology (see Table 2). Academic-research psychology grew somewhat more slowly. In 1940, for example, 75 percent of the members of APA were in academic professions; in 1962 by contrast only 47 percent were so employed.[6] By the 1970s the percentage of the APA membership engaged primarily in academic-research activities had stabilized at about 42 percent.

Not surprisingly, as the number of psychologists increased, so did the number of journals published. In 1946, for instance, the American Psychological Association published eight journals. In addition, there were a few privately published psychological periodicals and several psychiatric and psychoanalytic journals. From 1947 to 1975, however, over 120 new American psychological journals (not counting journals published by state societies) were founded. At the same time many new foreign publications appeared.

Although behaviorally-oriented journals reflecting the main theoretical stream of the field proliferated, publications on existential, humanistic, transactional, phenomenological, Jungian, Adlerian, Rankian, transpersonal, cross-cultural, mathematical, cognitive, thanatological, biological, community, school, counseling, family, instructional, psychosynthetic, population, and black psychologies also appeared, particularly in the 1960s and 1970s. In addition, journals concerned specifically with various therapies, religion, sex, history, homosexuality, autistic children, motor behavior, small-group behavior, creativity, death, vocational behavior, personal growth, altered states of consciousness, and aggression were published. Since the late 1960s, the magazine *Psychology Today* has provided a well-written popular account of developments in the field.

As an index of specific changes in American psychology, the proliferation of new journals affirms the following post-World War II developments:

a. Skinnerian psychology became a powerful force in American psychology by the late 1950s. The publication of the *Journal of Experimental Analysis of Behavior* and the *Journal of Applied Behavior Analysis* reflects this development.

b. Existential and humanistic viewpoints had, by the early 1960s, become influential enough to merit separate journals (1961, 1962). A separate journal on phenomenological psychology started publication in 1970.

c. The increasing importance of school psychology was indicated by the publication of journals in this area in 1963, 1964.

d. Mathematical psychology had become a significant specialty by the early 1960s.

e. Research on sex increased in the early 1960s. The *Journal of Sex Research* appeared in 1965 followed in 1974 by journals on sex and marital therapy, homosexuality, and in 1975 by a journal on sex roles.

f. Interest in the history of the behavioral sciences grew in the early 1960s; the *Journal of the History of the Behavioral Sciences* was first published in 1965.

g. There was a rekindling of concern with the study of death, suicide, and dying beginning in the middle of 1960s; *Omega* and the *Archives* of the Foundation of Thanatology appeared in 1970, and *Suicide* in 1971.

h. A significant number of new journals on child psychology, child psychopathology, and developmental psychology were published throughout the period signaling a step-up of work in these areas.

Table 2
Professionalization in Relation to Membership Growth of APA Divisions

Most academic				Academic and professional				Most professional			
	Membership				**Membership**				**Membership**		
Division	1948	1960	In-crease	Division	1948	1960	In-crease	Division	1948	1960	In-crease
1. General	541	596	10%	7. Developmental (Child-Adolescent)	350	616	76%	13. Consulting	189	232	23%
2. Teaching	186	538	189%	8. Personality and Social	339	1,346	297%	16. School	90	712	691%
3. Experimental 6. Physiological and Comparative	564	789	40%	9. SPSSI	393	806	105%	17. Counseling	467	993	112%
5. Evaluation and Measurement	392	638	63%	12. Clinical	821	2,376	189%	18. Public Service	111	227	105%
10. Esthetics	62	118	90%	14. Industrial and Business	186	734	295%	19. Military	234	276	18%
				15. Educational	419	555	32%	21. Engineering	—	273	New
				20. Maturity and Old Age	—	238	New				
				22. Disability	—	246	New				
Totals	1,745	2,679	54%		2,508	6,917	176%		1,091	2,713	149%

SOURCE: Robert C. Tyron, Psychology in Flux: The Academic-Professional Bipolarity, *American Psychologist* 18 (March 1963), p. 137. Copyright (1963) by the American Psychological Association. Reprinted by permission of the publisher.

     i. New journals on international and cross-cultural psychology marketed
during the early 1970s demonstrated a heightening interest in a broader
perspective.

The postwar flood of new journals was accompanied by an even greater
explosion of new books: in 1950, for example, about 11,000 books were
published as compared to over 36,000 in 1970.[7] Only ten years after
World War II, the sheer volume of freshly produced information was
making it difficult for journal editors to decide which manuscripts and
reports to reject and which ones to publish; one consequence was a
higher rejection rate and long lag times between the submission of articles and their publication.[8] More troublesome still has been the problem
of keeping up with new developments—that is, of retrieving information from books and journals. Again the problem was clearly manifest
by the middle 1950s; Cronbach, Farnsworth, and Bouthilet in their report on the status and prospects of the APA Publications Program (1955)
wrote:

As the volume of psychological publication increases, the percentage of psychologists who read the average article diminishes. The psychological profession
is in the sad position of the subscriber to the *New York Times* Sunday edition,
who never manages to read all that is interesting in one issue before the next one
is delivered. There was once a day when the psychologist could read every
paper as it appeared. With the first wave of expansion, he was forced to retreat
to skimming all the abstracts, reading only a few journals. Now even that is a
luxury beyond recall. In one discussion inspired by a Publications Board problem, a dozen capable research psychologists were asked to give some information about their own reading habits. Although these men are among the most
active and intellectually curious of psychologists, only one person in the group
could claim to read more than 25 percent of the materials in the journals he
subscribes to, let alone the remainder. This one exception claimed to read 50
percent of the material, and gave as his reason the fact that he was trying to keep
up-to-date while preparing a general textbook. It is evident that nowadays an
article is read chiefly by psychologists actively pursuing investigations on closely
related topics. For the rest of his knowledge, the psychologist depends heavily
on secondary sources such as handbooks and manuals in various areas of psychology, and on the *Annual Review*. Today's journal author does not really communicate his findings directly to the profession as a whole.[9]

The information-retrieval problem is today so serious that even with
the availability of rather well developed computerized library search
programs, improved abstracts, and micro-storage techniques, it is very
difficult to conduct a thorough search of the professional literature. As a
consequence psychologists tend to become extremely selective, or to
adopt the attitude that much of what is published is trivial. There is also
a tendency to redo much that has already been done.

Why did the rapid growth of the discipline take place? It occurred primarily because of the tremendous amounts of money invested by state and federal governments in higher education (see Table 3) and because Washington, mostly through the Veterans Administration, provided funds for the training of clinical psychologists. Since the middle 1950s, the National Science Foundation and the Department of Health, Education and Welfare have also increased the funds they give to support research in colleges and universities.[10] While there have sometimes been decreases from year to year in the amount of money allocated by state and federal departments and agencies to higher education and to psychology, the overall support has increased steadily. Psychology was uniquely favored, in part, because it is classified: as a science and is therefore eligible for monies from the National Science Foundation; as a helping profession and therefore supported by the Department of Health, Education, and Welfare; and, finally, as one of the humanities, making it eligible for programs sponsored by agencies assisting those disciplines.

Table 3
Expansion of Higher Education*

	MID-1940s	MID-1950s	MID-1960s	MID-1970s
Students enrolled	2,000,000	3,000,000	5,600,000	9,500,000
Staff	200,000	330,000	500,000	780,000
Degrees Award				
B.A.	140,000	290,000	540,000	1,000,000
M.A.	19,000	60,000	112,000	250,000
Ph.D.	2,000	9,000	16,500	34,000
Expenditures	1 billion	3 billion	12 billion	40 billion
Federal Funds			2 billion	6 billion
Junior College				
Enrollment		308,000	1,000,000	3,500,000

*Approximations based on *Statistical Abstracts of the United States* (1980).

The multiple labeling of psychology, while helping to bring funds to the discipline, also contributed to the confused view that many people have of psychology. Furthermore, it has most likely helped perpetuate the continual squabbling among psychologists as to the nature and purpose of the discipline. (See Table 4 for funding highlights.)

While most of the growth was in applied areas like clinical psychology, academic-research psychology benefited not only because of the general expansion of colleges and universities but also because applied psychologists are trained by academic psychologists. For example, as the Veterans Administration made money available for the training of clinical psychologists, academic departments were called upon to provide the training. The guidelines for the training of clinical psycholo-

Table 4
Government and Private Support of Psychology

I. PRE-WORLD WAR II

1917-1918   During the last year of World War I, when the U.S. was involved, psychologists were employed by the Army to develop and administer group intelligence tests.

1914-1945   Private organizations like the Rockefeller Foundation and the Carnegie Corporation provided the only non-university funding for psychological research and the support of graduate students or postdoctoral scholars. Such monies made it possible for foreign scientists to study in the United States; they also made possible large-scale studies like the Princeton Radio Project, and organizations like the Social Science Research Council (SSRC). (Early support for the SSRC came from the Laura Spelman Rockefeller Memorial; later support from a variety of private foundations.)

II. WORLD WAR II (1939-1945)

Much support of psychological research related to the war effort.

III. POST-WORLD WAR II

1946 -   Veterans Administration approved a four-year training program for clinical psychologists to be administered by qualified university departments.

1947 -   National Institute of Mental Health (part of the U.S. Public Health Service) sponsored training in clinical psychology.

1951 -   Ford Foundation began large-scale support of research in the behavioral sciences.

1952 -   National Science Foundation approved limited programs of support for the social sciences. In the years that followed, the monies allocated for research and educational purposes in the social sciences increased substantially.

1953 -   National Institute of Mental Health support broadened to research and training in areas of psychology other than clinical.

1957 -   Soviet Union launched first space vehicle (Sputnik); U.S. federal government increased funds for science and education. Psychology benefited through the middle sixties.

1963 -   President John F. Kennedy proposed a comprehensive community-based plan for helping the mentally ill and mentally retarded. Congress approved massive funds for these programs.

LATE 1960s - Congress became skeptical of large-scale federal support of science including the social sciences. Rate of increases reduced significantly from 1969 on.

EARLY 1970s - With a recession, federal research support was reduced drastically.

gists[11] were formulated in 1947. They supported a scientist-practitioner model and advocated that the graduate education of clinical psychologists include a solid foundation in experimental methods, statistics, test design and administration, and basic courses in the traditional areas of experimental psychology, personality theory, and psychopathology. As a result, the increasing demand for more courses in psychology, particularly in the late forties and fifties, which was in part a consequence of ever-growing college enrollments, was given an extra boost by the need to train more clinical psychologists and other applied psychologists. The growth continued through the 1960s with more and more teachers colleges becoming full-fledged universities and state legislatures generously supporting higher education. Only in the 1970s did societal enthusiasm for the academic enterprise start to wane. Enrollments stabilized and in some places commenced to decline, and the growth of psychology, like that of most other disciplines, moderated.

Rapid growth was also facilitated by the fact that, even in applied fields such as clinical psychology, masters' theses and doctoral dissertations were generally based on experimental studies. Since most experiments tend to take less time than clinical investigations or real-world field studies, students could complete the work for their graduate degrees fairly quickly; and professors were able to supervise more students. This emphasis on easy-to-design short-run experimental research unfortunately produced hundreds of narrowly trained technicians rather than broadly educated experts in human psychological functioning. Perhaps that is why most of American psychology's contributions have been technological rather than scientific.

Finally, the process of expansion was augmented by the development of labor- and time-saving teaching techniques, for example, automatically graded tests, photocopying facilities, information-retrieval services, and TV classes, and also by the gradual reduction of requirements and standards.

Possibly the most far-reaching outcome of the emergence of psychology as a major field of study during the postwar era has been the exposure of more and more people to at least a little formal psychology. Most college students take a minimum of one course in psychology; many school systems employ school psychologists; all mental hospitals utilize clinical or counseling psychologists; industries use the services of industrial psychologists; and psychological data is now sometimes referred to in making legal decisions.

The expansion of psychology along with the other social sciences, schools of education, and business programs also made it possible for universities and colleges to increase enrollments. Students not particularly interested in, or good at, the natural sciences or with little flair for writing or talent in the arts or the humanities could now major in psychology, sociology, education, physical education or business. These disciplines also permit individuals who are delayed in going to college because of a war, or a false career start, or those with poor elementary and secondary school training, a chance to work toward a higher degree. It is very difficult, if a person starts late or has a poor education through high school, to do well in college physics; with adequate motivation, however, he or she will probably be able to handle psychology.

Within psychology, the growth of the discipline allowed for more diverse interests and concerns. While the basic structure of the field has changed very little, all areas of psychology and research orientations are now much more adequately represented than they were in the 1940s. Seventeen new divisions have been added to the American Psychological Association, and there is a better balance of the major philosophies concerning the nature and purpose of psychology. There is still a strong feeling that psychology should be scientific, objective, rigorous, and empirical, but views as to what it means to be scientific have become less provincial. Existential, phenomenological, humanistic, and cognitive viewpoints have been incorporated into the discipline; and research areas such as parapsychology, psychohistory, imagery, homosexuality, death, and international affairs, which not too many years ago were considered either taboo or unproductive, flourish. As the discipline and its applications have grown, there has been less of a tendency to model psychology after the natural sciences.

Relative to other disciplines, particularly psychiatry, the expansion of psychology has resulted in some professional intrusion. By the 1950s and increasingly thereafter, clinical psychologists and to some degree counseling psychologists had, for example, broken the virtual monopoly of psychotherapeutic services formerly held by psychiatrists.

Technological Influences

Academic disciplines as well as individuals have been profoundly influenced by technological developments, particularly since World War II. While both world wars accelerated technological research, many of the advances made during World War II, especially in electronics, had an enormous influence on psychology and most other areas of study. Of special significance have been the high-speed electronic computer, television, audio equipment (for example, tape recorders), refined microelectrode techniques, versatile desk and hand calculators, copiers, and systems for machine-scoring tests. As is discussed in more detail in chapter 3 (World War II and Psychology), psychology was also influenced by the new perspectives gained by psychologists who worked on military research projects during the war with communication engineers and other specialists.

Computers The history of computing devices extends back at least 2,000 years to the time of ancient Greece. In the 1950s divers exploring in the Mediterranean found the remains of "a gadget with a complicated set of dials, gears, wheels, and inscribed plates"[12] used by the early Greeks as an analog computer of the solar system.

An analog computer is one that represents the elements of a problem by a physical variable; a simple example would be to represent the distance between two points by a stick. A more complex and contemporary example would be to represent an increase in learning rate by an increase in electrical voltage. The slide rule, invented in 1621, and the planimeter (1814), harmonic analyzers and synthesizers (1892), and differential analyzers (1930s) were all pre-world War II analog computers. Even the 1930s machines, however, were slow, relatively imprecise, special-use systems that required considerable time to change from one set of operations to another.

The other major type of computer is the digital machine, which has an even longer history than the analog computer. Digit means "finger," so a digital computation is literally one where each finger stands for a discrete event or thing. For obvious reasons, fingers as representations of discrete events are rather limiting, so people quickly learned to use other representations, in particular discrete numbers. The history of digital computers includes the abacus (devised hundreds of years before Christ and going through many modifications), the Napier Bones (1617), Pascal's calculating machine (1642), Leibniz's multiplication machine (1671), Hollerith's punched-card machines (1890), and Baggage's versatile Difference Engine which "was the true forerunner of the modern computer."[13] Baggage's machine, which looks like an elaborate watchworks, was a significant advance in computer technology because it not only calculated but also printed the results.

The first modern digital computer was the Mark I built by Howard Aiken of Harvard in 1937 with financial support from IBM. It was an electromechanical machine rather than an electronic computer but did have some versatility as it could receive instructions by means of punched paper tape. The first electronic computer was the ENIAC (Electronic Numerical Integrator and Calculator) built in 1946 by J. P. Eckert and J. W. Mauchly at the University of Pennsylvania. "A general purpose computer," according to Harold Borko, " it was designed to solve differential equations of the type used in calculating the trajectories of bombs and shells."[14] It was a cumbersome system, however, because the electrical connections had to be changed every time a new problem was introduced.

The first versatile electronic computer was the EDVAC (Electronic Discrete Variable Automatic Calculator) designed by John von Neumann, one of the immigrant intellectuals. It was based on the binary[15] number system and had an increased memory storage with the operating instructions internally stored in the memory. This system represented a tremendous technological advance because it could do any problem that it was instructed to do without changing the wiring. The EDVAC was built for the Army and was still in use in 1962. The University of Illinois, in 1952, was the first institution of higher learning to make a computer available for research purposes. The machine was a von Neumann type called ILLIAC (Illinois Integrator and Calculator). It was not until the early sixties, however, that computers had a serious impact on psychology.[16]

During the sixties most universities and many colleges acquired, or had access to, high-speed computers. By the seventies, as computer systems became more compact and modestly priced, probably every institution of higher learning and even many individual departments acquired computer facilities. Today, of course, it is not unusual for individuals to own computers.

Computers influenced psychology in several quite diverse ways. First, they made projects involving vast amounts of data and/or extensive mathematical analysis feasible. Factor analytic studies and large surveys, for example, can be run in a small fraction of the time it took before computers were available. Programs are now also on file to perform almost any type of statistical analysis of data.

Second, they facilitate the retrieval of information from libraries. It is now possible to go to any major library and ask for a computer search relating to a particular author or concept. If, for instance, an investigator wants to identify all articles and books published by Skinner since 1970, the search can be made in just a few minutes and at a small cost. Computer data banks and access terminals, in other words, save researchers considerable time.

Computers also enable researchers to automate experiments. For example, one can program a computer to control the conditions of any number of Skinner boxes simultaneously. If an experimenter is investigating the effects of a certain drug on the conditionability of rabbits under four different conditions, he/she can automate not only the events that take place but can also analyze the data as it is generated. Again much time is saved, and the entire operation is probably run with greater precision than would be the case if the study were conducted without computer assistance.

Insofar as data analysis is concerned, computers have been particularly useful in differentiating among response patterns. It is almost impossible, for instance, to detect subtle differences in brain-wave patterns by just looking at printouts on graph paper. Computers, however, can be programmed to make refined analyses and thus tell investigators whether or not an experimental manipulation of some sort has made a difference. This capability has been invaluable to physiological psychologists.

Computer technology has, in addition, provided intriguing models of cognitive functioning. Computer programs perform functions such as memory retrieval, problem solving, and sorting, which parallel human thought processes at least in terms of tasks accomplished. The principles of computer programming have, therefore, been looked to as models of human information processing.[17] The availability of computer models has, in fact, been partly responsible for the resurgence of interest in cognitive psychology since the 1960s. (See chapter 7, "Psychological Processes Return to American Psychology.")

Computers have, of course, played a role in instruction. Computers can interact with people and thus facilitate programmed learning. To illustrate, it is possible for a computer to present information or problems to students and then in a step-wise sequence test the learning process. Because of the expense involved, however, computer-assisted instruction is not yet widely used.

High-speed electronic computers also influenced psychology in more indirect ways. The space program, for instance, would not have been possible without computers capable of performing the calculations necessary for the design of the equipment or guiding the vehicles to their orbits or targets. The space program, in turn, facilitated research in human engineering psychology, generated a talent search, and led to a serious reexamination of our educational system to see why we had fallen behind the Russians in space technology. The talent search, subsequently, inspired research on creativity, the learning processes, and teaching techniques. This research is, in large part, conducted by psychologists.

Other Technology Television, which became an important force in American society by the 1950s, influenced psychology in three major ways: as a research tool (one can make a record of human or animal behavior or provide feedback to subjects); as a teaching aid (lectures and demonstrations can be made available to students by means of TV monitors); and as a societal phenomenon to be studied. (People became particularly interested in the effects of TV viewing on academic performance and the effects of TV violence on children.)

Tape recorders and other audio equipment played a consequential role in both academic-research and applied psychology. Tape recorders were particularly valuable in auditory studies and in research on attention. They have also been useful, of course, in any situation wherein it is important to provide subjects with consistent verbal instructions or projects wherein a record of what is being said is essential.

Refined electronic equipment—for example, micro-electrode setups, contributed to the progress made in the neurosciences (including physiological psychology) since World War II. Not only did procedures become increasingly more reliable but electronic advances made sophisticated equipment available to academic departments at modest cost. The mapping out of central nervous system and sensory processes would not have been possible without these technological developments.

Less obvious, but nevertheless important, were the manufacture of desk and hand calculators, photocopiers and the machine scoring of tests. Calculators facilitated the analysis of data; copiers made it possible to duplicate material necessary for writing articles and books or for instruction; and machine scoring facilitated both large-scale survey research and the teaching of large classes of students.

Overall technological developments have made it possible for increasing numbers of psychologists and students to perform many functions more quickly and precisely. It is doubtful that the dramatic growth of the discipline since the late forties would have been possible without electronic computers, calculators, copiers, test-scoring machines and so forth.

Even more important, however, is the fact that technological developments and procedural innovations in general tend to determine to a significant extent the particular research done within a discipline. Since the beginning of experimental psychology, for example, the following innovations have at various times played such a role (dates indicate when the technique or procedure was introduced): psychophysical techniques (to measure human sensitivity, 1860), reaction-time apparatus (to measure the time of mental operations, 1870s), nonsense syllables (to study memory, 1879), psychometric tests (to measure abilities, 1880s), classical conditioning apparatus (1890s), animal problem boxes (for the study of instrumental conditioning, 1890s), laboratory rats (used in psychological research, 1901), mazes (to study animal learning, 1901), intelligence tests (1905), stereotaxic apparatus (for neurophysiological research, 1908), Rorschach Inkblot Test (to measure personality, 1921), Skinner Box (for research on operant conditioning, 1930s), polygraph (to measure bodily processes, 1930s), automated research setups (1940s), electronic computer (multiple uses, 1950s), refined electronic hardware in general (1950s), and biofeedback equipment (1970s). Although technological advances usually derive from scientific discoveries, scientific progress also depends on technological creativity. Science and technology are, in fact, a reciprocal process.

Psychology's Impact on Society

In addition to making the educated public more aware of both the complexities involved in psychological processes and the activities of professional psychologists, the discipline has played a key role since World War II in the design, standardization, evaluation, and administration of tests of all kinds; provided new perspectives toward, and techniques for dealing with, human problems; contributed to our understanding of group processes and techniques; offered professional advice on how to raise children; taken part in consumer research; and provided important information on major social problems.

Test Construction and Administration While psychological testing in Western society goes back to at least the 1870s (Galton in England), the widespread use of tests in the United States did not begin until World

War I when psychologists were charged by the military with developing intelligence tests that could be administered to more than one person at a time. Since then hundreds of tests of all types have been constructed. World War II gave impetus to the development of easily administered personality inventories. Tests have for a long time been used routinely in schools, businesses, the military, mental hospitals, and other institutional settings.

Tests and testing have, however, come under severe criticism during the last twenty years or so on account of the questionable validity of many instruments, concern over the invasion of privacy, and because some minorities contend that tests discriminate against them. Despite this criticism there has been no noticeable decrease in either test construction or test use. Psychology's prime influence on American society, for better or worse, has probably come through its contribution to the test movement. (See chapter 9 for more on testing.)

New Perspectives on Human Problems and Intervention Strategies The second major influence of the discipline on society derives from the role psychologists have played in providing new conceptions and explanations of human psychological and emotional problems and new ways of helping people beset with such problems.

While many psychologists have made contributions in this area, Carl Rogers with his client-centered view of people and their problems, and B. F. Skinner who maintains that the consequences of behavior determine adult life styles, have probably had the most influence. Of course, Freudian ideas were also important, but Freud was not an American psychologist; nor were his most prominent followers, for example, Jung, Adler, Erikson, Fromm, and Horney.

Rogers brought an existential perspective to clinical psychology. He believes that people are born with the capability of solving their own psychological problems and making full use of their potential (self-actualizing) provided they are placed in a threat-free social environment.

Skinner, on the other hand, demonstrated in the laboratory that animal behavior patterns can be predictably controlled by the systematic manipulation of the consequences of particular actions. He, and others, applied this general principle to human behavior demonstrating that the frequency of almost any type of behavior can be increased or decreased provided the experimenter, therapist, or educator controls the consequences of the behavior. People in a mental hospital who refuse to feed themselves, for example, can be conditioned to go to the dining room; the frequency of delusional thinking can be reduced; autistic children can be made to embrace another person; bed wetting can be eliminated; school phobia can be cured; the learning process can be made more efficient through programming and other techniques, and so on. The Skinnerian (operant conditioning) approach, along with procedures deriving from Pavlovian (classical) conditioning, eventually became known as behavior therapy or behavior modification.

In the long run, the importance of Rogers, Skinner, and the others who provided us with new ways to view our lives and problems may not lie in any particular set of assumptions or prescriptions. What may turn out to be most significant for society is the demonstration that it is possible for people to view and conceptualize their experiences and trials in a variety of ways. The ability to do this is probably essential for successful adaptation to a complex, rapidly changing society such as ours.

Rather than being limited to ascribing depression, guilt, or anxiety to a sinful life (Christian view), a physiological anomaly (medical view), or unconscious and unresolved childhood conflict (Freudian perspective), a knowledgeable person can now ascribe these states to (a) long pent-up emotions; (b) inaccurate conceptions of people; (c) a false view of self; (d) a distorted perspective of the world; (e) conflicting reward systems; (f) factors inhibiting self-fulfillment or actualization; (g) a lack of clear boundary between self and world; (h) a sense of separation from the world; (i) inability to handle freedom; (j) no sense of future, and various other factors. We may, therefore, feel depressed, guilty, or anxious for a wide spectrum of reasons. Knowing this may provide insights into our problems.

Group Processes and Group Techniques "Groups have been used since time immemorial to help people deal with their problems," Richard D. James has observed. "Ancient healers, for instance, relied strongly on group forces. Modern group psychotherapy traces its roots back to around 1905, but it got its biggest boost during World War II when a shortage of psychiatric workers made individual treatment impractical."[18]

It is estimated that well over one hundred different types of group therapies or experiences currently exist. New approaches appear each year, but many are short-lived. Probably every major therapeutic orientation now includes group techniques. In addition, there are encounter groups, T (training) groups, sensitivity groups, and group meditation. Some encounters are conducted in the nude, some in silence, others involve touching exercises. Some groups analyze dreams. Some are highly directed, others are essentially leaderless. During the late 1960s groups became ways of life for a certain segment of the citizenry as they formed or joined communes.

Psychologists have not only contributed to the group therapy movement; they have, since World War II, also conducted much small-group research. While social psychological investigations were done in Europe and the United States prior to the 1940s, it was not until World War II and after that experimental studies of small-group processes were conducted. The pioneer in this area was Kurt Lewin who immigrated to this country from Germany in the 1930s. Lewin did small-group studies for the government during the war and was largely responsible for the creation of the group dynamics movement within social psychology during the immediate postwar years. See chapter 9 for more on group therapies.

Professional Advice on How To Raise Children Psychologist John Watson, the "Father of American behaviorism," wrote a child-rearing book in 1928 entitled *Psychological Care of Infant and Child*.[19] It was based mostly on classical conditioning principles and the assumption that children could, under the proper circumstances, be molded into any type of adult one wanted. The book was influential until the 1940s when it was replaced as a guide for child rearing by pediatrician Benjamin Spock's *The Pocket Book of Baby and Child Care* (1946).[20] By the 1970s, Spock's book had sold over twenty-four million copies. Spock's advice was based on Freud's assumption that personality development is largely a function of biologically-determined factors and that all parents have to do is provide a benign environment within which the developmental processes can run their course. This "permissive" approach to child rearing was in stark contrast to that of Watson who had stressed the importance of careful control by parents over the behavior of their children. Spock was eventually blamed for producing the rebellious youth of the late 1960s. Because of Spock's tremendous popularity, the professional influence on American parenting practices during the 1940s, '50s, and '60s came more from medicine than psychology.

Psychologists did play a role in what happened to children in the schools. Programmed learning derived from the conditioning tradition of B. F. Skinner, Fred Keller, and others. And the work of cognitive psychologists like Jean Piaget (a Swiss psychologist) and Jerome Bruner (an American now living in England) suggested new strategies for teaching children facts, concepts, and cognitive skills.

Consumer Research In the late 1950s John Kenneth Galbraith, a prominent economist, wrote a best-selling book called *The Affluent Society*.[21] Galbraith contended that the U.S. economy was based on the false assumption that economic vigor and growth depend upon the continual creation in people of new needs and desires through motivation research and advertising.

While Galbraith may or may not have overstated the significance of motivational manipulation through advertising, it is clear that the investment in consumer research, particularly since World War II, has been considerable. Work in this area involves individuals from a variety of professions including psychologists.

Walter D. Scott, on the staff at Northwestern University, was apparently the first psychologist to express an interest in applying psychological principles to advertising. He discussed this possibility in an address he delivered in 1901, and wrote twelve magazine articles that were brought together in a book entitled *The Theory of Advertising* (1903).[22]

World War I (1914-1918) and then World War II (1939-1945) boosted interest in applied psychology. Consumer psychology grew along with industrial psychology in general; and in 1962 a separate Division of Consumer Psychology was added to the existing divisional structure of the American Psychological Association.

Freudian principles, which ascribe an unconscious sexual basis to all motives, provided, at least for a while (1940s-1960s), an intriguing perspective on consumer needs. People did not buy powerful new cars for transportation, it was declared, but to satisfy unconscious sexual desires. Products should be designed, therefore, not so much for their utility as for their sex appeal. Interest in unconscious motivation generated the concept of subliminal perception, perceptual processes that are believed to operate below the level of consciousness. Attempts were made, for example, to motivate moviegoers to buy a particular soft drink by briefly flashing the name of the beverage on the screen during the show. The concept of subliminal perception, however, remains unsubstantiated.

Consumer research and the scientific manipulation of needs and wants itself became a popular interest during the post-World War II period. The most well-known exposé of the enterprise was probably Vance Packard's *The Hidden Persuaders* (1957).[23]

Psychological Data Used To Solve Social Problems The Supreme Court in deciding *Brown* vs *Board of Education*, Topeka, Kansas (1954) relied on, and referred to, social psychological data. The court concluded that on the basis of the available evidence, separate schools were by nature discriminatory and therefore unconstitutional. This case is usually considered the first one wherein the Supreme Court based its opinion, in part, on psychological findings.

Since then, much research has focused on major social problems. There have been studies of airplane high-jacking, TV violence and children, the effectiveness of various educational programs, child abuse, drug use, and so forth. Usually, however, the results have been equivocal, providing support for all sides of each issue. Unfortunately, government support for applied research on specific social problems frequently wanes before necessary long-run projects can be completed.

Psychology as a Symptom of a Free Society

In a sense, the mere existence of a free and separate discipline of psychology is important because it reminds us that situations can be viewed not only from various political, religious, social, aesthetic, and physical vantage points but also from the psychological. This is particularly important because the psychological perspective, more so than most other formal frameworks, is concerned with the thoughts, feelings, and motivations of the individual. A free psychology may, in fact, be symptomatic of a free society.

3

WORLD WAR II AND PSYCHOLOGY

Psychologists During the War

When the war started, there were only about 2,600 members of the American Psychological Association; by 1945 at war's end membership had climbed to a little over 4,000. Within this context it is a truly remarkable fact that, as John Flanagan has noted, "During World War II about 1250 psychologists were employed full time in psychological work related to the national emergency."[1] In addition to the 1,200 plus psychologists working full-time for the war effort, many worked part-time. For example, Edwin Boring, the most prominent American historian of experimental psychology, was involved in organizing and editing a small volume entitled *Psychology for the Fighting Man* (1943) which eventually sold about 380,000 copies. Boring later transformed the materials of the book into a text on military psychology appropriate for use at West Point.

Civilian concerns, of course, also continued and one of the most significant events to take place within American psychology during the war was the merging in 1943 of the American Association for Applied Psychology with the American Psychological Association. The merger facilitated the growth of psychology because the discipline as a whole was able to respond quickly following the war to the Veterans Administration offer to provide financial support for graduate students in clinical psychology and to institute programs to train them.

Findings of a survey study conducted in 1946 (Britt and Morgan) indicate that most of the psychologists in military service during the war spent some of their time administering tests, interviewing, classifying personnel, doing clinical counseling and consultation, conducting work of a nonpsychological nature, developing tests and training programs, analyzing statistical data, developing clinical and counseling techniques, and studying military tasks. Far fewer were involved at any time during their military careers in psychological warfare projects; research on vision, hearing, and fatigue in the performance of military tasks; and the design and testing of equipment.[2]

Interestingly, many of the personnel working on such psychological warfare projects as the use of radio broadcasts, films and leaflets for propaganda purposes, studies of morale, and research on rumor were not psychologists. The Office of War Information, for example, was placed under the leadership of radio commentator Elmer Davis, while author Robert Sherwood was in charge of the Foreign Information Service. Sherwood, Paul Linebarger recollects, "had a most extraordinary coterie of odd personalities assisting him: Socialist refugees, advertising men, psychologists, psychoanalysts. . . , professional promoters, theatrical types, German professors, a commercial attaché, young men just out of college, oil executives, and popular authors."[3]

The most well-known psychologist involved in psychological warfare work was Edwin Guthrie, who was senior psychological advisor to the secret psychological warfare office of the Military Intelligence Division. Other psychologists connected with psychological warfare projects who achieved some prominence during the postwar period were Robert C. Tryon and Leonard W. Doob.[4]

Psychologists were employed by all branches of the military, the National Research Council, the Office of Scientific Research and Development, the Department of Commerce, the Psychological Warfare Services, the Veterans Administration, the War Manpower Commission, the Department of Agriculture, the Federal Communications Commission, the War Production Board, and the Council of Personnel Administration. The following are representative examples of the types of projects that utilized psychologists during the war:

a. Clinical psychologists worked in Veterans Administration (VA) hospitals testing and providing therapy for military personnel.
b. Tests were developed, or existing tests modified, to screen recruits and place military personnel in appropriate positions.
c. Procedures were designed to select intelligence officers for the Office of Strategic Services. Candidates were observed under a variety of grueling situations simulating real conditions; they were given a battery of tests and interviewed extensively under both relaxed and stressful situations.
d. A systems analysis was made of a bomber; the bomber itself was treated as a system made up of many components including the men operating it; the airplane was also conceived of as a component of a larger system made up of bases, other planes, and support personnel. When all the components had been identified, systems analysis was employed to find the best combination of elements.
e. Research was directed toward maximizing the operational effectiveness of radar operators and the equipment they operated and observed. This task included developing selection and training procedures, de-

termining optimal operating conditions, and designing the equipment for maximum efficiency.

f.   A procedure needed to be devised for warning French citizens that their town, which was heavily occupied by German troops, would be bombed. After the bombing and subsequent occupation by American troops, ways of communicating effectively with the populace had to be established.

g.   New ways of gathering, analyzing, and evaluating information had to be worked out appropriate to a specific country or region of a country. Psychologists involved in psychological warfare were called in to assist the intelligence services.

h.   Psychological warfare specialists were asked to do research on the strengths and weaknesses of a particular people, so that effective propaganda measures could be initiated.

i.   Studies of leadership effectiveness and small-group communication were conducted to assist the military in carrying out their decisions most efficiently.

j.   Sitting for several hours in the darkened Combat Information Center of a ship watching a radarscope was extremely monotonous work; attention easily wandered, endangering the entire ship. Psychologists trained in perceptual research did studies to determine how to help radar operators maintain their vigilance.

k.   As airplanes became increasingly complex and sophisticated, pilots needed to attend to more dials and operate more switches and levers; cockpits turned into a veritable jungle of dials, meters, and controls. Human engineering psychologists worked with engineers and technicians to design and arrange monitoring and control devices so that pilots could operate their planes most efficiently.

l.   As new aircraft capable of faster speeds were developed, research was needed concerning visual perception under those conditions, particularly with regard to takeoffs and landings. James J. Gibson, a psychologist and perceptual specialist who had been working on visual perception since the late 1920s, served in the Air Force as an officer from 1942 to 1946. During that time he was director of the Motion Picture Research Unit in the Aviation Psychology Program. His research for the Air Force on visual perception was not only valuable to the military but it played a key role in Gibson's theorizing following the war. In the preface of his famous book, *The Perception of the Visual World*, published in 1950, he states: "The hypotheses I have adopted were precipitated by research in the field of military aviation, carried out during the war."[5]

m.   One of the more fascinating projects undertaken during the war, but in this case not within a military laboratory or setting, was that done by B. F. Skinner, Keller and Marian Breland, Norman Guttman, and William K. Estes, in training pigeons to guide missiles to targets. Work started initially in 1940 at the University of Minnesota with the experimental findings presented to the government the same year in hopes of obtaining funding. The military, however, was not interested at first. In 1942 General Mills decided to support the research and provided facilities and funds. The following year the results of the project, which had been very successful (pigeons could guide moving objects toward targets by being rewarded with food when they pecked at images of the targets), were again presented to the military. Finally in June, Skinner recalls, "the Office of Scientific Research and Development awarded a modest contract to General Mills, Inc., to 'develop a homing device'."[6] Six months later the award was terminated because electronic guidance systems were being developed. While the pigeons never had the opportunity to navigate missiles, the Naval Research Laboratory supported research on the use of animals to control delivery systems under a program called ORCON (Organic Control) following the war. The Brelands later went into the business of training animals for advertising and entertainment purposes. Guttman did important work in scaling. Estes developed a significant learning theory. Skinner, of course, continued to demonstrate the power of conditioning and to urge the use of behavioral engineering techniques to improve society.

Reviewing aviation psychology in 1948, J. P. Guilford observed, "[D]uring World War II the profession of psychology came of age. It is now recognized as having a distinct place among the professions and as having a number of unique services to offer."[7] Guilford was particularly impressed by "the continued and enlarged demand for psychological personnel by the federal government."[8]

The most well-known books describing the work done by American psychologists during the war include: *Psychology and Military Proficiency* (Charles W. Bray), *The American Soldier: Adjustment During Army Life* (Samuel A. Stouffer et al.), *The American Soldier: Combat and Its Aftermath* (Samuel A. Stouffer et al.), *Measurement and Prediction* (Samuel A. Stouffer et al.), *Personnel Research and Test Development in the Bureau of Naval Personnel* (Dewey B. Stuitt), *Assessment of Men* (U.S. Office of Strategic Services), *Human Factors in Military Efficiency: I. Aptitude and Classification. II. Training and Equipment* (Dael Wolfle), *Strategic Intelligence* (Sherman Kent), *Current Trends: Psychology in the World Emergency* (John C. Flanagan et al.), and *Army Air Forces Aviation Psychology Program Research Reports*.[9]

The Intellectual Migration

As indicated by Fleming and Bailyn in their book on the migration of European intellectuals to the United States during the 1930s and 1940s,

The exile holds an honored place in the history of Western civilization. Dante and Grotius, Bayle and Rousseau, Heine and Marx did their greatest work in enforced residence on alien soil, looking back with loathing and longing to the country, their own, that had rejected them. The Greek scholars from Byzantium who flooded the Italian city-states early in the fifteenth century and the Huguenot bourgeois who streamed out of France across Western Europe late in the seventeenth century brought with them energy, learning, and scarce, welcome skills; New England was founded by refugees who transformed a savage wilderness into blooming civilization. But these migrations, impressive as they are, cannot compare with the exodus set in motion early in 1933, when the Nazis seized control of Germany; the exiles Hitler made were the greatest collection of transplanted intellect, talent, and scholarship the world has ever seen.[10]

Included in the group were: physicists Albert Einstein and Enrico Fermi; writers Arthur Koestler, Thomas Mann, and Bertolt Brecht; management consultant Peter Drucker; architect Walter Gropius; painter Georg Grasz; orchestra conductor Bruno Walter, theologian Paul Tillich; philosophers Rudolph Carnap, Gustav Bergmann, Herbert Feigl, Herbert Marcuse, and Ernest Cassirer; political scientist Hannah Arendt, and many others.

The largest group of immigrants important to American psychology and psychological thought were the psychoanalysts. According to Laura Fermi, author of *Illustrious Immigrants: the Intellectual Migration from Europe 1930-41*, "the two areas in which the impact of the Europeans was most felt [were] atomic science and psychoanalysis."[11] In 1929, the year before psychoanalysts started leaving Europe, "there were a total of 205 active and associate members of [psychoanalytic] societies in Europe and Russia. (In comparison, the New York Society, which had been in existence since 1911, then the only such society in the United States, listed 38 active and 13 associate members; the American Psychoanalytic Association, which listed only active members, had 46.)"[12] Approximately 200 psychoanalysts, most of them Jews, came to the United States during the 1930s and early 1940s to escape the Nazi tyranny. The majority settled in the eastern urban centers of the United States and some on the West Coast. A few, however, went to out-of-the-way places like the Menninger Clinic in Topeka, Kansas, which became the center of psychoanalytic psychiatry and psychology in the Midwest.

Among the most well-known emigrés were: Wilhelm Reich (Austria), Otto Fenichel (Austria), Theodore Reik (Austria), Ernst Simmel (Germany), Beata Rank (Poland), Helene Deutsch (Poland), Rene Spitz (Austria), Karen Horney (Germany), Therese Benedik (Hungary), Erich Fromm (Germany), Frieda Fromm-Reichmann (Germany), Bruno Bettelheim (Austria), Erik Erikson (Germany), Ernest Kris (Austria), Fritz Redl (Austria). Other analysts, for example, Franz Alexander (Hungary), Sandor Rado (Hungary), and Hans Sachs (Austria) came to the United States before

1932 because they saw a receptive climate for psychoanalysis. They and the rest of the relatively small group of analysts already in this country when Hitler assumed power provided considerable help to those who came in the 1930s and early 1940s.

About 30 percent of the immigrant psychoanalysts were women.[13] This was an unusually high percentage, Laura Fermi has noted, because by 1958 "only 9 percent of all students in training institutions approved by the American Psychoanalytic Association"[14] were women. Some of the most famous have been mentioned previously. Others who are perhaps not as well known include Jenny Waelder-Hall, Berta Bornstein, Edith Buxbaum, Margaret Mahler, and Elizabeth Geleerd, all child analysts. The female psychoanalysts tended to specialize in the psychology of either women or children.

Among the psychologists emigrating from Europe to the United States who made the most important contributions to American psychology were (a) Wolfgang Köhler and Max Wertheimer, two of the founders of Gestalt psychology; (b) Kurt Lewin, also within the Gestalt tradition, who was primarily responsible during and following the war for bringing to American psychology research on group dynamics, a cognitive social psychological perspective and action research designed to investigate real-world problems; (c) Egon Brunswik, propounder of a probabilistic-functional theory of perception and ecologically valid research; (d) Else Frenkel-Brunswik, one of the researchers involved in the authoritarian personality study which was the most comprehensive postwar investigation of anti-Semitism; (e) Charlotte Bühler, whose humanistic and life-span perspective antedated both the humanist-existential-phenomenological movement within American psychology and the gradual emergence of a more comprehensive developmental psychology during the 1960s and 1970s; and (f) Rudolph Arnheim, who became one of the leading scholars of the psychology of art. Other European psychologists who achieved some prominence in the United States were Marie Jahoda and David Rapaport.

Social scientists Theodor Adorno, the primary investigator in the authoritarian personality study, and Paul Lazarsfeld, who established a social research institute at Columbia University in 1945, also influenced American psychology as did neurologist Kurt Goldstein, a proponent of a holistic model of man.

While the infusion of intellectual talent primarily from Germany and Austria was a gain for the United States, it was a terribly difficult experience for most of the immigrants. To be forced to leave home, position, friends, and country is tragic at any time; to have to do so during a world-wide depression is almost unimaginable. Some like Ernest Toller, a writer, and Karl Duncker, a psychologist, committed suicide. The great Hungarian composer Bela Bartok died penniless in 1945.[15] Karl

Bühler, whom Fleming and Bailyn call "the leading figure in Austrian psychology in the 1920s,"[16] failed to reestablish himself professionally in this country at all.

Of course, as Laura Fermi points out, there were also humorous incidents. For example, when Laszlo Moholy-Nagy, a Hungarian artist, was invited over by the Association of Arts and Industries of Chicago as director of a new school, the Association sent a cable that read: "MARSHALL FIELD OFFERS MANSION PRAIRIE AVENUE. STABLES TO BE CONVERTED INTO WORKSHOPS." The artist was in Paris when the cable arrived, but his wife who received it sent him a cable urging him to decline the offer. "The reason? *GERMAN EXAMPLE SHOWS FASCIST RESULTS WHEN FIELD MARSHALLS TAKE OVER EDUCATION. STABLES AND PRAIRIE SOUND JUST LIKE IT.*"[17]

Then there was the woman psychoanalyst who declined an offer to come to the Menninger Clinic because "she was afraid that her laundry would not be properly done in Topeka."[18]

Specific Influences of the War on American Psychology

Bertolt Brecht through his play "Mother Courage and Her Children," first produced in 1949, proclaims that "misfortune in itself is a poor teacher," and that people learn nothing from war. Whether or not psychologists learned anything substantive from World War II is debatable, but there can be no doubt that the war influenced the discipline in a variety of ways. The conflict, for example, had some bearing on each of the following events or developments:

    a. the accelerated growth of the discipline;
    b. the expansion of professional (particularly clinical) psychology;
    c. the spread of the psychoanalytic influence;
    d. the formulation of guidelines for research using human subjects;
    e. studies on anti-Semitism, prejudice, and rumor;
    f. analyses of concentration-camp experiences;
    g. research on peace, war, aggression, stress, and frustration;
    h. psychological projects solicited by the United Nations;
    i. increased interest in conducting interdisciplinary research;
    j. investigations suggested or made possible by technological developments;
    k. test development and validation;
    l. small-group research and the growth of social psychology, and;
    m. talent searches and work on creativity.

The Accelerated Growth of the Discipline Psychology's rapid growth in the postwar period was a function of the war to the degree that the conflict moved the country out of a severe depression; facilitated population growth because of improved economic conditions and the availability of home loans for veterans (G.I. loans); increased university and

college enrollments through G.I. educational benefits; led to the support
of graduate education in clinical psychology via the Veterans Administration (VA) programs; resulted in the hiring by the federal government
of more psychologists than ever before; and increased the support by
federal agencies of psychological research by civilian psychologists (mostly
in colleges and universities).

The Accelerated Professionalization of Psychology The need for more professionals was particularly acute in the mental health professions like
psychiatry, clinical psychology, and social work during the postwar decade. The rate of first admissions to mental hospitals increased rather
steadily through the thirties, forties, and early fifties; by 1955 it was
estimated that there were over 1,600,000 people in the United States
receiving some kind of treatment (both inpatient and outpatient) for
psychological problems.[19] Another equal number, while untreated, were
probably in need of some professional help; this did not include alcoholics, criminals, or the mentally retarded. At the same time there were
fewer than 10,000 psychiatrists in the country,[20] with only 450 new psychiatrists being graduated each year and some of them, because they
were resident aliens, returning to their native countries. The Veterans
Administration (VA), as indicated before, recognized the pressing need
for more highly trained professionals to help the large number of psychologically disabled veterans of World War II. During the war clinical
psychologists had demonstrated their ability to do research and conduct
therapy as well as to carry out their traditional role of administering and
interpreting psychological tests. In 1946, the VA, which was at that time
the largest single employer of clinical psychologists, initiated a four-year
training program for clinicians approved by the American Psychological
Association; in 1947 the U.S. Public Health Service inaugurated its own
program for training in clinical psychology and other helping professions; in 1950, the VA, Misiak and Sexton report, "made the Ph.D.
degree a requirement for employment as clinical psychologist."[21] By 1949,
some "1500 students were enrolled in doctoral programs in about 60
institutions." By the late fifties half the membership of the American
Psychological Association consisted of clinical psychologists or psychologists in closely related areas.[22]

In addition to clinical psychology, applied areas where growth was
most influenced by the war were human engineering psychology (essentially a new field), industrial psychology, and military psychology.
Other fields such as educational psychology, school psychology, and
counseling psychology were more indirectly affected by the war. The
fact that the Army, Navy, and Air Force continued many of their projects involving psychologists following the war helped maintain interest
during the 1950s in military psychology. In 1951, the Air Force, for
example, still had, according to Flanagan, "one or more active projects

in each of the following: detection, recognition, and interpretation of signals, objects and speech; psychomotor factors in personnel selection; systematic psychophysical analysis in the planning, development, and evaluation of weapons, countermeasures, and other equipment; psychophysical systems research; flying safety research; ground safety research; basic intellectual traits; basic personality variables; initial screening procedures for recruits and draftees; identification and selection of leaders;... classification procedures for officer personnel; analysis of the psychological requirements of jobs; criteria of performance; work modification; military manpower requirements; military management; strategic planning and intelligence; psychological warfare; techniques for the modification of knowledge and skills; research on the modification of personality characteristics; economical and effective methods of mass instruction; principles and procedures for selecting the content for military training programs; training of perceptual and sensory functions; conditions of efficient learning and retention of psychomotor skills; training devices."[23] The Air Force maintained the largest number and the Army the smallest number of in-service personnel working on psychological research during the postwar decade.[24]

The Spread of the Psychoanalytic Influence As has already been discussed in some detail, the migration of psychoanalysts from Europe to the United States in the 1930s and 1940s greatly contributed to the influence of Freudian ideas in this country. The expansion of clinical psychology which was a function, in part, of the war also facilitated the growth of the psychoanalytic influence. (See chapter 4 for details.)

The Formulation of Guidelines for Research Using Human Subjects In 1945-1946 an International Military Tribunal met at Nuremberg, Germany, to try the surviving top Nazi leaders accused of war crimes. They were charged with crimes against humanity, violations of international law, and waging aggressive warfare. It was hoped that by exposing the evils of nazism, Germany could be more effectively democratized. There were twenty-two defendants, nineteen of whom were found guilty with twelve sentenced to death.

Of the many atrocities committed by the Nazis, the most heinous was the torture and systematic extermination of about six million of the ten million Jews living in Europe before the war. The story of the concentration camps with their gas chambers and crematoria is a familiar one. What is equally horrifying is that, as reported by *Time*,

Leading Nazi medical men admitted at their trials the use of Jews as guinea pigs in every kind of pseudoscientific experiment. They were put to torture to test air pressures in planes, to determine the limits of starvation or thirst, to test out poisons. Their skin was taken for grafting operations on wounded German soldiers. The children were drained of their blood to supply the war blood banks. Here a military purpose was served. Apparently the purpose was purely ornamental when human skin was peeled off to make ingeniously tattooed lamp shades.[25]

Even in the context of the long history of atrocities committed by man against man, the feats of the Nazis are difficult to comprehend.[26]

While the Nuremberg trials apparently had no immediate direct effect on American psychology, the fact that a code of conduct concerning the use of human subjects in research was promulgated at the trials[27] indicated that society was concerned about the ethical issues involved in doing research on people. The 1953 code of ethics of the American Psychological Association, Wolf Wolfensberger observes, "was apparently the only one existent in 1963 that had been officially adopted by a scientific organization."[28] In 1966 the U.S. Public Health Service issued a policy encouraging those who sought grants from that agency to consider carefully the ethical implications of their research. More recently the Department of Health, Education, and Welfare (HEW), A. L. Otten notes, "has issued broad rules requiring HEW-financed research to try to eliminate all risks to human subjects."[29]

Research on Anti-Semitism, Prejudice, Propaganda and Rumor Anti-Semitism, prejudice, propaganda, and rumor all have to do with people's attitudes toward, and opinions of, each other. While some survey research on opinion was done in the last quarter of the nineteenth century in Europe, and studies of the effects of advertising go back to at least 1915, attempts to measure attitudes did not occur until the late 1920s. Opinion polls based on scientific sampling procedures were not initiated until the 1930s.

There was also some research before World War II on prejudice and propaganda directed toward blacks, Catholics, Communists, and other political types; but the upsurge of interest in the late forties and fifties in studying anti-Semitism and fascism was clearly a function of both the atrocities perpetrated on the Jews during the war and the fact that many Jewish scholars had immigrated to the United States. Research on rumor and propaganda was, understandably, also stimulated by the war.

The most extensive and well-known postwar investigation of anti-Semitism was that conducted by Theodor Adorno, Else Frenkel-Brunswik, Daniel J. Levinson, and R. Nevitt Sanford reported in a book entitled *The Authoritarian Personality* (1950).[30] While Adorno's interest in anti-Semitism goes back to the early thirties when he was on the staff of the "Institut für Sozialforschung" in Frankfort, Germany, the actual impetus to design and conduct a research project on the problem came in the early forties when he was with the Bureau of Applied Social Research[31] at Columbia University. When news of Nazi atrocities reached the United States, Max Horkheimer, director of the Institut in Frankfort while Adorno was there (Horkheimer migrated to Paris in 1933 and eventually to the United States in 1939), apparently initiated the anti-Semitism studies in 1940 or 1941. These led to the authoritarian-personality research and also to a series of articles published in *Harper's* magazine entitled "Studies in Prejudice."[32] Financial support for the project, which was conducted mostly at the University of California in Berkeley, was provided by the American Jewish Committee in New York. Horkheimer was director of the Research Division.

What made the joint project possible, according to Adorno, was "our common theoretical orientation toward Freud."[33] While the researchers recognized the importance of sociopolitical factors in the formation of anti-Semitic attitudes, the primary purpose of the project was to identify the psychological factors involved. They were, in other words, interested in finding out whether certain personality types suggested by Freud's theory tended to be pro-Fascist and anti-Semitic. Deviating from Freud, however, they designed attitude scales that provided quantitative data about their subjects; more in keeping with Freud's approach, they supplemented the quantitative data with qualitative information (case histories).[34] The F-scale (F for fascism) was the most substantive product of the investigation, being widely used in subsequent studies. One of the strengths of the authoritarian-personality research was the fact that the questions asked of subjects did not directly concern attitudes toward Jews. Instead questions providing information about the general rigidity of thought—the degree to which people are dogmatic or flexible—were employed. Thus, people who were administered the F-scale did not know that they were taking part in a study on anti-Semitism.

The results of the project were interpreted by Adorno, Frenkel-Brunswik, and their collaborators as demonstrating that a particular cluster of personality or behavioral tendencies comprised the foundation of the authoritarian personality and that these include

great concern with authority, involving deference to superiors and assertion over underlings; little personal regard for others; tendency to "manipulate and exploit" and the expectation of being similarly treated, conventionality, conformity, lack of "individuality"; strict "morality," self-righteousness, moral indignation; failure to accept one's own "immoral" impulses coupled with the tendency to attribute evil intent and actions to other groups, particularly minorities; stereotyped, inflexible "black-and-white" thinking; intolerance, bigotry, superstition; general hostility, destructiveness, cynicism; exaggerated concern with sex.[35]

The case study findings provide some evidence that child-rearing practices emphasizing strict morality, rigid obedience, and harsh punishment tend to produce authoritarian adults.

Several of the major criticisms of the work are that the study is based on Freudian personality types; the questions comprising the F-Scale are all worded so that a "yes" or agreement response always loads toward the high side of the scale (people who tend to agree with statements, therefore, automatically get a high score on authoritarianism); and the F-Scale only measures rightist (politically) authoritarianism, which assumes that leftists, for example, Communists, socialists, and liberals, can not be authoritarian.[36] Many of the general findings of the investigation, however, have apparently stood the test of time.[37]

Milton Rokeach, who as a graduate student at the University of California worked on the authoritarian personality research in order to eliminate the rightist bias of the F-Scale, designed what he called the Dogmatism Scale that reflects rigid, authoritarian predispositions regardless of political orientation.[38]

Another influential book that was directly inspired in the late forties by a deep concern over prejudice was *Research Methods in Social Relations* by Claire Selltiz, Marie Jahoda, Morton Deutsch, and Stuart Cook.[39] The events leading up to the publication of this work are of considerable interest.

The Committee on Intergroup Relations of the Society for the Psychological Study of Social Issues (SPSSI) was approached by Gordon W. Allport, an eminent Harvard psychologist, in 1948 with the suggestion that they produce a book on the measurement of prejudice. Allport himself did research on prejudice and rumor so this suggestion was certainly in keeping with his own interests.[40] The committee adopted Allport's idea, but in some of the early conferences it was decided that "the measurement of prejudice is not fundamentally different from the measurement of other social relations."[41] What is noteworthy is that while prejudice was the starting point for their work, a much more general book on social relations resulted. Financial support for the book came from the SPSSI, the Anti-Defamation League of B'nai B'rith, the National Conference of Christians and Jews, and the United Nations Educational, Scientific, and Cultural Organization. This indicates that there was a strong interest on the part of prominent Jewish organizations (and also some concerned Christians) in financing projects having to do with anti-Semitism, prejudice, and the dynamics of social relations in general.[42] Kurt Lewin also received support for some of his research on group dynamics from the American Jewish Congress.[43]

In a very real sense, then, concern over the prejudice toward Jews and other people acted as an important catalyst for social-psychological research on attitude formation and change during the 1950s and 1960s. Work done for the military on opinion, attitude, and propaganda also stimulated research in this area after the war.

Analyses of Concentration Camp Experiences By 1933, Hitler had set up over fifty concentration camps in Germany for political dissidents, Jews, and anyone else who displeased the leaders of the Third Reich. At first, most of the prisoners were beaten and then ransomed to their relatives or friends; some, however, were brutally murdered.[44] At any one time, before the war, there were probably never more than twenty or thirty thousand inmates in these German camps. After the occupation of Austria in 1938 and the invasion of Poland in 1939, large camps were established outside of Germany. By war's end, millions of people had been tortured and killed within the confines of those barbed-wire enclosures.

The most direct impact of the concentration camps on American psychology and psychological thought was through the writings of two men both of whom spent considerable time in the camps: Bruno Bettelheim, a Viennese psychologist and lay psychoanalyst who immigrated to the United States in 1939; and Viktor Frankl, a Viennese doctor and psychoanalyst who remained in Austria.

Bettelheims's 1943 article, "Individual and Mass Behavior in Extreme Situations,"[45] became a classic. In it he points out that the camps served a definite set of purposes for the Gestapo, namely to break the prisoners, spread terror in the populace, and provide a training ground and laboratory for the Gestapo. More interesting psychologically, however, was his analysis of the personality changes that such extreme environments produce and the defensive strategies people employ to avoid complete psychological disintegration. Bettelheim admits that he did this study to maintain his own sanity; it enabled him to hold onto his identity as a psychologist. Basically, he found that adjustment to the camp was a function of social class, the perceived reason for internment, and the length of time spent in the camp. In general, he found that prisoners tended to act childlike when minor punishments were carried out and apathetic and detached in more extreme situations. Most prisoners, according to Bettelheim, eventually became completely infantile in their dependence upon the guards; they even accepted the values of the Gestapo (for example, they identified with their masters and tormentors). The regression-to-childhood explanation, Bettelheim invoked, was basic Freud.

A radically different interpretation of the behavior of concentration camp internees was provided by Viktor Frankl. However, his writings, which were in German, were not brought to the attention of American psychologists until the late 1950s, mostly by Gordon Allport, who had a strong interest in European developments in psychology and psychiatry. Frankl's book *Man's Search for Meaning: An Introduction to Logo-therapy* (1962) is his most well-known work.[46] In it he describes his concentration-camp experiences and logo-therapy, which was an outgrowth of these experiences. Rather than ascribing the human ability to survive in extreme situations to regressive tendencies, as Bettelheim did, Frankl asserts that our resilience derives from the fact that we are free to choose whatever attitude we want toward any situation including those that make us suffer, experience pain, or face death. Survival, in other words, depends upon a frame of mind or outlook that makes a person want to find the meaning of each experience; this, in turn, provides a sense of future and gives life meaning. Basically, the logo-therapist tries to help people look at their experiences from new perspectives with the hope that they will perceive the meanings of these experiences for their lives.

The American discovery of Frankl in the late fifties and early sixties was part of the generally increasing influence of existential and phenomenological viewpoints during that time. Existentialism and phenomenology received important boosts in Europe right after World War II from French existentialist writers Jean-Paul Sartre and Albert Camus, who wrote about the absurdity of life and the meaning of death; and from Maurice Merleau-Ponty, who propounded the phenomenological method of examining human experience. There was understandably much interest among Europeans during and after the war in the nature of human experience, suffering, fear, and death. American psychology, however, was not influenced significantly by such concerns until about a decade later. Since the middle sixties, there has been a great surge of interest in death, suicide, aging, and dying, as well as existentialism and phenomenology. Research on human reactions to extremely stressful situations was also stimulated by the Chinese Communists' treatment of prisoners of war during the Korean conflict (1950-1953). The Chinese used "psychological" techniques to extract information from prisoners and to convert them to communism with a minimum of physical torture. These procedures were said to "brainwash" prisoners, for example, erase existing assumptions and beliefs, thereby making room for new perspectives.

Research on Peace, War, and Aggression Edward Tolman, one of the prominent learning theorists of the thirties and forties, wrote a rather inconsequential book in 1942 called *Drives Toward War*. There was also considerable theorizing and animal research on the relationship between individual frustration and aggression during the 1940s and after; and social psychologist Herbert Kelman helped found the Research Exchange on the Prevention of War in 1951. Surprisingly, however, very little systematic work was done by psychologists during the postwar years on war and peace. This was due in part to the fact that these phenomena are generally viewed as more relevant to political science, sociology, and anthropology. In addition, research on peace had, according to psychologist Charles Osgood, "become a highly emotionally charged topic. The university professor who becomes involved with political questions, as peace has now become, must know that he subjects himself to question and even suspicion."[47] While Osgood was writing about the late fifties and early sixties, aggression organized on a large scale (war) and peace were both conspicuously ignored by psychologists even in the postwar decade.

Osgood, however, became increasingly concerned over the possibility of a nuclear war in the late fifties and brought his training and research in experimental psychology to bear on the war-peace issue. He eventually devised a stratagem for international tension reduction (Graduated and Reciprocated Initiatives in Tension Reduction) which was taken note of by government officials.

Also indicative of the fact that psychologists were becoming more concerned with problems of war and peace was the formation in 1960 of a committee called Psychology in National and International Affairs and the publication in 1965 of a book edited by Kelman entitled *International Behavior: A Social-Psychological Analysis*.[48] Since the late 1960s, peace research on the part of psychologists and other social scientists has increased modestly.[49]

Research for the United Nations The formation of the United Nations in 1945 created new research opportunities for psychologists and other scholars. In general, projects solicited and supported by agencies of the UN such as UNESCO (United Nations Education, Scientific, and Cultural Organization) and WHO (World Health Organization) involve cross-cultural studies. This makes it necessary to look at problems such as mental illness, child-rearing, delinquency, and crime from a broader perspective than usual. Important books that have resulted from research done by psychologists for UNESCO include *Tensions that Cause Wars* (1950)[50] edited by Hadley Cantril and *In the Minds of Men* (1953)[51] by Gardner Murphy. Perhaps the best-known work generated by a project supported by WHO is *Maternal Care and Mental Health* (1951)[52] by John Bowlby. Many noteworthy studies supported by UN agencies, however, have been published, particularly in the area of mental health. There is no doubt that one of the most important products of World War II was the international perspective brought to bear on psychological problems largely as a result of the research done for the United Nations. Such projects also facilitated interdisciplinary investigations which, as indicated before, increased for a while after the war.[53]

Anthropologists and sociologists have been actively engaged in cross-cultural work since the beginning of the twentieth century. Their findings are based primarily on what they observed as they lived with the peoples they were investigating. Psychological investigation across cultures did not begin in earnest until the 1940s when, as Otto Klineberg has observed, "more and more young anthropologists who went into the field took with them the Rorschach ink blots, Murray's TAT or other projective techniques, or they used the biographical or clinical-psychological approach with their individual informants."[54] Psychoanalytic assumptions concerning early childhood experiences and personality development provided a strong incentive for cross-cultural investigation from the 1930s through the 1950s; however, most of the studies were conducted by social scientists other than psychologists. Klineberg, who published a book entitled *Race Differences* in 1935, was one of the first American psychologists to encourage a systematic cross-cultural perspective within the discipline. Few psychologists, though, were engaged actively in cross-cultural research until the 1960s. Since that time studies have been conducted in areas ranging from perception, cognition, and language to personality development, social processes, and psychopathology. Reflecting the growth of cross-cultural psychology during the last twenty years has been the publication of the *International Journal of Psychology* and the *Handbook of Cross-Cultural Psychology* (1980).[55] Many of the articles published in the *Journal of Social Psychology* also concern cross-cultural studies.

In addition to projective techniques, the psychological instruments or tasks most frequently used in cross-cultural investigations include Charles Osgood's Semantic Differential which measures the connotative meaning of concepts; Jean Piaget's problems for children designed to reflect cognitive development; certain so-called culture-free intelligence tests; the F-Scale to measure authoritarianism; and imbedded figure tests to determine subjects' dependence on visual contexts.

Interdisciplinary projects World War II as well as the United Nations contributed to the development of interdisciplinary projects. The problem-centered research done by social and natural scientists during the war was usually interdisciplinary in nature. It was not unusual for psychologists, sociologists, anthropologists, and linguists to be brought together to deal with problems having to do with propaganda or military intelligence or for engineers, physicists, and experimental psychologists to work jointly designing a new man-machine system or for psychiatrists, psychologists, and social workers to join forces to provide mental health services in a military hospital. In addition, the intrusion into psychology of psychoanalysis, new models of human mental processes, and so forth, which resulted from wartime developments, tended to remind psychologists that most of the problems they are concerned with are by definition multidisciplinary.

In some universities, interdisciplinary programs were created; at Harvard in 1945, for example, the Department of Social Relations was formed. At the same time many university and college departments developed interdisciplinary courses and curricula. There was, in addition, a feeling among many academicians that, with the various fields expanding rapidly, increasing fragmentation was inevitable and that the only way to counteract such divisiveness was to design coordinated educational programs.[56] Some called for coordinated research within psychology on significant problems[57] and for the integration of research program planning.[58] Clyde Kluckhohn, a famous anthropologist, saw in Lewin's field theory "a possible framework for the creation of a basic social science which would unify much of psychology, psychiatry, sociology and anthropology."[59]

Wartime work on sophisticated communication and monitoring devices and high-speed electronic computers also contributed to the feeling after the war that integrated multidisciplinary approaches to problems should be maintained. For example, general systems theory, which, according to James G. Miller, it was hoped would develop into "an empirically testable general theory of behavior,"[60] emerged in the late forties. In 1949 a group of scholars at the University of Chicago started meeting regularly to see if enough was known to develop a comprehensive theory of behavior. The meetings, which continued for several years, were truly multidisciplinary. There were historians, anthropologists, economists, political scientists, sociologists, psychologists, mathematical biologists, physicists, and philosophers. The complexity of the problem soon became apparent and work within the context of general systems theory is still continuing.

The military, too, was directly involved in the integration of psychological research. In the early fifties, the Bureau of Naval Personnel, for instance, developed a plan for coordinating programs of personnel research and development.[61]

The creation during the war of research bureaus or centers associated with universities but funded chiefly by outside monies and research facilities like the Group Dynamics Laboratory at the Massachusetts Institute of Technology (MIT) also tended to foster multidisciplinary projects.

To summarize, the war brought people together to work on common problems. This resulted in a cross fertilization of ideas and some attempt to engage in cooperative thinking and research. After the war, however, most scholars and scientists gradually moved back into the folds of their own disciplines. One notable exception has been in the area of brain research. During the late fifties, the general area of "neuroscience" was created; the term subsumes all professionals studying the brain or analogs of the brain whether biologist, chemist, physicist, engineer, or psychologist.[62] Neuroscience represents a coordinated attack on the mysteries of brain function. The degree to which the war or military support of research during the postwar decade contributed to this development is uncertain, but the climate and funding for multidisciplinary research were, at least partly, products of the war.[63]

The Impact of Wartime Technological Research on Psychology While efficient means of mechanized transport and mass destruction had been developed by the time of World War I, it was not until World War II that highly sophisticated electronic systems of communication, target detection and tracking, and destruction-delivery were perfected. The automotive engineer and chemist are appropriate symbols of World War I, but the physicist, electrical engineer, and mathematician better symbolize World War II.

Communication, detection, and control, as basic aspects of human functioning, are essentially psychological processes. Psychologists, therefore, and young men who later entered the profession of psychology, were frequently involved in research on these phenomena during the war or perhaps afterwards while working on projects for one of the military services. Consequently, such promising new conceptions as information theory, detection theory, decision theory, and cybernetics were imported into psychology from communications engineering, electronics in general, physics, and mathematics. At the same time, the increasingly sophisticated and refined electronic hardware that was developed provided psychologists with many new research tools.

Information theory is a way of quantifying information and uncertainty and of conceptualizing the relationship between the input to a receiver and output of a transmitter. It is possible, for example, by using the theory to specify the amount of information in a situation, provided the number of yes-no questions, each reducing the uncertainty by one half, can be specified. The formulation seemed promising for psychology because it offered a way to quantify the complexity of certain stimulus presentations. It appeared to have particular relevance for perceptual and cognitive studies. The implications of the theory for the discipline, however, did not become apparent until the late 1950s. Within about a decade much of the enthusiasm for information theory had diminished, mostly because the theory, while appropriate for passive information transmission systems like radio, did not provide a reasonable model for human psychological functioning.[64]

George Miller, a professor of psychology at Harvard University who was one of the first to introduce information theory to psychology, worked at Harvard's Psycho-Acoustic Laboratory on voice enunciation during the war. It was not until 1948, three years after the war, that Claude Shannon of the Bell Telephone Laboratories published his classic paper[65] on information theory. Although this paper stimulated Miller to examine the theory's implications for psychological research, his interest in information transmission goes back to his doctoral research during World War II. Similarly, Fred Attneave, who also recognized the potential of information theory for psychology and wrote a useful short volume in 1959 entitled *Applications of Information Theory to Psychology*,[66] served in the Army Signal Corps during the war and later did research for the Air Force. Finally, Norbert Wiener, a noted mathematician who played an important role in the development of information theory and cybernetics (the study of self-controlling mechanisms), worked on electronic systems for controlling antiaircraft guns.[67]

World War II brought psychologists in contact with scientists, engineers, and technicians employing new communication concepts and techniques, but many of the basic ideas involved in information theory were developed before the war and had nothing to do with military research. In mathematics, for instance, there had been a turn toward probability theory and applied statistics (mathematics of the imprecise real world) since the beginning of the century.[68] Furthermore, research on communication processes had been going on at the Bell Telephone Laboratories for many decades; Shannon's ideas on information theory were developed in connection with his work there on telephone circuitry and switching problems.

In addition to communication studies, psychology was influenced by research on detection systems like radar and sonar. Radar was an English invention and extensive work was conducted in England as well as in the United States on ways of making the equipment and the operators as efficient as possible. Some of Norbert Wiener's research on radar-controlled gunnery systems resulted in a technique for maximizing the visual signal and reducing background illumination (noise), making it easier for radar operators to detect ships and planes.

There were three direct spin-offs for psychology of detection research: (1) signal detection theory itself; (2) decision theory; and (3) the study of long-term attentional processes in the context of extremely monotonous conditions (vigilance research). Since the 1870s, psychologists have been interested in the ability of people to detect changes in the environment. Experimental psychology, in fact, emerged in about 1860 when a few German scientists tried to determine how bright a light, how loud a tone, or how heavy a weight is required before it is detected; or to find out how much different stimuli must be before the differences are sensed. This kind of research is called "psychophysical" because it is concerned with the relationships between changes in the measurable aspects of the physical environment and perception.

In studying the ability of radar operators to notice signals, it quickly became apparent that detection depends on more than sensitivity to light. The length of time viewing the radar screen, the frequency of signals, the motivation and fatigue levels of the operator, the nature of the immediate environment, and so forth, all have a bearing on whether or not a particular "blip" on the screen is noticed. Detection theory assumes that sensory excitation varies continuously so that even if all environmental conditions are kept constant, sensitivity changes within certain limits. Decision theory, at least insofar as it is associated with detection problems, recognizes the fact that variables like expectation (both as a function of what has happened before and relative to expected payoffs or rewards) influence the detection task. Detection theory was compatible with the general interest in statistical or probability models of real-world phenomena which became prominent in science in the forties and which by the fifties had been imported into academic-research psychology. The theory recognizes the variability of human functioning and tries to account for it. Detection and decision theories also assume that prediction can only be approximate and that one must look for ways to reduce error to a minimum.[69]

A very general but important postwar development that was to some degree a function of research done during the war on communications, target detection, and gunnery control was cybernetics. Cybernetics comes from the Greek word meaning steersman and refers to control processes or mechanisms. More precisely, cybernetics has to do with the guidance of processes by means of systems that feed back to relevant control centers information concerning the current state of those processes. Any nonrandom activity, in other words, is by definition guided by something; cybernetics has to do with the nature of guidance systems.

Cybernetics is mostly a conception of Norbert Wiener. According to his own explanation, Wiener's ideas on cybernetics came from a variety of professional experiences: "Because I was interested in the theory of communication, I was forced to consider the theory of information and, above all, that partial information which our knowledge of one part of a system gives us of the rest of it. . . . Because I had worked in the closest possible way with physicists and engineers, I knew that our data can never be precise."[70] He went on to say that he wrote his book on cybernetics in order to provide "an account of the new information theory which was being developed by Shannon and myself, and of the new prediction theory which had its roots in the prewar work of Kolmogoroff and in my researches concerning anti-aircraft predictors," as well as to introduce the educated public "to the long series of analogies between the human nervous system and the computation and control machine which had inspired the joint work of Rosenbleuth and me."[71] Rosenbleuth was a Mexican physiologist and colleague of the great Harvard physiologist, Walter Cannon.

The impact of cybernetic models was particularly significant in physiological psychology, perceptual and cognitive research, and language and communication studies. It also provided the basis for general systems theory which in turn was seen by some as affording a comprehensive model of all organismic functioning.[72] The book *Plans and the Structure of Behavior* by Miller, Galanter, and Pribram (1960) presents the first well thought out application of cybernetic ideas to psychology.[73]

As mentioned before, many psychologists worked with engineers and technicians during the war designing the control systems of complex machines like jet airplanes or monitoring stations such as the Combat Information Centers of naval vessels or control towers at airports. As military vehicles became increasingly sophisticated and capable of greater speed, more and more demands were placed on the operators. Consequently dials, meters, buttons, knobs, radarscopes, levers, and so forth had to be designed and positioned so that human operators could exercise maximum control with a minimum of effort and fatigue. Research on communications, detection and decision making, in the context of cybernetics, was all integral to control-system design. In addition, studies of perception under high-speed conditions of the type done by James Gibson were also required.[74]

One of the direct consequences of man-machine research was the formation after the war of a research specialty called Human Factors or Human Engineering. The Society of Engineering Psychologists became a division of the American Psychological Association in 1958.[75] Human factors research was maintained, in part, because the military continued to provide financial support.[76] In addition, human engineering psychologists found employment in industrial firms. The space program of the late fifties and sixties also inspired work in this area because psychologists helped design the interiors of space capsules.[77]

The war stimulated computer development by generating problems of such complexity, for example, those involved in designing gunnery control systems, that extremely rapid computations were essential. As mentioned earlier, the first versatile electronic computer, the Electronic Discrete Variable Automatic Calculator (EDVAC), was designed and built for the Army in the late 1940s by John von Neumann. The space program, in turn, was possible only because of the availability of increasingly efficient computers.

To summarize, in a highly industrialized society, war tends to accelerate technological developments; this was certainly the case during World War II. Advances in electronics, communication systems, guidance control mechanisms, and aviation placed military personnel in new man-created environments which frequently required them to analyze and respond quickly to much more information than had ever been necessary before.

Psychologists played an important role in designing these special environments. By working closely with engineers, communication specialists, and other professionals they were introduced to detection theory, decision theory, information theory, and cybernetics. After the war they brought these perspectives back to psychology. Many of the technological developments, particularly in electronics, found immediate use within the discipline.

Test Development and Validation American psychology owes much of its growth and vigor to "the test" because most test development and administration has been done by psychologists. This is particularly true with regard to tests of intelligence, personality, psychopathology, interests, and values. Psychologists preempted test construction and administration because of the emphasis placed on quantification, psychometrics, and applied statistics in their training. Of all socio-behavioral scientists, psychologists tend to receive the most intensive instruction in quantitative techniques.

It was natural, therefore, that when the Army asked for group intelligence tests to screen military conscripts during World War I, psychologists were employed to do the job. The results of their work included the extensively used Army Alpha intelligence group test. Work on test design, development and standardization continued during the 1920s and 1930s, and when the United States entered World War II in 1940, psychologists were again pressed into service to develop and administer psychometric instruments.

Psychologists, however, had little time during the war to do basic research on test design and construction; mostly they modified and administered existing tests. When new instruments were developed to fit a particular group of servicemen or a particular task, they were either short forms of old tests or tests consisting of standard items. There was little innovation, and no new approaches to testing were forthcoming. The specific work that was done included (a) the development of useful abbreviated versions of some of the standard intelligence and personality tests; (b) large-scale validation projects;[78] (c) studies that provided better understanding of the fact that tests developed for one group of people (for example, urban middle-class whites) cannot legitimately be used to evaluate members of a different group (for example, lower-class blacks); and (d) the construction of paper-and-pencil personality inventories.[79]

Personality inventories were used rather successfully to identify individuals unfit for military service because of psychological problems.[80] The Minnesota Multiphasic Personality Inventory (MMPI), which is still considered one of the best personality tests, was widely used by the military and, indeed, first gained wide acceptance during World War II. Projective tests,[81] in particular the Rorschach Inkblot Test (including some short forms) and the Thematic Apperception Test (TAT), were also fairly extensively administered to military personnel. Many clinical psychologists, however, questioned their usefulness as screening devices.[82] During the late forties and fifties there was a trend both toward the widespread use of projective techniques and toward research trying to determine the validity of these techniques.[83]

In addition to testing intelligence and personality, psychologists and sociologists also sampled opinions and attitudes. Social scientists working for the Research Branch of the Army's Morale Services Division, including psychologists Samuel Stouffer, Leonard Cottrell, and Carl Hovland, for example, did studies on military and civilian morale and on the efficacy of orientation films for military personnel. While the methodologies involved in opinion and attitude measurement differ in some ways, both have to do with psychological assessment, and both share problems of reliability[84] and validity.

Concerning attitude and opinion research and testing, Quinn McNemar, a well-known expert in psychometrics, stated: "[N]o marked contributions to methodology were made during the first 30 months of the war effort."[85] McNemar goes on to say,

Minor advances have been made. The Census Bureau and Likert's group in the Department of Agriculture have...succeeded in ironing out biasing bugs of sampling, but this was being done before the United States entered the war. Likert has made progress in refining open-end question interviewing. Guttman's scaling method originated in connection with his work as consultant to the Research Branch of the Army's Morale Services Division....All the major agencies have carried out studies of a methodological nature, but the striking thing is the fewness and limited nature of such studies. One looks in vain for work on the fundamental problems of reliability and validity.[86]

McNemar saw Guttman's unidimensional scaling technique as the single most important advance in attitude measurement to result from government work during the war.

To recapitulate, World War II (a) facilitated the development of many useful short forms of existing intelligence and personality tests; (b) produced a number of large-scale validation studies; (c) made psychologists more aware of the danger of giving tests to people different from the group used to standardize the instruments; (d) demonstrated the usefulness of some tests as screening techniques; (e) contributed to the rise of interest in projective methodologies (see also chapter 4 on psychoanalysis); and (f) in a modest way led to some advances in the measurement of attitudes and opinions. Much of the enthusiasm for social psychological research following the war was due to wartime work on attitudes and opinions and small-group dynamics.

Research on Small Groups Most investigations prior to World War II on the behavior of people in small groups concerned coacting groups. A coacting group is one wherein the individuals involved work together side by side without really communicating or interacting. The point of such research might be, for example, to find out what happens to efficiency when people perform the same task individually but in each other's presence.

It was not until after World War II that face-to-face, small groups, for example, groups wherein people communicated and interacted with each other for a particular purpose, were extensively studied. The person most responsible for this upsurge of interest in group dynamics was immigrant psychologist Kurt Lewin. While Lewin is known for a variety of contributions including a theory of personality and research on children, goal tensions, social climates, interrupted tasks, frustration, aggression, level of aspiration, conflict resolution, altruism and leadership, his most far-reaching and enduring influence has probably been in the areas of group dynamics and action-research. Action-research has to do with "the experimental use of social sciences to advance the democratic process."[87] Having escaped from Nazi tyranny,[88] Lewin was much interested in investigating what happens to people under democratic and nondemocratic conditions. Some of the research he supervised or inspired directly concerned group behavior within the contexts of authoritarian and democratic leadership styles.[89]

When World War II broke out, Lewin, who was then at the University of Iowa, turned his attention to questions of morale, psychological warfare techniques, military leadership, civilian acceptance of reduced food rations and substitute foods, human relations and industrial productivity, the psychological rehabilitation of those injured in combat, and other wartime problems. This was action-research of the utmost urgency, and it is not surprising that Lewin, along with other social scientists experienced in real-world research, for example, Margaret Mead (anthropologist); Samuel Stouffer, Paul Lazarsfeld, and Rensis Likert (public-opinion researchers); and Henry Murray and Donald MacKinnon (psychologists) served in a consulting capacity or worked directly for the government during the war. Lewin traveled back and forth between Iowa City and Washington during the war years, mostly as a consultant for the Office of Strategic Services.

As the war progressed, Lewin apparently felt increasingly that psychologists should spend more time trying to discover how people can change their attitudes and outlooks and as a consequence behave more civilly. His interest, therefore, turned more and more toward action-research and group dynamics.

When the war ended in 1945, Lewin left Iowa and established the Research Center for Group Dynamics at MIT. He lived only two more years, and the center was then moved to the University of Michigan which became an important center for graduate work in social psychology.

It is difficult to determine the degree to which the war stimulated research on face-to-face, small groups; perhaps such research would have been done in any case. It is certain, however, that without Lewin's studies this area would have been much slower in developing. It is also evident that wartime projects and Lewin's work directed toward fostering democratic leadership and institutions through action-research largely generated the tremendous interest in studying small groups that characterized the postwar decade. Lewin, as founder and director of the Commission on Community Interrelations of the American Jewish Congress, played a direct role, too, in initiating research on anti-Semitism, prejudice in general, and minority-group problems. In addition, the commission, under his direction, did studies on effective community leadership, gang behavior, and group loyalty. Finally, Lewin "invented" sensitivity training and the T-group, which are still used in one form or another to help people work together more effectively.

To summarize, research on the dynamics of small task- or problem-oriented groups was inspired primarily by the thinking and studies of Kurt Lewin. His genius, however, went beyond new insights and techniques; he also had the ability to interest others in his approach. The impressive list of people who worked, studied, or frequently conferred with him includes: Roger Barker, Dorwin Cartwright, Tamara Dembo, Karl Duncker, Sibylle Escalona, Fritz Heider, Mary Henle, Sigmund Koch, Boyd McCandless, Donald MacKinnon, Neal Miller, Gardner Murphy, Robert Sears, Edward C. Tolman, Alex Bavelas, John R. French, Leon Festinger, Isidor Chein, Gordon Allport, Morton Deutsch, Harold Kelley, Albert Pepitone, Stanley Schachter, John Thibaut, Alvin Zander, Ronald Lippitt and R. Duncan Luce. There is certainly strong support for Tolman's statement that "Freud the clinician and Lewin the experimentalist—there are the two men whose names will stand out before all others in the history of our psychological era. For it is their contrasting but complementary insights which first made psychology a science applicable to real human beings and to real human society."[90]

Talent Searches and Research on Creativity As Wolfle has aptly observed,

World War II marks the time at which there began to be clear recognition that the need for resources of land and capital had been surpassed by the need for resources of human talent....It was in World War II that we were pinched for men and brains. It was then that we also began to recognize that invention could be deliberately planned. The scientific and engineering achievements of the war period provided dramatic evidence that some major problems could be solved and some major new inventions produced when imaginative and talented men set their minds to the task.[91]

World War II also led to the Cold War, which involved intense technological rivalry between the Soviet Union and the United States. This competition has kept pressure on both nations to maintain parity with each other technologically. Thus, there has been a continuing concern in both countries over the use and development of human resources, human talent, and more effective educational processes. American and Russian psychologists have been involved in talent searches because research on the learning processes has for a long time been central to both psychologies. By the 1950s, creativity had also become a notable area of study in the United States.[92]

The concern over human talent was intensified by the diminished pool of college graduates during the late forties and early fifties because of the lowered birth rate in the thirties (the depression years) and also because a high percentage of talented high school students did not go on to college.[93] By 1950, the shortage of scientists, engineers, and educators had become so acute that a commission on Human Resources and Advanced Training was established by the American Council of Learned

Societies, the American Council on Education, the National Academy of Sciences, and the Social Science Research Council. The commission published an influential report in 1954 concerning the need for talent and ways of increasing the talent pool.[94]

The importance of identifying and nurturing promising students also led to the establishment of the "discovery of the talented" annual lectureship by Dr. Millicent Todd Bingham, under the auspices of the American Psychological Association in memory of Dr. Walter Van Dyke Bingham, her husband and a famous industrial psychologist.

In 1957, when the Soviets launched the first earth-orbiting satellite (Sputnik) and it appeared as if the United States were lagging behind technologically, the call for better educational techniques and talent utilization intensified. By the early sixties, after our space feats had surpassed those of the Russians and a high percentage of young people was going to college, less and less was heard about talent searches. Research on creativity, however, continued at a modest pace.

The war further contributed to the shortage of highly trained professionals by transforming a seriously depressed economy into a vigorous one; the 1946 to 1957 period was a particularly prosperous time. Prosperity, however, created an increased demand for scientists, engineers, and other professionals. Furthermore, the baby boom of the late forties, which was, of course, related to a high level of prosperity, intensified the need for more educators. Finally, there were not enough clinical psychologists and other helping professionals to provide adequate psychological services for war veterans.

The talent shortage and search in combination with the demand that gifted people be better educated and encouraged to go to college stimulated the following types of psychological research: the design of new tests of creativity; investigations of the relationship between creativity and other variables like intelligence; studies of talented groups (scientists, artists, novelists); research on educational techniques, basic learning processes, problem solving, concept formation, and memory; and projects concerned with the influence of such factors as anxiety, fatigue, sleep, rewards, and punishment on the acquisition and retention of information or knowledge.

4

THE FREUDIAN INFLUENCE

Introduction

In 1895, Sigmund Freud, a Jewish physician living in Vienna, introduced the term "psychoanalysis" to refer to a technique for eliciting from neurotic patients repressed information about their past lives. Eventually, however, psychoanalysis came to refer to the complex theory of personality, therapeutic approach, and research orientation developed by Freud and his followers.

It is a dreadful irony that the two men who perhaps had the most influence on American psychology during the 1940s and 1950s were Freud and Adolph Hitler, whose policies forced most European psychoanalysts, along with many psychologists, to flee to the United States, and who, more than any other person, started World War II.

Interestingly, both Freud and Hitler lived in Vienna in 1909, as Vincent Brome has noted, "each totally unaware of the other's presence. They occupied different quarters of the city but their daily life frequently took them into identical streets to sit occasionally in the same cafes."[1] Hitler was only twenty at the time when Freud was fifty-three. For different reasons both were rather unhappy with their lives in Vienna: Hitler because he had to scrape out a living as a casual laborer; and Freud because of what he called "the bad mood of the Vienna surroundings."[2] Hitler hated and feared the Jews even then; he felt among other things that they were a clear threat sexually to young Germanic maidenhood.

While the Freudian influence on American psychology (as a discipline) reached its height during the 1935-1955 period, Freud's impact on psychiatry, the child development movement, sociology, social work, literature, political science, art, drama, and even formal psychology was considerable by the early 1920s. Freud's first major book, *The Interpretation of Dreams*, was published in 1900; and he came to the United States in 1909 to lecture on psychoanalysis at Clark University. The first reference to psychoanalysis in the American psychological literature was apparently made in 1894 by William James, who published an article in *The Psychological Review* that referred to a paper authored by Breuer and Freud.[3] It was the rise to power of Hitler in the 1930s which drove many psychoanalysts, along with other professionals, out of Europe, however, and World War II which catalyzed the Freudian influence on American psychology.

One of the most intriguing aspects about the literature on Freud is that there are so many different ways of describing his major contributions. Sundberg, Tyler, and Taplin (1973),[4] for example, state: "The most pervasive of Freud's ideas is the conception of personality as the *interplay of intrapsychic forces.*" On the other hand, Kazin (1956) writes, "Freud's extraordinary achievement was to show us, in scientific terms, the primacy of natural desire, the secret wishes we proclaim in our dreams, the mixture of love and shame and jealousy in our relations to our parents, the child as father to the man, the deeply buried instincts that make us natural beings and that go back to the forgotten struggles of the human race."[5] Murphy (1956) says, "I believe that the insights of Freud, with reference to human motivation, impulse control, reality testing...are among the most profound ever vouchsafed to an investigator."[6] Bruner (1956) believes that "Freud's contribution lies in the continuities of which he made us aware. The first of these is the continuity of organic lawfulness. Accident in human affairs was no more to be brooked as 'explanation' than accident in nature."[7] And Hacker (1956) comments in this way: "Both psychoanalysis and Marxism represent, despite all their acknowledged predecessors, fundamentally novel and original viewpoints. Intellectually seductive and appealing in their consistency and ability to pierce through random irregularities of the surface to the depth of the grandiose logic of the hidden, they share a radical distrust of appearance."[8]

In my opinion psychoanalysis influenced American society by (*a*) providing a model of man which acknowledges that, because of unconscious motivation, one can be successful and wealthy without being happy and content; (*b*) affording an intriguing new perspective on human nature for novelists, dramatists, artists, and historians; (*c*) instilling at least in the educated public a deeper concern over the rearing of children, particularly during early infancy; (*d*) creating an atmosphere which led to a new openness toward sexuality; (*e*) presenting a view of human motivation emphasizing sexual drives which stimulated consumer research and influenced the advertising industry; and (*f*) providing theoretical support for the idea that criminals, juvenile offenders, alcoholics, and drug addicts should be rehabilitated rather than punished.

The work of Dr. Benjamin Spock probably represents the most direct and far-reaching vehicle for broadcasting Freudian ideas to American society, particularly during the 1940s, 1950s, and 1960s. Ten months after the publication of the paperback edition of Dr. Spock's *The Pocket*

Book of Baby and Child Care (1946),[9] over 500,000 copies had been sold; by 1949, a million copies a year were coming off the presses; by the 1970s over 24 million copies had been purchased, making the book the world's all-time best seller after the Bible and Shakespeare.[10] It was revised in 1957, 1968, and 1976 and has been through more than 200 printings.

Obviously a book with such a wide and extensive readership[11] over a thirty-year period, particularly one on child-rearing practices, has had some effects on contemporary American society. The rebellious youth of the late sixties and the strangely unmotivated young adults of the seventies are, in fact, blamed on, or credited to, Spockian recommendations to their parents. Since the child-rearing practices advocated by Spock are based primarily on Freudian views of human development, the book was perhaps the single most important disseminator of psychoanalytic philosophy to the American people as a whole.[12] The philosophy was, incidentally, presented without using many formal Freudian concepts. Spock gave his advice in terms of ordinary everyday language; most people had no idea that the counsel he provided was largely based on Freudian prescriptions.[13]

In general, Spock agreed with the following psychoanalytic assumptions: (*a*) the infant and child are primarily directed by basic biological drives; (*b*) psychological development is a function of the interaction between genetic and social factors; (*c*) the period from birth to young adulthood involves five psychosexual states of development (oral, anal, phallic, latency, and genital); (*d*) the interpersonal activities which occur between the infant-child and the other members of the family at each stage of development are the primary determiners of adult personality; and (*e*) the resolution of the Oedipus complex is an essential part of normal psychological development. Since Spock, like Freud, believed that the sequence of human development was basically under the control of a biological (genetic) program, Spock's message to parents was to let the baby or child do things, for example, become toilet trained, when he is ready—that is, don't try to force him to do things before he is capable of doing them and before he wants to do them.[14]

Spock encouraged parents to relax and enjoy their children and to be as permissive as was practicable.[15] In his later editions, he modified his views somewhat and he now feels that parents can be too permissive. He advises that they set clear rules for their offspring and help them develop a sense of responsibility toward other people and society as a whole.

While Spock's ideas have been widely acclaimed, they have also been criticized, not only because his views of child rearing may have had something to do with producing the radical youth of the late sixties and the passive young adults of the seventies, but because his advice was mostly for middle-class Americans. Spock was also admonished by women with liberated perspectives as being sexist; he tried to remedy this fault in the 1976 edition of his book.

Overall, Spock's major contribution has probably been the humanizing of American child-rearing practices by emphasizing the built-in potential of infants and children to tell parents what they need and when they need it and by assuring parents that if they provide an atmosphere of care and love, normal psychological development will occur naturally. Freud's views provided Spock with a comprehensive theoretical basis for this prescription.

Psychoanalysis influenced psychiatry, clinical psychology, and the other psychological helping professions by providing (*a*) the first comprehensive theory of personality development and structure and neurosis; (*b*) a set of therapeutic techniques logically related to theory; (*c*) support for the idea that psychological and emotional problems can be treated by talking privately with a trained professional; and (*d*) a common psychological language. This was particularly important when clinical psychology was expanding after World War II. Everyone working in VA hospitals, for example, learned to use the concepts of id, ego, super ego, Oedipal complex, repression, and defense mechanism. This facilitated the team approach to diagnosis and therapy which evolved in the 1940s. There were, of course, also limitations to placing almost the entire therapeutic enterprise within the framework of psychoanalytic thought. As a result, new outlooks, for example, client-centered therapy, quickly emerged.

Psychoanalytic perspectives were also imported into industrial psychology by Harry Levinson, Erich Fromm, and others. The details of the Freudian influence on American psychology are presented later.

Major Freudian Assumptions

Freud's psychological writing extended over a period of more than forty years (1880s-1930s). While he modified some of his ideas as he went along, most of his basic tenets concerning personality, psychological development, psychopathology, and therapy remained fairly constant throughout his career. The most significant change he proposed in his theory of personality (and motivation) concerned human instincts. Late in his career (following World War I) he argued that there were two basic instincts instead of one. He had originally believed that all human activity was directed toward the preservation of life (the life instinct); later, however, he felt life was also characterized by a built-in tendency to self-destruct (death instinct). Most psychoanalysts prefer his original one-instinct theory.

Freud's major assumptions include the following:

a. Psychological determinism No human behavior is accidental; even dreams and slips of the tongue represent underlying continuities in personality. There is a logic and explanation for everything that we do; there is no such thing as chance behavior.

b. Unconscious processes Many of the determinants of behavior operate outside of or below consciousness; we are not fully aware of the forces controlling, or the reasons for, our behavior. These forces include repressed wishes and conflicts as well as primitive biological drives and certain aspects of ego and superego functioning.

c. Components of personality Personality consists of three processes: id (primitive biological drives which operate entirely in the unconscious); ego (processes structuring perception and thought, operating partly in consciousness and partly in the unconscious, which serve the dual function of orienting us to the real world and mediating between the id and superego); and superego (conglomerate of introjected values, "dos" and "don'ts" which, like the ego, operates both in consciousness and in the unconscious).[16] Adult behavior is always a function of the interactions among id, ego, and superego.

d. Behavior is purposive While behavior is a function of the interplay of id, ego, and superego, the overall purpose of these dynamics is to preserve the species. There is a life instinct, guided by pleasure, much of it associated with sexual activity, which provides a relentless overall purpose to human behavior.[17] We learn to be attracted to certain people, objects, and activities and repelled by others as a function of the amount of *libidinal energy* we invest. Libidinal energy (a controversial and ambiguous term) apparently provides feelings and emotions with their power and intensity. The more strongly you feel toward someone, for example, the more libidinal energy you have invested in that person.

e. Personality development is a function of the interaction between genetically-determined stages of development and experience The period from birth through adolescence is divided into five psychosexual stages (oral, anal, phallic, latency, and genital) with the first three stages characterized by the rise to eminence of a particular area of the body (mouth, anus, genitals) as the locus of pleasure. Early personality development (birth to about age five) is a function of the interplay among the child's attempts to experience pleasure, the realities of his world, and the "dos" and "don'ts" imposed upon him by his parents or parent substitutes. Each of the five states provides special challenges that must be dealt with if the child is to reach psychological adulthood after adolescence and take his place in society relatively independent of his parents and ready to start a family of his own.

f. Defense mechanisms Since the id, ego, and superego are usually in conflict, people are frequently beset with uncertainty and anxiety. Anxiety is unpleasant, and, therefore, we develop strategies to avoid and manage it. Some of these strategies, called defense mechanisms, are adopted unconsciously and include denial, repression, dissociation, regression, reaction formation, and sublimation. Neurosis can result if a person is burdened with too many unresolved childhood conflicts and is forced into an overly rigid use of particular defense mechanisms.

g. Personality differences Adult personalities vary as a function of specific infantile and childhood experiences. People are classified as oral, anal, and phallic with each type having particular preferences, predispositions, and life styles.

h. The nature of psychological inquiry Psychological inquiry must be directed toward understanding the unconscious forces (which include repressed wishes and conflicts as well as primitive biological drives) directing a person's behavior. Free association, dream analysis, and projective techniques, within the context of a one-to-one clinical setting, are the primary methods available for fruitful psychological inquiry. Experiments, group tests, and quantitative approaches to research are irrelevant insofar as psychoanalytically-oriented investigations are concerned.

i. The nature of therapy Therapy must be long-range, intensive, conducted by a trained psychoanalyst, and include a period when the patient has the same intense feelings, through a process called transference, toward the therapist that he had as a child toward his parents.

The Compatibility of Psychoanalytic and Research Psychology's Major Assumptions and Prescriptions

The behavioral orientation of American psychology is in many ways compatible with the psychoanalytic emphasis on the naturally determined nature of behavior, the functional strain of the discipline with the psychoanalytic proposition that behavior is purposive and goal directed, the Gestalt emphasis on innate, unconscious organizing tendencies and tension systems with the psychoanalytic emphasis on unconscious motivational factors, the pleasure principle, and the recognition that temporal context (for example, psychosexual stage) is relevant to behavioral and psychological development and function. Psychologists also tend to believe in the general continuity of human development from infancy through adulthood, which is perhaps the main theme of psychoanalysis. Furthermore, during the forties and fifties in particular, a comprehensive theory like psychoanalysis fit in well with the strong feeling within American psychology that all behavioral and psychological processes are interrelated and that interdisciplinary studies should be encouraged. There was, as we have previously indicated, much interest in constructing integrated theories or models of human functioning.

Psychoanalysis and mainstream American psychology tend to differ most with regard to methodological matters. Psychoanalytic research takes place primarily in the context of therapeutic sessions, while research psychologists prefer highly controlled experimental studies. In general, American psychologists with their emphasis on the study of animal behavior in contrived laboratory settings and their faith in operationally defined concepts and statistical analyses of data tend to disclaim many of the specific assumptions of psychoanalysis with regard to personality development, internal conflicts, and the nature of neurosis because they are based on *post hoc* interpretations of behavior observed in therapy sessions. In addition to the relatively uncontrolled nature of encounters between therapist and patient, there is also the danger that the expectancies of the psychoanalyst elicit the very reactions predicted by psychoanalytic theory. Psychoanalytic research is unscientific if one uses as a model for the scientific method the procedures employed by physicists and chemists, a model that many American academic-research psychologists have strongly embraced since the discipline started late in the nineteenth century.

Unfortunately most psychologists have not kept pace with changing conceptions of science and the scientific method during the last several decades. Of particular relevance is the fact that the scientific approach has become more probabilistic, supplanting to some degree the radical determinism that research psychology modeled after.

Freud envisioned psychoanalysis as the only truly scientific approach to the study of human behavior because it is based on the careful observation and interpretation of human behavior over long periods of time and assumes that natural causes underlie behavior. Experiments, he felt, with their short-run focus and concern with the measurable aspects of behavior are apt to deal with trivial rather than truly significant aspects of human life.

Both psychoanalysts and American research psychologists have been interested in creating a scientific psychology;[18] there are serious differences of opinion, however, concerning the nature of such a discipline.

Obstacles to the Importation of Psychoanalytic Thought into American Psychology prior to 1935

As indicated earlier, while Freudian ideas made a major impression on the American intellectual community and some disciplines and professions during the 1910-1930 period, the impact of psychoanalysis on American psychology was rather minimal for a variety of reasons until about the middle 1930s. To begin with, Freud was a medical doctor in private practice rather than an academician. At first his ideas were not accepted even by other medical doctors. When others did join the psychoanalytic movement, Freud and his followers tended to be viewed by most of the medical and academic community as unscientific and in some instances blasphemous and immoral. Psychoanalysis, as a movement, was almost like a secret society before World War I. The psychoanalytic perspective only gradually influenced philosophy, literature, art, the social-behavioral disciplines, and cultured society in general.

Since about 1910, applied areas like psychiatry, social work, and the mental health, child guidance, and child development movements and disciplines concerned with people in society, such as sociology, anthropology, and political science have been significantly changed by Freudian ideas. Psychoanalytic perspectives were less relevant to pre-World War II psychology which was mostly concerned with the measurement of behavior and processes like learning, perception, and sensation.

Psychologists' strong faith in experimentation, psychometrics, laboratory science, operationally defined concepts, and animal research as well as their suspicion of data and theory derived from clinical observations were the most important inhibitors of the Freudian influence in American psychology. The fact that a majority of American psychologists before the 1940s were academicians rather than applied practitioners also served to delay the impact of Freud.

Other factors that restrained the impact of Freudian thought on pre-World War II American psychology were the lack of accurate English translations of most of Freud's major works, the fact that many of Freud's writings were problem-oriented rather than systematic, and the continuing development of Freud's ideas. It was difficult, in other words, for American psychologists to know precisely what Freud had written and meant.[19] Adding to the problem was the fact that many translations and interpretations were inaccurate either because of ignorance or bias. Even today, there is a tendency to view Freud's contributions in ways that are compatible with our particular attitudes toward psychoanalysis.

The Accelerating Influence of Freudian Thought on American Psychology during the 1935-1955 Period

While there were obstacles to the importation of psychoanalytic ideas into American psychology during the first third of the twentieth century, Freudian concepts and principles did not go entirely unnoticed. Many prominent psychologists of the 1900-1940 period, for example, G. Stanley Hall, Edwin B. Holt, John B. Watson, Calvin Stone, L. L. Thurstone, Gardner Murphy, Henry A. Murray, Edna Heidbreder, Clark L. Hull, Hobart Mowrer, Neal Miller, and Robert Sears, found something positive to say about psychoanalysis.[20] But the influence of Freud within academic-research psychology was rather minimal until the late thirties.

During the 1930s and 1940s, the Freudian influence was encouraged by the expansion of clinical psychology, which was accelerated by World War II[21] and the massive government funding of graduate students and programs in clinical psychology following the war. The growth of clinical psychology magnified the Freudian influence because only Freud's theory provided a comprehensive and interrelated view of personality, neurosis, and therapy. The fact that personality had become an important area of study by the 1930s also increased the compatibility of psychoanalysis and mainstream academic psychology.

In terms of professional articles listed in the *Psychological Abstracts* from 1930 to 1975, the highest annual percentages of articles on psychoanalysis occurred during the early 1950s. From 1935 to 1945 and from 1956 to 1975, the percentages tended to hover around 2 percent; during the 1946 to 1955 period, however, the average percentage of all articles concerning psychoanalysis was slightly over 3 percent.

The Psychoanalytic Influence on American Psychology

Most of this section deals with the 1935-1955 era because it was during those two decades that American psychologists actively investigated the relevance of psychoanalytic ideas and procedures for the discipline. Psychoanalytic perspectives have, of course, continued to be manifested within psychology, particularly in courses and programs having to do with personality, abnormal psychology, and clinical psychology; even in 1975 Freud was still the most highly cited individual in the psychological literature.[22] Others within the psychoanalytic tradition who continue to be highly cited are Erik Erikson, Carl Jung, Erich Fromm, and Anna Freud.

The two most important developments within psychoanalysis during the forties and fifties were the appearance of neo-Freudianism, which emphasized cultural and interpersonal rather than biological or sexual factors in personality development, and the emergence of ego psychology, concerned with the strategies people develop to adapt to the world rather than the dynamics of intrapsychic conflicts which Freud emphasized. The neo-Freudians (Karen Horney, Erich Fromm, Erik Erikson, and Harry Sullivan)[23] generally accepted Freud's assumptions concerning psychological determinism, unconscious motivation, and the importance of childhood experience; but they took issue to varying degrees with the importance Freud placed on infantile sexuality. The ego psychologists (Anna Freud, Heinz Hartmann, Rudolph Loewenstein, Ernst Kris, and David Rapaport),[24] agreed with Freud's basic view of personality development and structure, but felt that Freud had failed to address the strategies people develop to deal with and adapt to the real world. Ego psychology was, therefore, much concerned with perceptual and cognitive styles.

Another development within psychoanalysis which had some importance for psychology was the application of Freudian ideas to the explanation and treatment of psychotic individuals. Particularly significant was the work of Frieda Fromm-Reichmann who demonstrated that psychoanalytic therapy could be done with seriously withdrawn schizophrenic patients.[25]

Perhaps the most important theoretical development within psycho-analytic thought since the early 1960s has been Ernst Kris's principle of "regression in the service of the ego." To regress in this way means to allow oneself to experience the primitive infantile part of one's psychological makeup with as few restrictions and inhibitions as possible, for creative purposes. The basic uncivilized aspect of everyone's nature is viewed as a rich source of new perspectives for the artist, poet, or novelist. One needs a strong sense of self and reality, however, in order to return from a regressed state, for entrapment there is by definition insanity.

Erikson's developmental theory, which derives from the psychoanalytic tradition, also continues to be influential. It was the first comprehensive theory of human development which dealt with the entire life span. Freud's theory, for example, encompasses only the period from birth to adulthood. Erikson's perspective contributed significantly to the recent emergence of life-span developmental psychology.

Ego psychology continues to be concerned with the identification and study of the perceptuo-cognitive strategies involved in coping with the real world. However, there have not been any apparent advances or breakthroughs in this area for some time.

The psychoanalytic model of personality and to a lesser degree Freud's model of psychopathology are still important to clinical psychology and psychiatry. Psychoanalysis as a therapy, however, has steadily declined in importance because of its questionable effectiveness, the time involved, and the cost.

Finally, there has appeared since the early 1970s a renewed interest in psychohistory, due in part to the publication of the *Journal of Psychohistory* founded by psychoanalytically-oriented scholars. There are several types of psychohistorical research, but, in general, it involves using psychological theory to analyze historical figures or historical developments.

Psychoanalytic thought influenced American academic-research psychology by enriching personality theory; stimulating child psychology; converging with and bolstering dynamic (motivational) psychology; contributing to the "new look" in psychology; providing a theory compatible with projective testing; playing a role in the research on the authoritarian personality (discussed in chapter 3); transforming abnormal psychology into a more comprehensive speciality; inspiring changes in the classification of psychological problems; and leading to the attempt on the part of Clark Hull and some of his colleagues and students (the Yale Group) to transform Freudian concepts into more precisely defined and testable behavioral terms.

The Enriching of Personality Theory by Neo-Freudian Ideas Personality was not recognized as a significant area of study within mainstream academic-research psychology until the middle 1930s. By the early forties, however, psychologists of every inclination (behaviorists, field theorists, Gestaltists, functionalists) had written on personality. Much of the research and most of the major statements on personality development emphasized social and environmental factors. With the exception of British psychologist William McDougall, psychologists largely ignored the role of heredity.

While Freud's views had an influence on personality theory during the twenties and thirties, it was the neo-Freudianism of Horney, Fromm, Erikson, and Sullivan with its cultural and interpersonal, rather than genetic, emphasis which best meshed with the American tendency to view man as a product more of his environment than his genes. Horney concentrates on our efforts to adjust to a society characterized by conflicting ideals while Fromm presents a detailed approach to the integration of social and psychological complexities. Erikson relates individual psychological development to the needs and options provided by societies and the ways individuals, particularly the young, take their places in the adult world, in the process influencing the course of history. Sullivan presents a complex theory of the emergence of a sense of self and others out of the interaction patterns occurring between infant/child and parents. Of all the neo-Freudians, Sullivan was the most seriously concerned with the world as experienced by developing human beings, including adults. In that sense he was compatible with existential psychologists and therapists, like Rollo May, Carl Rogers, and R. D. Laing.

The Stimulation of Child Psychology by Psychoanalytic Theory Freud postulated a direct relationship between infant experiences and adult personality. Moreover, he believed that biological maturation forces everyone to face the same psychological challenges in a predetermined order as we develop from infant, to child, to adult. It is natural, therefore, that psychoanalytic theory enriched child psychology and provided additional incentives for the study of children, not only in Western industrialized societies but in primitive cultures as well. Psychologists, along with sociologists and anthropologists, wanted to find out if Freud's views on the psychological dynamics of infancy and childhood and the relationships between early experience and adult personality were correct.

In order to appreciate the role played by psychoanalytic theory within child psychology, one must realize that before Freud, human development was explained either in terms of simple conditioning (J. B. Watson)[26] or in terms of the natural biologically-controlled emergence of perceptual, cognitive, and motor capabilities (A. Gesell).[27] Freud claimed that psychological development involves complex interactions between environmental and genetically controlled factors; and he offered a general formula for the nature of this interaction. Furthermore, he had a greater interest than either environmentalists like Watson or maturationists

like Gesell in the dynamics of human emotion, motivation, and personality as a whole.[28]

Particularly important in bringing the psychoanalytic orientation to
child psychology during the postwar decade was the publication starting in 1945 of the *Psychoanalytic Studies of the Child*. Founded by Anna
Freud, Erik Erikson, and other psychoanalytically inclined psychologists,
this journal published many articles on the techniques infants and children develop to cope with the environment.

The work of the Yale Group (Hull, Sears, Dollard, N. Miller, and
Mowrer) also brought psychoanalytic perspectives to bear on child psychology. While primarily behaviorists, they were interested in the integration of S-R theory and Freudian dynamics and in objectively testing
out psychoanalytic propositions. Sears believed that psychoanalysis contributed to child psychology by replacing measuring devices with human
observers, by increasing the use of projective techniques such as doll
play and finger painting in the study of children, and by inspiring cross-
cultural research. Sears was, for a while, director of the Iowa Child
Welfare Station founded in 1917 and sponsored by the Women's Christian Temperance Union. Lewis P. Lipsitt, current director of the Walter
S. Hunter Laboratory at Brown University and one of the initiators of the
newborn laboratory at the Providence Lying-In Hospital, which has since
the late fifties conducted important research on the sensory and conditioning capacities of young infants, also feels that he was much influenced by Freud's emphasis on the early childhood determinants of adult
behavior, the Freudian belief that all behavior has causes, and the Yale
Group's attempt to accomplish "a rapprochement between psychoanalytic and learning theories."[29] Finally, Albert Bandura, one of the founders
of social learning theory and an investigator of the role of imitation and
modeling in child development, says: "I was very much influenced by
the Miller and Dollard writings."[30]

The Freudian influence also extended to therapy with autistic children, for example, Bruno Bettelheim's work; the understanding and
care of severely disturbed children, for example, Fritz Redl's experiences
with "children who hate";[31] Rudolph Ekstein's work with borderline
children; and Rene Spitz's research on the impact of institutionalization
on young children. Bettelheim, Redl, Ekstein, and Spitz, however, were
not directly part of mainstream academic-research child psychology.[32]
Some of the studies on family dynamics were also generated by psychoanalytic theory.

Convergence with and Bolstering of Dynamic (Motivational) Psychology According to Edwin Boring, the famous historian of scientific psychology,
"Dynamic psychology is a field, the psychology of motivation."[33] Boring
devotes an entire chapter to the topic pointing out that dynamic psychology is not a cohesive school but rather includes theories from a

variety of orientations, in particular psychoanalysis, McDougall's hormic or purposive psychology, Tolman's purposive behaviorism, Woodworth's explicitly dynamic point of view, Lewin's field theory with its vectors and tensions, Hullian tension-reduction theory, Murray's dynamic view of personality, and the theoretical inclinations of a variety of other psychologists concerned with the problems of motivation.

Boring states: "The principal source of dynamic psychology is, of course, Freud."[34] Other antecedents of dynamic psychology, however, include activity psychology (Leibniz, Herbart, Brentano, Ward) with its emphasis on mind as process; and hedonism (Hobbes, Locke, Hartley, Bentham, James Mill, John Stuart Mill, Thorndike) with its focus on the motivational power of pleasure.

Boring also makes this interesting point: "The dynamic principle—the specific determinant of the psychological event—has been obscured under the camouflage of a diversified vocabulary,"[35] including at different times and in different contexts the concepts of attention, expectation, preparation, predisposition, set, instruction, determining tendency, attitude, instinct, drive, incentive, purpose, and need. All of these terms refer to the readiness of an organism or person to act in a certain way, and all assume that behavior is under the control of more than external stimuli. In that sense, dynamic psychology is incompatible with radical forms of behaviorism, which view behavior as being directly under the control of the environment.

The influence of psychoanalytic thought during the forties and fifties contributed to an increasing interest within American psychology in motivation. While the roots of dynamic psychology extend back to the dawn of psychological thought and certainly back to the beginning of scientific psychology in the middle of the nineteenth century, motivation as a separate field of study was slow in emerging. David McClelland, who has worked in the area for many years, said in 1955 in the preface of his edited book on motivation, "The psychology of motivation is in its infancy. In fact, it can hardly be said to exist as a separate discipline or field of study within psychology today."[36] The importance of psychoanalytic perspectives on motivation is demonstrated by the fact that fifteen of the fifty articles included in McClelland's book are psychoanalytic or psychoanalytically inclined. There are papers by Freud, Murray, Spitz, Flugel and McClelland himself; they deal mostly with unconscious motivation, the motivating aspects of sexuality, and the use of projective tests to identify various motives.

The intrusion of psychoanalysis into dynamic psychology during the forties is further illustrated by the fact that Percival Symond's widely used textbook, *Dynamic Psychology*, published in 1949, is almost entirely psychoanalytic in its organization and emphasis. By far the most references are to psychoanalysts followed by Kurt Lewin, the Yale Group excluding Hull (Dollard, N. E. Miller, Mowrer, Sears, and Doob), and Albert Maslow, who proposed a hierarchical arrangement of needs.

Another sign that interest in the study of motivation had increased significantly by the 1950s, in part because of the importation of psychoanalysis into mainstream academic-research psychology, was the publication in 1953 of the *Nebraska Symposium on Motivation*, which became an annual series. In order to maintain perspective we must remember, of course, that the increased interest in motivation during the postwar decade was also a result of other developments such as research on instincts by ethologists; drive in animals by psychologists like Harlow, Hull, and N. E. Miller; the reinforcement of behavior by selective brain stimulation (Olds); social factors and motivation (Paison, Riesman, Kardiner); and the effects of values, attitudes, and expectancies on perception and cognition (directive state research).

Psychoanalytic Influences on the "New Look" in Psychology (Directive State Theories of Perception, Perception as a Key to Personality) One of the most distinctive developments in American psychology during the postwar decade was the emergence of directive state or "new look" theories of perception. Directive state refers to any bodily process or condition, for example, a motive, value, expectancy, or past experience, which has the potential to determine or modify what we see, hear, feel, taste, smell or experience generally. "New look" referred to the assumption that perception, motivation, affect, and learning are interrelated processes or different aspects of one basic process; as a consequence, the study of individual differences in perceptual or cognitive styles (ways of organizing information about the world and ourselves) was seen as a way to study personality. Bruner and Krech's *Perception and Personality* (1949); Blake and Ramsey's *Perception: An Approach to Personality* (1951), and Witkin *et al.*, *Personality through Perception* (1954) are the primary references on the postwar "new look" in perception. F. H. Allport's *Theories of Perception and the Concept of Structure* (1955) contains three detailed chapters analyzing directive state theory.

Allport identifies six main propositions associated with directive state theories: (1) "Bodily needs tend to determine what is perceived."[37] (2) "Reward and punishment associated with the perceiving of objects tend to determine what is perceived. They also tend to determine its apparent magnitude and its speed of recognition."[38] (3) "The values characteristic of the individual tend to determine the speed with which words related to those values are recognized."[39] (4) "The value of objects to the individual tends to determine their perceived magnitudes."[40] (5) "The personality characteristics of the individual predispose him to perceive things in a manner consistent with those characteristics."[41] (6) "Verbal stimuli that are emotionally disturbing or threatening to the individual tend to require a longer recognition-time than neutral words, to be so misperceived as radically to alter their form or meaning, and to arouse their characteristic emotional reactions even before they are recognized."[42]

Also associated with directive state research are such inferred processes as perceptual defense (the tendency not to notice taboo information as easily as neutral information) and subception or subliminal perception (sensory information processing that takes place in the unconscious). Both of these processes generated much research, but the findings are still controversial.

The "new look" movement represents a serious attempt to integrate or unify three of the main concerns of academic-research psychology, namely perception, motivation, and learning. As such the development, along with the Yale Group's attempt to bring psychoanalysis and S-R theory together and the authoritarian personality researchers' effort to bring Freud and social psychology to bear on the problem of prejudice, manifested a general feeling that psychology should be unified. This outlook was generated in part by the fact that wartime projects forced professionals and specialists from different disciplines and research areas to work together; as a result, some psychologists were at least temporarily jarred loose from narrow theoretical and methodological biases. The "new look" also resulted from an interest on the part of social and clinical psychologists in exploring new, more systematic ways of studying personality.[43] Since clinical psychology was expanding dramatically in the forties and fifties, clinicians exerted more and more influence on academic-research psychology.

Krech saw as the primary catalyst or vehicle for integration the thinking of Kurt Lewin, who represented the Gestalt tradition; he also saw considerable integrative potential in Tolman's cognitive-behavioral conceptualizations.[44] Gardner Murphy, on the other hand, traces the "new look" back to psychoanalysis with its comprehensive view of personality dynamics and the development of "more sensitive instruments, such as projective tests,"[45] for the evaluation of personality.

What role did psychoanalysis play in the emergence of "new look" psychology? In the most general sense, psychoanalysis contributed to the increasing interest, starting in the 1930s among American psychologists, in the study of personality. More specifically, the psychoanalytic emphasis on unconscious or underlying directing forces (motives, values, instincts) most certainly contributed to the "new look's" focus on directive states. In addition, the Freudian concept of defense mechanisms (unconscious strategies for warding off anxiety) clearly linked perception and cognition as particular states of consciousness to directive state assumptions. Moreover, the ego psychologists' interest in identifying perceptual and cognitive styles and relating them to more general personality characteristics was an integral part of the "new look" movement. Finally, and of key importance, was the psychoanalytically inspired assumption that ambiguous stimuli like inkblots or vague pictures (projective tests) offer a systematic procedure for identifying personality structures.

Projective techniques, in particular the Rorschach inkblot test and the Thematic Apperception Test (TAT), may have been the single most important psychoanalytic contribution to "new look" psychology, though the work of the ego psychologists (most of whom were at the Menninger Clinic in Topeka, Kansas) also played a direct role. The two psychoanalytically oriented psychologists most directly involved in the "new look" movement were George S. Klein (Menninger Clinic), and Else Frenkel-Brunswik (Institute of Child Welfare, University of California). Frenkel-Brunswik was also one of the primary collaborators in the authoritarian personality research.

Returning briefly to the theme that "new look" or directive state psychology resulted from an attempt to unify research psychology and in the process make it more relevant for social and clinical psychology, it is interesting to note that James G. Miller, who in the early fifties became part of an interdisciplinary group at the University of Chicago to develop a general theory for the behavioral sciences based on systems theory,[46] was a speaker at the 1949-1950 Clinical Psychology Symposium held at the University of Texas. This symposium generated the papers comprising Blake and Ramsey's "new look" book *Perception: An Approach to Personality* (1951).

To this same volume Urie Bronfenbrenner[47] contributed a paper entitled "Toward an integrated theory of personality" that reviews the theories of Lewin, Freud, Otto Rank, McDougall, and H. S. Sullivan. Like Miller, Bronfenbrenner argues for a "systems" view of human processes and interactions, which conceives of personality as a hierarchical organization of physical systems. In order to test out this model, including many subsidiary propositions, a long-range program of research involving professionals in child development, experimental psychology, clinical psychology, social psychology, sociology, anthropology, psychiatry, and social work was initiated at Cornell University.[48] Over the years many important findings have emanated from this comprehensive study.

The Role of Psychoanalytic Thought in Projective Testing As indicated earlier, one of the major developments of the forties and fifties was the increasing use of projective techniques, particularly the Rorschach inkblots and the Thematic Apperception Test (TAT).[49] The availability of projective instruments for identifying personality characteristics, in fact, played a major role in the growth of clinical psychology during the same period. Even today projective methodologies comprise one of the main approaches to clinical diagnosis; there are now, of course, many more tests to choose from, though the TAT and Rorschach are still apparently the most widely used.[50]

Ambiguous stimuli were recognized as potential indices of human mental functioning (creativity, imagination) as far back as the sixteenth century. It was not until the early twentieth century, however, that the potential of ambiguous designs as indices of personality was explored. Credit for developing a personality test incorporating ambiguous presentations is usually given to Hermann Rorschach, a Swiss psychiatrist who published his inkblot test in 1921. Carl Jung, who at first joined Freud's group but later broke away from Freud, was at least indirectly involved in the development of the Rorschach test. Jung, in the early 1900s, had developed a word association test (a verbal projective instrument), and Rorschach worked with Jung at a mental hospital in Zurich for a few years.

Neither the Rorschach inkblots, however, nor any other test for that matter, was called a projective technique until the late 1930s when Henry Murray and Lawrence K. Frank used Freud's concept of projection to explain the way in which ambiguous stimuli serve as indices of personality. The concept of projection cast the Rorschach, the TAT, and other similar tests within the conceptual framework of psychoanalytic theory, although some psychologists, for example, Marguerite Hertz and Samuel Beck, saw the Rorschach as a useful technique for personality assessment only if it was divorced from psychoanalytic interpretations.

While not all users considered the Rorschach or the TAT as psychoanalytic tests, the enthusiastic acceptance of projective techniques during the 1940-1960 period was undoubtedly a function, at least in part, of the general waxing of the psychoanalytic influence. Aside from the fact that prominent clinicians like Bruno Klopfer and David Rapaport interpreted Rorschach results and TAT responses psychoanalytically, the Freudian emphasis on unconscious motivation and the symbolic meaning of dreams provided a compatible theoretical framework within which to view all projective testing.

The growth of clinical psychology, the increased use of projective techniques, the cresting of the psychoanalytic influence, and the emergence of directive state ("new look") theories, particularly during the period from 1940 to 1960, were all interrelated, mutually supporting developments. Psychoanalytic thought played a key role because it provided a comprehensive theoretical framework for the other developments.

The Influence of Psychoanalysis on Abnormal Psychology in the Forties and Fifties According to Roback (1955),

Abnormal psychology is not talked of so much now as in the teens of the century, when courses and textbooks on the subject were relatively plentiful. Has there been less abnormality since? That can hardly be the answer; for we know that nervous disorders have increased, or at least, they cry for help more than in the past. What has happened is that psychoanalysis has liquidated the

distinction between normal and abnormal, and, then too, clinical psychology
has established its empire, in many cases absorbing the practical phase of abnormal psychology.[51]

Psychoanalysis "liquidated the distinction between normal and abnormal" by emphasizing the role of early childhood experience rather
than heredity in personality development and by proposing that a neurotic differed from a normal person not in kind but in degree; the former
was less happy and perhaps less effective socially and on the job than
the latter only because his burden of unresolved infantile and childhood
conflicts was heavier. These conflicts remained a burden, according to
psychoanalysts, because they and the anxiety they produced could only
be kept from consciousness by an elaborate set of defense mechanisms.

The two most widely used textbooks on abnormal psychology during
the postwar decade were Robert W. White's *The Abnormal Personality*[52]
and James C. Coleman's *Abnormal Psychology and Modern Life*.[53] White's
book was clearly psychoanalytic in orientation, the 1948 edition being
strongly influenced by Karen Horney's views and the 1956 edition adding some of the perspectives of Fromm and Sullivan. It was, in fact, a
thoroughly neo-Freudian text. Coleman's book, on the other hand, while
st_ongly influenced by Freudian ideas, particularly with regard to the
neuroses, was more holistic in approach. By "holistic" is meant that man
is considered a unified whole: his biological, psychological, and sociological aspects are viewed as interrelated. While psychoanalysis is completely compatible with a holistic perspective—Freud's thinking definitely
inspired a more holistic view of man—Coleman's text went beyond
psychoanalysis to include more on situational problems, family dynamics, interpersonal relations, societal factors, and biological influences.[54]
The early editions (1948, 1956) were more explicitly psychoanalytic than
the two most recent editions (1964, 1972).

*The Influence of Psychoanalysis on the Classification of Psychological Disor-
ders* The psychoanalytic influence was also felt within abnormal and
clinical psychology by playing a role in bringing about important changes
in the psychiatric classification systems of mental and emotional disorders. While the Freudian perspective was evident within American psychiatry during the entire first half of the twentieth century and some
psychiatrists, for example, Smith Ely Jelliffe, William A. White, and, in
particular, Edward J. Kempf, devised and recommended classification
systems reflecting psychoanalytic dynamics, it was not until the late
1940s that a widely accepted taxonomy of human psychological problems indirectly incorporating Freudian views appeared.[55] William Menninger, who had long been dissatisfied with the static, disease-entity,
Kraepelinian view of psychological disorders[56] upon which the standard
classification was based and who was much influenced by both Freud

and Adolph Meyer, succeeded, while serving in the Army during World War II as chief of the Neuropsychiatry Consultants Division of the Office of the Surgeon General, in having accepted by the Army (1945), the Veterans Administration (1946), the Navy (1947) and during the late forties at least much of psychiatry in general, a system of classification which he considered to be "consistent, practical, and in line with the newer (Freudian) theories of personology and psychodynamics."[57] In 1951 the Veterans Administration formally adopted a somewhat modified version of Menninger's system, and the 1953 official classification system of the American Psychiatric Association, while rather cumbersome and still strongly emphasizing the disease model of psychological disorders, clearly bore the stamp of psychoanalytic perspectives.

The attack on static, disease-entity conceptualizations of psychological and emotional problems mounted by psychoanalysts and holistic psychiatrists and psychologists, which finally in the forties and fifties resulted in important modifications of the formal psychiatric classification system, has since then grown into an increasingly powerful challenge to some of the basic assumptions of mainstream psychiatry. Not only has the disease-medical model been criticized by psychiatrists like Thomas Szasz and the Menningers and by such psychologists as Leonard Ullman and Leonard Krasner, but the very act of placing labels on people has received strong criticism. Interestingly, behavioral, humanist, and existential social scientists have all participated in the attack which, incidentally, has been only partly effective.

During the past few years there has been a sort of backlash against nonmedical views of psychological problems. There is again much talk about chemical and other somatic "cures" of the psychoses and neuroses. The pendulum will probably swing the other way once more in a few years.

The "Yale Group's" Attempt To Transform Freudian Concepts into Testable Behavioral Language Perhaps the most systematic and influential attempt on the part of American research psychologists to integrate Freudian and behavioral psychologies was that undertaken during the late thirties and forties by the "Yale Group," the most prominent members of which were Clark Hull, Neal Miller, John Dollard, Hobart Mowrer, and Robert Sears.[58] Starting as a series of seminars organized by Hull and running from 1936 through 1943,[59] the group's efforts resulted in 1950 in the publication by Dollard and Miller of *Personality and Psychotherapy.* This book helped perpetuate within American research psychology a high level of interest in both Hullian and psychoanalytic viewpoints for the next ten years or so.

The seminars were inspired, in part, by the atmosphere generated by the Yale Institute of Human Relations which was dedicated to the integration of the behavioral and social sciences.[60] Primarily, however, the meetings reflected Hull's interest in translating the main psychoanalytic concepts into the stimulus-response (S-R) language of his theory of conditioning and learning. Hull, even when it became apparent that such a transformation was going to be difficult, continued to feel with regard to psychoanalysis that "there is something important in that theory."[61,62] Hull had integrated, to his satisfaction, Pavlov's reflexology with Thorndike's law of effect. This integration provided Hull's theory with the motivational processes necessary to make conditioning more than a random, push-button affair. Pavlov's theory seemed to imply that the reflex arc alone could account for all learning; anything consistently associated with a reflexive action, it was argued, would become conditioned—that is, capable of eliciting the response. But how, Hull asked, could this indiscriminate modification of behavior help an organism survive? Hull believed that conditioning had to be a function of motivational states (hunger, thirst, etc.) as well as reflexive actions. Motivation, in other words, gave conditioning some direction.[63]

In any case, Hull's concern with the motivational aspects of his theory, as well as his previous interest in hypnosis and a general desire to transform other major theories into more testable Hullian concepts and principles, resulted in the aforementioned seminars.

While the importation of psychoanalysis into American research psychology was facilitated even in the late 1930s and throughout the 1940s by the work of some of the members of the Yale Group, in particular Sears and Miller, the most significant manifestation of the group's work in terms of generating interest in Freud's ideas among American research psychologists was the publication of Dollard and Miller's *Personality and Psychotherapy*.[64] The subtitle proclaimed that the contents represented "An analysis in terms of learning, thinking, and culture"; the book was, however, dedicated to "Freud and Pavlov and their students."

Dollard and Miller indicate that the main purpose of the book was to "attempt to aid in the creation of a psychological base for a general science of human behavior,"[65] by bringing together psychoanalysis, the work of Pavlov, Thorndike, Hull and other experimentalists, and modern social science with its emphasis on social variables. They state, "The ultimate goal is to combine the vitality of psychoanalysis, the rigor of the natural-science laboratory, and the facts of culture."[66]

They proposed that the study of psychotherapy should be encouraged because it provided a sort of "window to mental life"[67] and personality. The person in therapy was seen as being more motivated than a nontroubled "normal" individual to talk honestly for a long period of time about his past, his problems, and his outlooks. Therefore, clinical data was viewed as a rich source of information about personality. Dollard and Miller selected the Freudian approach to therapy and the psychoanalytic theory of personality and personality disorders because the psychoanalysts "have advanced the most fruitful hypotheses which exist in the field."[68] What they believed needed to be done was to transform the data, concepts, and speculations of psychoanalysis into the language of systematic learning theory and into the form of hypotheses that could be tested experimentally. They were particularly interested in detailed analyses of neuroses and the process of psychotherapy as practiced by psychoanalysts.

An examination of the book's general structure indicates that much of what is said about the development and rearing of infants and children, as well as the nature of neurosis and the therapeutic process, is based on Freudian thought. The actual transformation of psychoanalytic concepts into what Dollard and Miller considered to be more experimentally testable terms included: (a) replacing Freud's pleasure principle with the principle of reinforcement; (b) substituting for the broad concept of ego strength exact descriptions of the higher mental processes, learned drives and skills that relate a person to the world; (c) defining the mechanism of repression as "the inhibition of cue-producing responses which mediate thinking and reasoning";[69] (d) conceptualizing the therapeutic process of transference as an example of generalization; (e) explaining intrapsychic conflict in terms of basic learning principles; and (f) specifying more precisely than Freudian theory the nature of reality in terms of physical and social variables. While these transformations did lead to more testable hypotheses (mostly with animals), psychoanalysts generally believed that the original meaning of much of Freud's thinking was lost or distorted in the process.[70]

Whether or not Dollard and Miller succeeded in integrating psychoanalysis and the predominantly Hullian learning theory of the 1940s and 1950s, however, is not as significant as the fact that their efforts represented a serious attempt to legitimize Freud for experimental psychologists. The attempt itself clearly contributed to the rise in importance of psychoanalytic thought within mainstream academic-research psychology during the postwar decade.

5

THE HULLIAN ERA (1940-1960)

Period of Primary Influence

In his article, "On Skinner and Hull: a Reminiscence and Projection," (1977) Guttman has commented,

While it is unlikely that anyone who has followed recent American psychology would doubt the dual fact of the rise of Skinner and the decline of Hull, some hard data may add conviction. If one tabulates references in the *Journal of Experimental Psychology* to Clark L. Hull, together with references to his closest systematic collaborator Kenneth W. Spence, one finds the following enumeration by decades: in 1940, 4% of the 107 papers published refer to one or the other of these men. By 1950, 7 years after the publication of Hull's *Principles of Behavior*, the figure is a remarkable 39% of 86 papers. By 1960 the peak influence had passed and the figure is 24% (N = 131), and in 1970 it is back to 4% (N = 196).[1]

Hull's importance within American psychology during the fifties is also reflected by the fact that from 1951 through 1961 the terms "Hull" and "Hullian" were included as major headings in the index of *Psychological Abstracts*. The *Abstracts* list all the psychological books and articles published in major journals each year along with brief summaries.

Melvin Marx, in his book *Learning: Theories* (1970), reiterates the same theme when he states: "[T]he Hull-Spence approach was undoubtedly the major force evident in general behavior theory within psychology throughout the late 1940s and the early 1950s."[2]

Biographical Sketch

Clark L. Hull (1884-1952) was an American psychologist best known for trying to develop a comprehensive theory of behavior based on experimental research, formal logic, and mathematical modeling. Brought up in a log cabin in Michigan, he attended a one-room school and

aspired to a practical profession such as mining engineering. He con-
tracted poliomyelitis, however, and was forced to prepare for a less
physically demanding occupation. Inspired by William James's famous
textbook, *Principles of Psychology*, he decided to become a psychologist.
He received his Ph.D. in 1916 from the University of Wisconsin and
upon graduation joined the faculty of that institution. Hull remained at
the University of Wisconsin until 1929 when he accepted an appointment at Yale University in the Institute of Psychology. The year prior to
going to Yale he had served as visiting lecturer at Harvard teaching a
course in aptitude testing.

Hull's professional interests were diverse. In 1920 he published a book
on the evolution of concepts, followed in 1924 by a volume on the
influence of smoking tobacco on mental and motor efficiency. In 1928 his
book on aptitude testing brought him an invitation from Harvard to
serve as visiting lecturer. Then in 1933 he wrote a book on hypnosis and
suggestibility.

His most influential work, however, centered around the application
of the mathematico-deductive approach to behavioral phenomena. This
effort led first to a book on rote learning entitled *Mathematico-Deductive
Theory of Rote Learning* (1940),[3] followed by three books on a general
theory of behavior (*Principles of Behavior*, 1943;[4] *Essentials of Behavior*,
1951;[5] and *A Behavior System*, 1952).[6]

Hull's Theory

The mathematico-deductive approach to theory building involves identifying the best substantiated facts of a particular research area (Hull, for
example, first selected rote learning because the phenomenon had been
vigorously researched for many years), creating appropriate concepts
and postulates, and then deriving, mathematically, if possible, specific
hypotheses to test experimentally. If the hypotheses are supported by
experimental data, they and the postulates originally generating them
are retained. If the hypotheses are not supported by experimental data,
then the relevant postulates are modified or eliminated. As we have
indicated before, this approach involves careful experimentation, formal
logic, and the mathematical expression of relationships, procedures that
are at the heart of a classical, but somewhat idealized, view of the scientific method.

Hull described his approach as follows:

I came to the definite conclusion around 1930 that psychology is a true natural
science; that its primary laws are expressible quantitatively by means of a mod-
erate number of ordinary equations; that all the complex behavior of single
individuals will ultimately be derivable as secondary laws from (1) these primary

laws together with (2) the conditions under which behavior occurs; and that all the behavior of groups as a whole, i.e., strictly social behavior as such, may similarly be derived as quantitative laws from the same primary equations. With these and similar views as a background, the task of psychologists obviously is that of laying bare these laws as quickly and accurately as possible, particularly the primary laws.[7]

Hull's most influential book was *Principles of Behavior* (1943). In this work he confidently presented his mathematico-deductive theory of behavior, which was based on the ideas of Pavlov (the famous Russian psychologist who conditioned salivating dogs), Thorndike (a prominent American learning theorist in the early part of this century), and Darwin (a British naturalist famous for his monumental theory of evolution).

Ivan Pavlov (1849-1936), the Russian physiologist whose conditioning research so much influenced not only Hull but American psychology in general, wrote (1903), "In observing the normal working of the salivary glands one cannot but be amazed by the high degree of adaptability."[8] He noticed that when a dog is given dry food, he salivates profusely; but if given liquid food, he salivates only a little. Pavlov also observed that dogs will salivate to all sorts of external objects associated with their food—for example, the food bowl, the room they are fed in, the people who bring the food, or the sound of the footsteps of the food bearers. He decided, therefore, to study the process whereby formerly neutral stimuli became associated with the salivary reflex; in doing so, he devised the procedure that became known as classical conditioning. As Skinner has said, "Pavlov was a specialist in conditioned salivation."[9]

A dog was prepared for classical conditioning by first performing minor surgery to divert the salivary duct to the outside so the saliva could be collected and measured; the subject animal was then placed in a restraining apparatus located in a room shielded from extraneous noise. Typically, Pavlov or one of his assistants would then present a neutral stimulus like a light which produced no salivation. Immediately afterwards the dog would be given some food which, of course, produced copious salivation. Light-followed-by-food would be presented repeatedly until the light alone made the dog salivate. This basic paradigm for classical conditioning may be depicted as follows:

Light $\longrightarrow$ Food $\longrightarrow$ salivation

(repeated until)

Light $\longrightarrow$ salivation

Classical conditioning represents a relatively unambiguous stimulus-response (S-R) process. The phenomenon is sometimes referred to as stimulus substitution in that a formerly neutral stimulus is made to substitute for the original unlearned stimulus in producing the response. Classical conditioning usually involves reflexive rather than voluntary behavior.

One of the reasons Pavlov's work influenced Hull was because of Pavlov's theoretical explanations of classical conditioning. Hull was in particular influenced by Pavlov's concept of delayed or trace conditioned reflexes. Hull's attempt to apply the hypothetico-deductive approach to rote learning was, in fact, triggered by the suggestion in 1931 by William M. Lepley, then a graduate student, that Ebbinghaus's concept of excit-atory tendencies in rote learning was identical with Pavlov's delay or trace conditioned reflexes.[10] The concept of trace refers to physiological activities, brought about by a stimulus, which continue after the offset of the stimulus. Both Pavlov and Hull believed that this process pro-vided an associative link with the response that follows. This concep-tion, or some variant of it, forms the very basis of all S-R theories.

Edward Lee Thorndike (1874-1949), an influential American learning theorist particularly during the first third of this century, derived what he called the "law of effect" from his studies of animals, primarily chickens and cats, in puzzle boxes. In a typical puzzle box (really a pen with a top) experiment, a cat would be given the opportunity to escape and get to a bowl of food by clawing a rope or pushing a bobbin. The law of effect states:

Of several responses made to the same situation, those which are accompanied or closely followed by satisfaction to the animal will, other things being equal, be more firmly connected with the situation, so that when it recurs, they will be more likely to recur; those which are accompanied or closely followed by dis-comfort to the animal will, other things being equal, have their connections with that situation weakened, so that when it recurs, they will be less likely to occur. The greater the satisfaction or discomfort, the greater the strengthening or weak-ening of the bond.[11]

Hull admitted that one of his key formulations, the law of primary reinforcement, "is closely related"[12] to Thorndike's law of effect. Hull's law states (symbols removed): "[W]henever a reaction takes place in temporal contiguity with an afferent receptor impulse resulting from the impact upon a receptor of a stimulus energy, and this conjunction is followed closely by the diminution in a need (and the associated diminu-tion in the drive, and in the drive receptor discharge), there will result an increment in the tendency for that stimulus on subsequent occasions to evoke that reaction."[13]

Hull's theory was dependent for empirical verification mostly on exper-iments done with white rats in mazes at Yale University. Hilgard and Bower, in their widely used learning text, describe the procedure as follows:

In experiments we measure environmental influences upon the organism (the input), and then measure the organism's responses (the output). These measures provide firm anchorage for the data in the environment, where objectivity can be achieved and maintained. Input and output are not comprised exclusively of the experimentally studied stimuli and responses. Other influences upon the organism can be treated as experimental variables, such as prior history of training, deprivation schedules, injection of drugs, and these influences can be described as objectively as stimuli and responses. What goes on inside the organism we have to infer, and in the course of making these inferences we postulate certain *intervening variables* or *symbolic constructs*. If we tie these inferences firmly to the input-output terms by way of quantitative mathematical statements, we lose nothing in objectivity, and gain something in convenience, understanding, and fertility of deducing new phenomena.[14]

In general terms, Hull's theory states that certain characteristics of responses such as their latency and amplitude depend on the number of prior reinforcements (number of times a stimulus and response occurred together previously when a drive stimulus was reduced), drive, stimulus intensity, amount of reward, strength of habit, and work involved in responding. To account for the observed relationships between input variables and responses, Hull inferred a myriad of interrelated internal processes (intervening variables) including habit strength ($S^H R$), drive (D), stimulus-intensity dynamism (V), incentive motivation (K), reactive inhibition ($^I R$), reaction potential ($S^E R$) and so forth. It is one thing, of course, to identify variables that influence behavior and another to generate meaningful and valid equations involving such variables. For example, Hull believed that the effect of drive or drive stimuli like pain and pleasure on habit strength was multiplicative, that is, that the relationship between habit strength ($S^H R$) and drive (D) was expressed by the formula $S^H R \times D$. On the other hand, inhibitory effects, caused by responding or conditioning were, Hull proposed, subtractive; that is, they tended to reduce the probability of a particular response occurring.

Influence of Hull's Theory

Hull's theory was influential because it provided an almost limitless supply of hypotheses to test experimentally. Psychologists concerned with the learning processes were naturally interested in working out the many implications of the theory, and graduate students found it easy to derive dissertation research topics from Hullian theory.

What were these studies about? The following represents a sampling of research articles appearing in the 1950 volume of the *Journal of Experimental Psychology* (the most important journal in experimental psychology at that time) which were generated by Hullian theory: "A combination of primary appetitional need with primary and secondary emotionally derived needs"; "Reactive inhibition as a factor in maze learning: I. The work variable"; "Acquisition of a simple spatial discrimination as a function of the amount of reinforcement"; "Studies in motivation and learning: II. Thirsty rats trained in a maze with food but no water, then run hungry"; "An experimental test of the selective principle of association of drive stimuli"; "A study of simple learning under irrelevant motivational-reward conditions"; and "The effect upon level of consummatory response of the addition of anxiety to a motivational complex."

Although Hull died in 1952, his influence continued not only because of the many investigators who tested out his assumptions but also because of the work of a small number of creative and prolific "Hullians." Foremost among these were Kenneth Spence (1907-1967), who was Hull's chief advocate even though he modified Hull's theory considerably; Neal Miller (1909-   ), whose research on conflict, motivation, and, more recently, biofeedback was originally inspired by Hull; Hobart Mowrer (1907-   ) who proposed a two-factor learning theory (sign learning and solution learning) taking Hull's views into account; Janet Taylor Spence (1923-   ), who developed a widely used manifest-anxiety scale inspired by the Hull-Spence views of drive; John Wolpe (1915-   ), a clinical psychologist who developed a technique based on Hullian theory for desensitizing people to anxiety-producing situations; Albert Bandura (1925-   ), whose social-learning theory has roots in Hull's ideas; Leonard Berkowitz (1926-   ), whose research on frustration and aggression derives from a Hullian framework; and Robert Zajonc (1923-   ), who has employed the Hull-Spence habit strength model to account for social facilitation effects. Hull's attempt to express mathematically the relationship among those variables he hypothesized as interceding between stimuli and responses also inspired others (for example, Estes, Bush, Mostellar) to build mathematical models of certain behavioral processes. Of lesser scope than Hull's work, these attempts were, nevertheless, in the spirit of Hull.

In 1936, at Yale, Hull organized an open seminar with the help of Miller, Mowrer, and John Dollard, a sociologist, to discuss, according to Boring et al., "the essential identities lying in conditioned reflexes and behavior laws generally on the one hand, and, on the other, in the phenomena considered by Freud and his psychoanalytic associates."[15] Dollard and Miller eventually wrote a book entitled *Personality and Psychotherapy*[16] in 1950 which did much to legitimize psychoanalysis for experimental psychologists. (See chapter 4 on Freud for more details.)

Spence's role in perpetuating Hullian psychology was particularly important because his contributions, more so than anyone else's, as Howard Kendler has observed, "can be viewed as a continuation and extension of Hull's work."[17] However, Spence was more of an experimentalist than Hull. Spence preferred to study intensively discrete phenomena and was less concerned than Hull with devising a comprehensive theory of behavior. He is known particularly for his careful analysis of Hullian and other learning theories, his theory of discrimination learning, his elaboration of Hull's fractional anticipatory response concept[18] to bridge some of the differences between his and Tolman's theoretical perspectives, and his eyelid conditioning research.

According to Sigmund Koch, editor of the seven volume series *Psychology: A Study of a Science*, who by the early 1950s became one of Hull's strongest critics (Koch, 1954),[19] Hull's contributions include (*a*) clarifying the role of scientific theory for psychologists; (*b*) recognizing the complexity of psychological phenomena (other S-R theorists tended to oversimplify); (*c*) providing many useful hypotheses to test; and (*d*) improving experimental design. What he did not do, Koch pointed out, was to develop a comprehensive theory of behavior.

In a more practical vein, Hull's theory was important because it provided psychologists and graduate students with a rich source of research ideas at a time when the discipline was undergoing vigorous growth.

By the early sixties, however, most psychologists had lost interest in the specifics of Hullian theory because the system was cumbersome, imprecise, and failed to predict behavior in many situations. Even those who claimed to be Hullians recognized that Hull did not develop a workable theory of behavior; what they still held to were one or another specific hypothesis and perhaps an approach to research inspired by Hull's work.

Other Neobehavioral Learning Theories

Hull's theory of learning was by no means the only formulation of consequence during the 1940s and 1950s. The behavioral theories of Edward Tolman, Edwin Guthrie, and B. F. Skinner were of considerable significance at that time. Hull, Tolman, Guthrie, and Skinner, in fact, are all referred to as neo-behaviorists, following in the tradition of Thorndike and Watson.[20] In addition, Wolfgang Köhler's Gestalt view of learning, which emphasized perceptual and cognitive restructuring (insight) rather than conditioning, provided psychologists with an important alternate view of the learning process. (See chapter 7 for more on Gestalt psychology.)

Purposive behaviorism, the theory advanced by Edward Tolman (1886-1959), was a blend of behavioral, cognitive, and functional orientations. This approach was behavioral in the sense that he rejected introspection as a method, believing, instead, in the observation of people and animals. It was cognitive because he believed that learning involved the formation of cognitive maps rather than stimulus response bonds. (He was influenced by Gestalt theory.) It was functional, Hilgard and Bower note, because he "recognized that behavior is regulated in accordance with objectively determined ends."[21] Unlike Hull, Tolman further believed that learning was not dependent on reinforcement (drive, or drive stimulus reduction). Tolman, in other words, was a contiguity theorist rather than a reinforcement theorist. According to Tolman, information became associated with repeated exposure whether or not reinforcement occurred.

Edwin Guthrie (1886-1959) proposed only one law of learning, namely: "A combination of stimuli which has accompanied a movement will on its recurrence tend to be followed by that movement."[22] Like Tolman, he believed that learning is not dependent on reinforcement. He furthermore proposed that: "A stimulus pattern gains its full associative strength on the occasion of its first pairing with a response."[23] His position seems to ignore the fact that in learning and conditioning the acquisition of a response is stepwise, frequently taking many trials. For Guthrie, however, the stimuli involved in learning were not those presented by experimenters; rather they were the events produced within organisms by the movement of animals or people in the context of new situations. Like Watson, Guthrie was concerned with patterns of muscle movements rather than the outcomes of particular activities.

For a discussion of Skinner's orientation, see chapter 6.

Overview of Neobehaviorism

To summarize, the period of neobehaviorism in American psychology extends from about the late 1920s until the beginning of the 1960s. Guthrie was the earliest of the neobehaviorists, followed by Tolman, Hull, and Skinner. Hull's influence was greatest from around the early 1940s until the late 1950s. His most serious rival in the 1940s was probably Tolman, but eventually (by the 1960s) Skinnerian behaviorism became predominate.

Neobehaviorism has its immediate roots in the work of John B. Watson (1878-1958) and Edward L. Thorndike (1874-1949), who together represent the period of "classical behaviorism" in American psychology. Watson, in turn, was strongly influenced by the conditioning research of Pavlov. The entire behaviorist and neobehaviorist movement was, in part, a revolt against mentalistic psychology which was based on introspective analyses of consciousness and which saw animal research as irrelevant to psychology.

Bolstering the neobehaviorist orientation during the 1930-1960 period was the introduction of operationism into American psychology by Tolman and others.[24] Operationism in essence proclaims that wherever possible only concepts definable in terms of observable operations should be employed in science. Traditional concepts like mind, consciousness, will, and feeling, therefore, are relegated from psychology because they do not refer to observables. Stimulus, response, hunger, thirst, and so forth are legitimate concepts in the context of operationism but only if an experimenter publicly links them to performed operations.

Overview of Behaviorism in General

The behaviorist movement in psychology can be divided somewhat arbitrarily into the following periods: classical behaviorism (1900-1930), neobehaviorism (1930-1959), Skinnerian behaviorism (1960-1969), and cognitive behaviorism (1970-present). Behaviorism really started formally, however, in 1913 when John B. Watson, a psychologist disillusioned with traditional psychology, proclaimed that human and animal behavior, rather than mind and consciousness studied introspectively, were the only legitimate concern of psychologists. Behaviorism in its most general sense is, therefore, defined as an orientation based on the idea that psychology is the study of the behavior of animals and people rather than the study of mind and/or consciousness.

The behaviorist does "third person" research, observing the behavior of other people and animals and reporting what they did. Conversely, the mentalist, that is, the psychologist who studies mind or consciousness introspectively, examines his or her own experiences and reports "I saw this" or "I felt that." The mentalist, in short, does "first person" research.

While behaviorists generally share the common belief that psychologists should investigate behavior and avoid introspection, there are many different types of behaviorists. Some believe only in describing what they and their subjects do, (for example, Skinner), others advocate the search for comprehensive theories (for example, Hull), and still others concentrate on working out miniature systems (for example, Spence, Estes, Miller). There are also those who try to bridge the gap between behavioral and physiological activities (for example, Karl Pribram), and increasingly some who, as Tolman did, work within the framework of a cognitive behaviorism (for example, Albert Bandura).

Conclusion

Hull's major contribution to behaviorism and psychology in general was to attempt to apply the hypothetico-deductive method to behavior; in the process he created a framework that served as a catalyst for much fruitful research. Critics who feel that Hull's attempt to construct a comprehensive behavior theory set psychology back a number of years ignore the Zeitgeist of the 1930s and 1940s which was characterized by a tremendous enthusiasm for applying the scientific method in all its forms to psychological problems. Within that Zeitgeist it was natural that someone would proselytize for a mathematico-deductive approach to psychology.

6

THE RISE OF SKINNERIAN BEHAVIORISM

Skinner's Fame

Burrhus F. Skinner is without question the most famous American psychologist in the world. He is, for example, the only post-World War II psychologist to be featured on the cover of *Time* magazine.[1] He is also the only U.S. psychologist included in Robinson's book, *The 100 Most Important People in the World Today*.[2] Furthermore, a 1975 survey of American college students indicated that he is the best known of all U.S. scientists.[3] Finally, American psychologists see his work as the most important contribution within psychology during the post-World War II (1945-1978) period.[4] Norman Guttman in his review of Hull and Skinner states: "Skinner has become a symbol; he has become more than himself. Skinner is, as it were, the leading figure in a myth already made in the popular imagination and awaiting a new occupant. He has succeeded to the role of the scientist-hero, the Promethean fire-bringer, the master technologist and instructor of technologists."[5] Striking a similar theme, David Cohen in his introduction to an interview with Skinner writes: "Whatever psychologists think of Professor Burrhus Skinner's work, he has become something of a legend."[6]

Rise to Prominence

As indicated in chapter 5 on the Hullian influence, Skinner's rise to prominence in American psychology became clearly apparent by the early 1960s. In 1958, a new publication, *Journal of the Experimental Analysis of Behavior*, appeared. It specialized in Skinner's type of research. A second such journal, the *Journal of Applied Behavior Analysis*, followed in 1968. It publishes papers concerned with applications of operant conditioning procedures in the context of real-world settings. Both journals helped widen Skinner's influence. A look at the *Psychological Abstracts* also shows that Skinnerian research articles increased dramatically in 1959, the first year following the publication of the *Journal of the Experimental Analysis of Behavior*.

Skinner's influence had also spread to other disciplines by the middle sixties. As Guttman demonstrates, for example, the number of entries under the headings *reinforcement* and *behavior modification* in the *Education Index* increased significantly from about 1964 to 1974.[7] During the last fifteen years or so, Skinner's ideas and procedures, largely through the behavior modification movement which is discussed later, impacted upon all professions engaged in changing human behavior. Operant conditioning techniques have been tried with criminals, retardates, psychotics, alcoholics, juvenile delinquents, neurotics, autistic children, the physically handicapped, as well as with so-called normal children and adults. The procedures have, in fact, been implemented in every type of institution from jails to kindergartens.

Skinner became known to college students in general during the turbulent late sixties not only because many of them took at least one introductory course in psychology but because his novel *Walden Two* (1948),[8] describing life in a fictional small utopian society (commune) based on operant conditioning principles, was assigned reading in a variety of courses on campuses all over the country. *Beyond Freedom and Dignity* (1971),[9] wherein he describes the behavioral engineering techniques now available for the alleged betterment of society, further brought Skinner's ideas to the attention of the educated public. His most recent nontechnical book, *About Behaviorism* (1974),[10] along with his two-volume autobiography,[11] have also helped make Skinner a household word, at least among college graduates.

Background

Skinner (1904-) grew up in the Pennsylvania railroad town of Susquehanna. His father was a lawyer, his mother was "bright and beautiful," and his homelife "warm and stable."[12] He attended the same school for all twelve years and graduated from high school with seven other classmates. As a child, he enjoyed building things (wagons, sleds, rafts, bows and arrows, model airplanes), and he liked school.

Skinner majored in English literature at Hamilton College in New York State where he acquired a fairly typical liberal arts education. As an undergraduate, he aspired to become a writer. Within about a year after graduating from Hamilton, however, during which time he lived in Greenwich Village and then Europe, he decided that his attempts at a literary career were a failure because he felt he had nothing important to say.

He became interested in psychology after reading Pavlov's *Conditioned Reflexes* and Bertram Russell's *Philosophy*. Russell's critique of Watsonian behaviorism inspired Skinner to read Watson's *Behaviorism* and *Psychological Care of Infant and Child*, a book by Watson that was used by many Americans in the 1930s as a child-rearing guide.

Skinner enrolled in the graduate program in psychology at Harvard University in 1928 fully convinced even then that a behavioral approach to psychological inquiry was what he wanted to pursue. He got little support at Harvard for his point of view but doggedly set out to study the reflex that soon included operant as well as respondent behavior.[13] He was awarded the Ph.D. in 1931 and stayed on at Harvard until 1936 conducting research while supported by fellowships. During the period 1930 through 1936 at Harvard, he published twenty papers on his research, many of them in the prestigious *Proceedings of the National Academy of Science*. These papers, plus two published in 1937, formed the basis of his first book, *The Behavior of Organisms* (1938).[14]

In 1936 he took a faculty position at the University of Minnesota where he remained until 1945 at which time he accepted the chairmanship of the psychology department at the University of Indiana. He stayed at Indiana until 1948, then returned to Harvard University as a regular faculty member. He has been at Harvard ever since.

Professional Publications

Skinner's professional career extends from about 1930 to the present. His major technical publications in addition to *The Behavior of Organisms* include *Science and Human Behavior* (1953), *Verbal Behavior* (1957), *Schedules of Reinforcement* (1957) coauthored by C. B. Ferster, *Cumulative Record* (1959), *The Analysis of Behavior* (1961) written with James G. Holland, *The Technology of Teaching* (1968), and *Contingencies of Reinforcement: A Theoretical Analysis* (1969).[15]

Skinner considers *Verbal Behavior* his most important professional publication because it represents a systematic attempt to apply operant conditioning principles to a complex real-world human activity. Linguist Noam Chomsky's critique of this book is discussed later in this chapter.

Orientation

Both Hull and Skinner as behaviorists, or more accurately neobehaviorists, have shared a belief in studying behavior rather than mind and consciousness; and the work of both is in the tradition of Pavlov, Watson, and Thorndike. Also both have believed that "[s]cientific progress would be further facilitated. . . [if] 'simple' phenomena such as classical and instrumental conditioning were studied first."[16]

Hull and Skinner, however, have differed radically in their approaches to the study of behavior. Hull, as we have seen (chapter 5), recognized the importance of careful observation and experimentation, but placed high priority on deducing hypotheses from general postulates. Skinner, on the other hand, in the spirit of Francis Bacon,[17] emphasized the careful observation of behavior coupled with cautious induction. Skinner pointed out that the behavioral phenomena one observes are never wrong; only hypotheses, principles, postulates, and theories can be in error.

From Pavlov, Skinner learned that if you "control the environment. . . you will see order in behavior."[18] Insofar as Thorndike is concerned, Skinner admits that he was merely carrying on Thorndike's puzzle-box experiments. What Skinner has called operant conditioning is virtually identical with Thorndike's concept of instrumental conditioning. (See chapter 5 on Hull for more about Thorndike.) Skinner also believes that Tolman's concept of intervening variable, that is, an abstraction linking a stimulus and a response, is similar to what he (Skinner) had referred to in his thesis as a "third" variable.

In addition, Skinner has been opposed to linking behavior with physiological processes or changes. In the first place, he feels that not enough is known about the physiological correlates of behavior to make such a linkage possible, and secondly he points out that invoking physiological or pseudo-physiological concepts to explain behavior is usually no more enlightening than ascribing behavioral changes to mind, soul, feelings, thoughts, or other nebulous entities. Skinner does not believe that feelings and other mentalistic states are nonexistent as is sometimes thought; he states, for example: "I have no hesitation in saying I feel my own body, I feel happy, I feel tired, I feel exhausted, I feel cheerful. But I don't behave in any way *because* of my feelings. . . . Feelings are by-products of behavior."[19]

Operant conditioning

Skinner first used the concept of "operant" in his reply in 1937 to two Polish physiologists, Konorski and Miller, who had challenged some of Skinner's earlier work.[20] The function of the term, according to Skinner, is "to identify behavior traceable to reinforcing contingencies rather than to eliciting stimuli."[21] Since all of Skinner's major contributions derive from his work on operant conditioning, let us examine this phenomenon or procedure in some detail. In the process, operant is differentiated from Pavlovian (classical, respondent) conditioning, discussed in chapter 5 on Hull.

By the time Skinner started his experimental work in the late 1920s, it had been well demonstrated by other researchers that Pavlovian conditioning was an effective technique for associating reflexive behavior with formerly neutral stimuli such as bells, buzzers, and lights. When, in 1930, Skinner proposed that some behavior was not elicited by specific stimuli, as is the case in classical conditioning, he was roundly criticized by Konorski and Miller, who believed that all learning involved classical conditioning.

According to Skinner, "An operant is an identifiable part of behavior of which it may be said, not that no stimulus can be found that will elicit it...but that no correlated stimulus can be detected upon occasions when it is observed to occur. It is studied as an event appearing spontaneously with a given frequency."[22]

Most behavior, particularly human behavior, then, is of the operant type; that is, it is behavior that is not caused by specific antecedent stimuli. A teenager turning on his stereo, a parent going to work, a dog begging for food, or a rat pushing a bar in a Skinner box (see picture on page 102) are all examples of behavior which is not automatically and regularly elicited by a particular stimulus but which is maintained instead by the consequences produced. The relevant stimulus in operant conditioning follows the response; it is the change in the environment, the consequence of an action, which maintains the behavior rather than a preceding stimulus.

Any consequence that increases the probability of a response occurring in the future is called a reinforcer. The basic formula for operant conditioning is simply:

$$R \text{ (response)} \longrightarrow S \text{ (reinforcer)}$$

In general, then, operant conditioning entails selecting a particular voluntary (non-reflexive) behavior and, by controlling the consequences, increasing the frequency of that behavior. Ideally, the person doing the conditioning has complete control over the consequences in the sense that food, drink, social reward, etc., occur only when the desired behavior is produced. In research, the organism to be conditioned is usually deprived of the reinforcer prior to conditioning in order to facilitate the reinforcing properties of the consequences. Abraham Maslow, an important humanistic psychologist, has defined behavioral psychology as the study of semistarved rats.

Operant conditioning can involve either positive or negative reinforcement. While the goal of conditioning is always to increase the frequency of a response, the use of positive reinforcement entails providing a reward when the desired behavior is emitted. Negative reinforcement, on the other hand, allows the person or animal being conditioned the opportunity to avoid or escape from an aversive stimulus such as electric shock by performing the desired behavior. Punishment, which is not a conditioning procedure, also involves aversive stimuli; but the goal of punishment is to reduce the frequency of a particular response by presenting the electric shock or other painful stimulus whenever the undesirable behavior occurs.

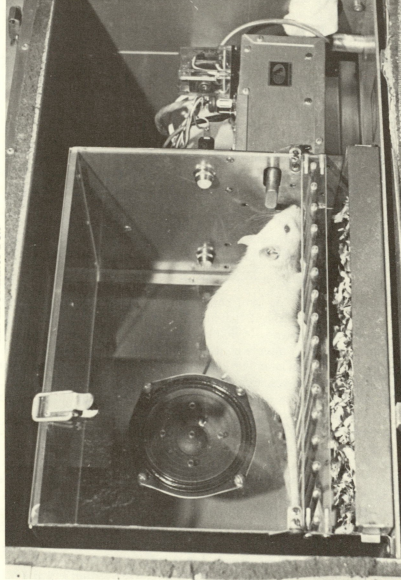

Illustration 1.
Rat in Skinner Box

It is also possible to vary the schedule of reinforcement. A rat may, for example, be required to press a bar five times before food appears (ratio schedule); or the reinforcer may appear on the average every ten seconds provided the bar has been pressed during each interval (interval schedule).

The basic R——> S (reinforcer) procedure may be rendered more complicated by making the appearance of the reinforcer following the response contingent upon some antedating stimulus: A pigeon, for instance, may be given a food pellet only if it pecks at a spot in a Skinner Box after a small light (discriminative stimulus, S^D) has gone on. The paradigm then becomes:

$$S^{D(light)} \; R \text{————}> S^{\,(reinforcer)}$$

Or conditions may be arranged so that the reinforcer appears only when a response is given after the onset of a red light instead of an orange light. The animal must make a discrimination before it is reinforced.

These and other modifications have made operant procedures useful in the study of the sensory and perceptual capabilities of animals and human infants. Infants, of course, are not able to tell us directly whether or not they can perceive the difference between a red and an orange light, or a square and a triangle, or something that smells like a pineapple or a banana, or the sound of a violin or flute, and so forth, so we have to use indirect procedures, including operant discrimination techniques, to find out what it is that preverbal humans can identify.

Operant conditioning research has involved both studying various procedural modifications (different schedules of reinforcement, situations involving positive and negative reinforcement, discrimination paradigms, and so forth) using increasingly more refined equipment, and applying available techniques to new problems. As just indicated, operant procedures have been productively employed in the study of infants' sensory and perceptual capabilities. The procedures have also become a standard part of psychopharmacological research. There are, in fact, no major research areas wherein operant conditioning techniques have not found significant application.

The most significant contribution Skinner may have made to academic-research psychology is to provide a set of techniques for producing reliable behavioral baselines. Before one can accurately assess the effect of a new drug on behavior, for example, one needs a way to produce a consistent response rate (a baseline); only then can the effect of the introduction of the drug be detected. The applications of operant conditioning are discussed in more detail later in the section on behavior modification.

To summarize, operant conditioning generally involves selecting a voluntary activity, identifying a consequence (a reinforcer) that will change the frequency of occurrence of that behavior, and providing the reinforcer on some sort of predetermined schedule. Response rate and response pattern are the relevant measures of operant conditioning.

Classical (Pavlovian, respondent) conditioning, in contrast, involves selecting a reflexive behavior and pairing a neutral stimulus with the stimulus regularly producing the reaction until the formerly neutral stimulus elicits that response all by itself. The relevant measure of classically-produced responses is the number of times the response appears to the now-conditioned stimulus, along with response latency and amplitude. Resistance to extinction (the reduction in response frequency over time after the reinforcer, in operant conditioning, or the unconditioned stimulus, in classical conditioning, is no longer presented) is also a measure of response strength for both types of conditioning.

On the surface it looks as if Skinner and perhaps Pavlov, too, contributed very little to basic knowledge. We knew that animals salivate when they anticipate food long before the advent of classical conditioning, and we recognized that the consequences of behaviors increase or decrease the frequency of those behaviors prior to Skinner's operant conditioning studies. Animal trainers have for many years used operant conditioning techniques to teach elephants to haul logs, dogs to serve as Seeing Eye companions, and circus animals to perform all sorts of tricks.

When we look at the research of Pavlov and Skinner, we find that what distinguishes their work from others is that they both developed systematic ways to modify behavior and furthermore that they and those who carried on their work have carefully identified the effects on conditioning of various important variables. Skinner, for example, determined the types of response patterns associated with different schedules of reinforcement as well as the effects of different amounts of reinforcement. In addition, he pointed out the relevance of behavior modification techniques for language learning, teaching, and the treatment of individuals who behave psychotically. Skinner's research is important, in part, because it produced techniques with almost limitless application. His work is significant also because he developed a simple conceptual system involving mostly descriptive terms that he has used consistently regardless of the context (laboratory or applied setting) within which operant procedures have been employed.

Hull's hypothetico-deductive theory system serves as a good contrast to Skinner's atheoretical descriptive system. While Hull tried to construct a highly complex abstract conceptual system to account for the relationships between stimuli and responses, Skinner has attempted to avoid interspersing any abstractions between response and stimulus. Both men have contributed to psychology through their very different attempts to relate environmental and behavioral events. Hull's influence diminished because he failed to develop a valid behavioral theory. Skinner's approach has endured because it is simple and yet provides a set of powerful procedures for modifying behavior predictably, especially in situations where the experimenter, educator, clinical psychologist, or other authority has a high degree of control over relevant variables.

The major criticisms of Skinner's basic research are that (a) the study of single subjects fails to take individual differences into account (many of Skinner's findings are based on experiments employing only one subject); (b) his focus on the frequency of responding diverts attention from other characteristics of behavior; (c) his insistence on not abstracting from the data and a concern only with observable changes in response frequency and environmental manipulation are unscientific because science requires theory as well as description; (d) his definitions of "stimulus," "response," and "reinforcer" are circular (tautological)—that is, a stimulus is identified as a reinforcer if, as a consequence of a response, it increases the frequency of that response, whereas the increasing frequency of the response is then said to be a function of reinforcement; (e) his work really tells nothing about the learning processes; all it does is to provide techniques for increasing the frequency of behaviors the animal or person is already capable of; (f) his system excludes cognitive (thinking, imaging, remembering), affective (feeling, emoting), and physiological modes of analysis; and (g) recent research has shown that for each species only certain behaviors are conditionable.

The major critique of Skinner's attempt to account for verbal behavior, in his book of that name, in terms of operant conditioning was written by linguist Noam Chomsky at MIT.[23] Chomsky pointed out that, while the notions of stimulus, response, reinforcement, and so forth "are relatively well defined with respect to bar-pressing experiments and others similarly restricted,"[24] Skinner's terms, if taken literally, cover "almost no aspect of verbal behavior....The terms borrowed from experimental psychology simply lose their objective meaning with this extension, and take over the full vagueness of ordinary language."[25] In Chomsky's view, Skinner oversimplifies the nature of those environmental factors determining verbal behavior, ignores the innate characteristics of human beings which make complex language possible, and similarly, fails to recognize the fact that "all normal children acquire essentially comparable grammars of great complexity with remarkable rapidity [which] suggests that human beings are somehow specially designed to do this."[26] Chomsky, in short, believes that, while environmental factors operating sometimes through the application or withholding of positive reinforcements play a role in determining the specific words used, the rules (grammar) by which word usage is governed are a function of inborn characteristics of the human being.

Behavior Modification

Concerning behavior modification, Skinner states: "One cannot use the term today without adding a caveat and a definition. I do not mean the modification of behavior by implanted electrodes or psychotropic drugs. I do not mean Pavlovian conditioning with vomit-inducing drugs or electric shock. By 'behavior modification' I mean what the term was introduced to mean—changing behavior through positive reinforcement."[27] In spite of Skinner's attempts to limit the concept of behavior modification to techniques employing positive reinforcement, a look at the literature indicates that the term has a variety of meanings. Stolz et al. (1978) describe the situation succinctly: "Behavior modification is a diverse field, and behavioral techniques comprise a family of quite different methods. Most behavioral techniques are based on the principles of classical and operant conditioning. Some behavioral professionals restrict themselves to environmental manipulations; others give causal status to cognitive factors and other private events, emphasize cognitive mediation and vicarious and symbolic learning processes, like modeling, or use drugs as an adjunct to therapy."[28]

In fairness to Skinner, it is important to understand that most critiques of behavior modification concern the use of punishment to modify behavior, a procedure he does not advocate.[29] His major argument, in fact, is that if we use reinforcement techniques wisely we can discontinue punishing procedures entirely.

The term "behavior modification" did not occur in the *Psychological Abstracts*, even as a subheading under "behavior," until 1967. The term "behavior therapy," with one reference listed, first appears in 1960. Publications concerning behavior therapy began to increase during the late sixties, with behavior modification noted as one type of behavior therapy. It was not until 1973 that "behavior modification" was included in the *Psychological Abstracts* as a category separate from "behavior therapy." Since then the number of articles and books noted under "behavior modification" have far exceeded those listed under "behavior therapy." The latter term is now mostly reserved for therapies based on classical conditioning; the former, in line with Skinner's view, refers almost exclusively to techniques based on operant conditioning.

Although behavior modification was, at first, classified as a type of behavior therapy, the approach is more than a therapeutic technique because operant conditioning procedures can be applied in any situation wherein the goal is to change behavior. A quick scan of any university library card catalog shows that behavior modification strategies have been employed in schools, businesses, and governmental settings, as well as mental hospitals, psychological clinics, prisons, nursing programs, and counseling facilities. The techniques have been used with parent groups, school personnel, social workers, exceptional children, retarded people, alcoholics, juvenile delinquents, and individuals classified as neurotic or psychotic.

In line with operant conditioning principles, behavior modification involves (*a*) identifying the behavior one wants to either increase or decrease; (*b*) observing and determining the frequency of that response; (*c*) identifying an appropriate reinforcer if the goal is to increase a behavior or identifying the reinforcer already maintaining a response if the person wants to reduce or eliminate a particular response; (*d*) arranging conditions so that the therapist or educator has control over the reinforcer; and (*e*) manipulating the reinforcers in such a way that the selected behavior can be modified.

One of the main problems with the approach concerns the control necessary for efficient behavior change. The real challenge is to modify the behavior of those individuals who control the reinforcer or reinforcers. If a child is being worked with, then the task is to get the parents and/or teachers to provide and withhold the reinforcer according to the schedule set up by the therapist. If the person being helped is an adult in a mental hospital, then the therapist must get the cooperation of the hospital staff or the program cannot be implemented.

One of the most interesting developments within the behavior modification movement is behavioral contracting. As DeRisi and Butz explain, "Contracting is a technique used to structure behavioral counseling by making each of the necessary elements of the process so clear and explicit that they may be written into an agreement for behavior change that is understandable and acceptable to everyone involved. It is also a means of scheduling the exchange of positive reinforcements . . . between two or more persons."[30]

Contracting has also been applied to educational settings in the sense that a group of behavioral consultants will contract in writing with a school system to implement a program designed to bring the competency of students in a particular area (for example, science, mathematics, grammar) to an agreed upon level with the understanding that the consultants will be paid only to the degree that the goal is met. The unique feature of this approach is that payment is contingent upon the success of the program.

Another development that Skinner subsumes under the heading of behavior modification is programmed instruction. In 1954, Skinner gave a paper at the University of Pittsburgh entitled "The Science of Learning and the Art of Teaching" and, he recalls, "demonstrated a machine designed to teach arithmetic, using an instructional program."[31] About two years later, Skinner designed the teaching machines used in his undergraduate course at Harvard. He and James G. Holland created the

programmed materials for the course. They were published in 1961 as
The Analysis of Behavior.[32]

Skinner's work on programmed learning became an important part of
an educational specialty usually referred to as instructional technology.
It includes the use for educational purposes of TV, radio, film, audio
tapes, overhead projectors, slide projectors, and computers as well as
teaching machines and programmed learning. Whether or not programmed
learning, or any of the other technologies, has made a substantive
contribution to education, however, is still a matter of considerable
controversy.

It is interesting to note that in a recent survey, American psychologists
viewed behavior modification as one of the most important developments in psychology during the post-World War II (1945-1978) era.[33]

The following are some of the major criticisms leveled at behavior
modification, that is, the application of conditioning procedures to real-
world problems: (*a*) the approach, unless used with the utmost sensitivity, can be dehumanizing; (*b*) because procedures based on operant
conditioning are on the surface deceptively simple, they are sometimes
implemented by individuals with only a cursory understanding of both
the problems being dealt with and the procedures themselves; (*c*) behavior modification techniques overemphasize immediate results whereas
the long-range effects of a program may, in fact, be negative; and (*d*)
similarly, there is some question as to whether or not educational or
therapeutic programs designed for *efficient* behavior modification are
beneficial to society as a whole. With regard to this last point, there is
agreement among most evolutionists that diversity of experience en-
hances the survival of the species. Therefore, a variety of approaches is
preferable to any single approach no matter how efficient.

Skinner as Social Philosopher

As stated before, Skinner wrote a number of nontechnical books to
explain his work and position to the educated public. Of these perhaps
the most controversial has been *Beyond Freedom and Dignity*, wherein
Skinner proposes that the concept of freedom, and along with it what he
calls the "autonomous man," are generated in a society by the existence
of aversive situations. A sense of freedom or the absence thereof, he
feels, exists only because some people are oppressed or punished. If we
controlled human behavior with positive reinforcement, instead of punishing procedures like forced confinements, people would, Skinner believes, not develop an exaggerated view of their freedom from environmental
forces.

The concept of dignity, Skinner claims, is produced by the mistaken
belief that we are responsible for what we do. Skinner believes that our

behavior is a function of our experiences (encounters with the environment, reinforcement history) rather than an internal guiding entity (the autonomous man), so we should not give credit to a person when he/she behaves in what we view as a good way; or assign blame if an individual misbehaves in our eyes. Ascribing credit is what creates the concept of dignity. Credit, blame, and freedom, in turn, create in us a false sense of autonomy. As always, Skinner's main assumption is that the environment determines and controls behavior; therefore, it is the task of the behavioral engineer to structure the environment in ways that reduce or eliminate the need in a society for punishment or aversive situations in general.

Noam Chomsky, whose critique of Skinner's book *Verbal Behavior* has already been discussed, also critically reviewed *Beyond Freedom and Dignity*.[34] Chomsky's reservations about the book are that (*a*) people may not be as malleable as Skinner thinks;[35] (*b*) Skinner uses the terms "freedom" and "dignity" in idiosyncratic ways and really has very little to say about the concepts as generally employed; (*c*) there is not nearly the consensus Skinner claims concerning present-day knowledge of the control of human behavior in society (Punishment, in contrast to what Skinner thinks, may sometimes be a useful way to modify behavior.); (*d*) contrary to Skinner's view, we really know very little at this time about designing cultures; (*e*) Skinner's assertion that, as a science progresses, it increasingly ascribes cause to external rather than internal factors is false; (*f*) Skinner in a very unscientific way makes *a priori* judgments about the results of future research in the behavioral sciences; (*g*) survival value may not, as Skinner claims, always be the primary consideration in the design of a society—people sometimes put freedom and dignity above survival; (*h*) Skinner tends to adhere to an oversimplified view of both man and his environment; (*i*) Skinner tries to give his views credibility by saying that his is a scientific approach; (*j*) while not advocating totalitarian forms of government, Skinner's prescriptions for ways to move efficiently toward a better world are as appropriate for dictatorships as democracies; and (*k*) it is not clear how Skinner would deal with those people who for a variety of reasons do not want to conform to the established order.

Gordon Harrington, a psychologist at the University of Northern Iowa, in an interesting critique of Chomsky's review, points out that, while Skinner may be more technician than scientist, as Chomsky suggests, we should not rule out the possibility of a society controlled in many significant ways by leaders invoking operant conditioning techniques. Harrington reminds us, "The first steps have already been made in schools, clinics and factories."[36]

Summary of Skinner's Contributions

Skinner may be more technician than scientist because he has perfected ways of modifying behavior without constructing a theory of what goes on inside the organism or person, and his views of man and society are perhaps naive; but there is no question that his work has led to important developments within academic-research psychology, professional (applied) psychology, and in other disciplines.

For researchers, his systematic investigations of various schedules of reinforcement have provided ways to generate reliable response patterns so that the effects of other variables (environmental, organismic, pharmaceutical) can be determined. Operant conditioning techniques also provide ways of researching the sensory and perceptual capabilities of animals and human infants. This has been of tremendous significance. (See chapter 8 on developmental psychology.) Finally, Skinner's procedures have led to important advances in the study of monkey language and the learning processes in general.

For applied psychologists and workers in other applied fields, Skinner's work, in the context of the behavior modification movement, has been of primary importance in the better treatment of people who are retarded, or psychologically impaired, and the more effective handling of problem children at home or in school. Programmed learning, to which Skinner made a fundamental contribution, has also provided educators with another important instructional tool.

Perhaps the most significant impact of Skinner's work, however, has been to make both researchers and applied professionals go at their work more systematically. The Skinnerian approach requires that the objectives, procedures, variables, measurements, and so forth, be clearly identified before an investigator begins an experiment or project. This requirement, when implemented, raises the standards of both behavioral technology and psychological science.

Since Skinner is without question the single most influential post-World War II American psychologist and he is a behaviorist, does that mean that behaviorism as a philosophy for doing psychological inquiry has been a success? The answer is probably both yes and no. On the one hand, the behavioral orientation encouraged a rigorous definition of concepts and research procedures and the study of animals as well as people. On the other hand, no single theory of behavior has been forthcoming nor have the behaviorists succeeded in excluding introspection and the study of mind, consciousness, and mentalistic states and processes (thoughts, images, memories, dreams, feelings, and so forth) from research psychology. During the last ten to fifteen years, in fact, mentalistic psychology has made a vigorous comeback. (See chapter 7). For a list of criticisms most frequently leveled against behaviorism in general, see Skinner's *About Behaviorism*. The book is essentially his response to these criticisms.

7

PSYCHOLOGICAL PROCESSES RETURN TO AMERICAN PSYCHOLOGY

Psychological Processes

In chapter 1, psychology was defined as the study of all those processes that orient living things to their surrounds and make guided activity (behavior) possible. These processes, as indicated, include sensing, perceiving, thinking, imaging, and remembering, which are sometimes referred to as cognitive, or mentalistic, processes and feeling, or affect. Therefore, a psychological process is, by definition, any process that is part of the guidance system of an organism. The cognitive, or mentalistic, aspect of the human guidance system is usually called the mind. Mind and feelings operating together underlie motivation.

While Hull tried without success to build a model of organismic guidance systems using behavioral and environmental, rather than psychological, concepts and Skinner excluded whatever went on in the organism from his system, research on sensation, perception, and the other psychological processes continued rather vigorously throughout the entire post-World War II period. On the surface, however, the work was subordinate to behavioral research because, first, no single figure predominated, and second, most of what was done did not have widespread application.

What, briefly, are the distinguishing characteristics of sensing, perceiving, imaging, thinking, remembering, and feeling? We shall assume that, with the possible exception of thinking and remembering, each process generates specific changes in consciousness which are referred to respectively as a sensation, a percept, an image, and a feeling. While we speak of thoughts and memories as events in consciousness, it is not clear that we are directly aware of thinking and remembering. Both processes may be nothing more than sequences of percepts, images, and feelings. Incidentally, there are also states of consciousness such as illusions[1] and hallucinations,[2] which are essentially misperceptions, and dreams, a type of imaging, which we consider residual products of psychological functioning.[3]

In order to understand the distinguishing characteristics of the various psychological processes and states, it is necessary to consider the nature of consciousness in general. While consciousness has been defined many ways, I find it useful to conceive of consciousness as a three-dimensional representation generated by an organism of its surround characterized by changing foci (things in attention) and multiple changing backgrounds (contexts, frameworks, fields). From this viewpoint any creature capable of generating for itself a three-dimensional representation is, by definition, sometimes conscious. I also accept the functional assertion that the capability to be conscious, wherever it evolved, helps species survive.[4]

With these general assumptions in mind, we are, it seems, aware of a particular sensation when the focus of consciousness is on an experience associated with a specific sensory system. If, for example, our attention is on a particular odor, color, or sound rather than the source of the odor, color, or sound, then we say that we are sensing. Sensation has a one- or at best a two-dimensional character.

If, on the other hand, we are attending to objects-in-the-world, then we are perceiving. A percept is an awareness event wherein the focus is on a three-dimensional object in three-dimensional space. Percepts tend to be highly structured, have the quality of being about things external to us, and are of the same set of awareness foci as what we call our own body.

Images are similar to percepts in the sense that they are highly structured and are three-dimensional, but their location can be either out there in the world or inside the head. Furthermore, when we imagine, we are aware that the focus of attention is on something which is not in the same set as our perceived body.

Finally, feelings are relatively diffuse (unstructured) experiental events which usually concern the person as a whole. It is my total being that feels bad, good, joyful, or apathetic. Unlike a sensation that is specific to a certain sensory system, a feeling refers to the overall tone of a person.

What, then, are thinking and remembering? Thinking, we infer from our experience, appears to be a process that orders percepts, images, and conceptual information in a certain way. The process starts with a specific focus, say a definition in a crossword puzzle, and then generates sequences of awareness events which either lead to an answer or which fail. At that time attention reverts back to the definition being considered or shifts to something else. Remembering and thinking are interrelated, but the remembering process may be more relaxed—that is, have a different feeling tone. We may, for example, be casually remembering, that is creating images of past encounters with the environment, without trying to solve a problem as in thinking.

There are no pure sensations, images, percepts, or feelings; there are only changes in awareness with a shifting attentional focus and changing background. At any moment the focus may be primarily perceptual, or imaginal, but there is always a complex background that includes changing affective tones.

Background

Experimental psychology emerged as a separate discipline of study about one hundred years ago when attempts were made to investigate mind and consciousness scientifically in the laboratory. The mentalistic processes of most concern were sensation and perception, though there was some interest right from the beginning in higher cognitive processes such as thinking and remembering. Most investigations involved people reporting their experiences in special experimental situations. Introspection was the primary technique for gathering pychological data.

Early in the twentieth century, experimentalists gradually became disillusioned with the study of mind and consciousness. Increasingly, the behavior of animals was researched rather than introspective reports of people's experiences. By the 1920s functional-behaviorism had become the most promising general approach within psychology.

So promising has been this orientation that it continues to predominate in American psychology. During the entire functional-behavioral period, however, research on sensory, perceptual, cognitive, and affective processes continued, and since about the middle 1960s, interest in cognitive and psycholinguistic phenomena has increased significantly. Even the concepts of mind, consciousness, and introspection have regained some of their former respectability.

Steady progress has been made since World War II in all areas of research having to do with one or more of the psychological processes. The most consequential developments within these areas to be discussed. Since the impact of World War II on psychology is considered in chapter 3, suffice it to say here that the war influenced research on the psychological processes primarily by speeding up technological developments that provided more refined equipment for the study of vision, audition, and other sensory and perceptual processes and by leading, in some cases, to financial support of research having to do directly with sensation, perception, problem solving, and other such topics.

Developments During the Postwar Decade (1946-1955)

Included among the most important influences and developments during the immediate post-World War II period were (a) Gestalt psychology with its emphasis on innate organizing tendencies; (b) research and theories concerning the influence of past experience and motivation on perception; (c) research and theory on bodily tonus and perception (sensory-tonic theory); and (d) Gibson's theory of perception which proposes that there is specific information in stimuli for every aspect of visual perception (theory of psychophysical correspondence).

Gestalt Psychology The starting point of Gestalt psychology was the study of apparent movement conducted by Max Wertheimer in Germany in 1912. The fact that two lights a short distance from each other shown repeatedly in succession look like one light moving back and forth (the phi phenomenon) indicates, Wertheimer pointed out, that visual information is organized in some way in the brain. The flashing lights are not recorded passively and the information sent to the brain; rather the brain immediately organizes the visual information so that we see one moving light rather than two flashing lights.

Utilizing many other demonstrations, the Gestaltists showed convincingly that innate organizing processes act automatically upon all information received by the various sensory reception systems (the eyes, ears, skin, and so forth). As Allport puts it, "The central idea of gestalt theory is *form*, both in psychological phenomena and in nature generally. Form is a fundamental law; it is the way things appear to the perceiver...and forms establish themselves and persist, independently of the stimulus, as a property of the perceiving organism."[5]

In the context of the long-standing argument between nativists (those who believe that the structure of consciousness is to some degree a function of innate organizing tendencies) and empiricists (individuals who propose that most of the structure of consciousness is a function of experience), the Gestalt orientation is clearly nativistic.

Methodologically speaking, the Gestalt psychologists are phenomenologists—that is, they believe in describing conscious experiences in everyday language as these experiences appear naturally to observers. To illustrate the Gestalt laws of form, wholeness, transformation, symmetry, closure, organization and so on, they have devised many ingenious demonstrations. Closure, for example, can be demonstrated by drawing incomplete figures or letters and then demonstrating that most observers tend to remember the designs as complete. A law of organization, on the other hand, is demonstrated by presenting patterns of dots (See Illustration 2) and showing that people automatically organize them into groups. Columns A and B go together, as do C and D, and E and F.

The Gestalt theorists also speculated about the brain processes associated with the various phenomena they investigated. They proposed, for example, that perceived forms are brought about by fields of brain activity. Each presentation perceived by a viewer, it was felt, has in the brain a configuration that is isomorphic (identical in form) with it. This pseudo-

Illustration 2.
A Law of Organization Shown by Dot Patterns

```
 . .      . .      . .
 . .      . .      . .
 . .      . .      . .
 . .      . .      . .
 . .      . .      . .
 . .      . .      . .
 A B      C D      E F
```

physiological theory resulted in some interesting critical research on brain functioning.[6]

Gestalt theory and research have extended beyond perception. Wolfgang Köhler, who along with Max Wertheimer and Kurt Koffka founded Gestalt psychology, studied chimpanzees in the process of solving various types of problems;[7] and Wertheimer,[8] Duncker,[9] and other Gestaltists did extensive research on human problem solving. Motivation, too, was treated from the Gestalt perspective (incompleted tasks were found to be remembered more than completed tasks, suggesting that the interruption of an activity creates a residual tension directed at task completion).[10] Kurt Lewin, whose work is discussed in chapter 3, was also influenced by Gestalt thought. His theory of personality, in particular, is based on Gestalt assumptions.

The most important contributions of Gestalt theorists have been their demonstrations of what appear to be unlearned organizational tendencies insofar as psychological processes are concerned and their defense of phenomenological research during a time when psychology was in danger of being overwhelmed by behavioral perspectives. The Gestaltists pointed out that there was still a need to study the conscious experiences of people and that research on behavior alone could not deal with all psychological phenomena.

The Effects of Past Experience and Motivation on Perception While it is not clear whether or not past experience acts to modify perceptual processes as such or whether the influence arises immediately after such processes organize information coming to the brain from the various sensory systems, it is obvious that our previous encounters with the world do effect in some fashion the manner in which we perceive that world. Past experience manifests itself in many ways, and the concept as used here includes our values, expectancies, frames of reference, and predispositions to look for or at certain things in our surround. In a sense, even our momentary motivational states such as hunger, thirst, or sexual desire are determined by what we have been doing recently, that is, our past experiences. During the immediate postwar period, theories that tried to identify the various effects of past experience on perception were called directive state theories, or the "new look," in perception. (See chapter 4 on Freud.)

The individuals most directly associated with this new look were Jerome Bruner, James and Eleanor Gibson, Harry Helson, Adelbert Ames, and Egon Brunswick. The basic viewpoint of these theorists was functional since it was assumed that the various directing states or determining tendencies underlying perceptual organization are adaptive.

Bruner, who went on to become an important figure in perceptuo-cognitive theory, demonstrated in 1947 that the perceived value of coins, which is a function of past experience, influences the perceived size of coins. Poor children, for example, saw coins as larger than did rich children.[11]

Gibson and Gibson (1955) proposed that past experience operated on the perceptual processes by making it possible to identify things with less information. Before we have experience differentiating faces, complex figures, and the like, we have to take a good look in order to tell one stimulus from another. Once we have more familiarity with particular forms, however, just a little bit of the total information is sufficient for recognition or differentiation.[12] (See chapter 8 for a more detailed discussion of perceptual learning.)

Harry Helson did extensive work involving judgments of various series of stimuli or objects and proposed that our evaluation of a particular set of things is determined in part by past experience with such items. If, for example, an individual has extensive experience looking at and judging oil paintings by established artists, his/her view of what constitutes an outstanding, average, or poor painting is very different from the perspective of a person with little experience judging oil paintings. Past experience creates a frame of reference against which we judge new things relevant to that framework. Helson's central concept is the "adaptation level" which is a sort of neutral point in a relative scale of judgment.[13] Paintings you would consider neither good nor bad would, for example, constitute the adaptation level for paintings.

Adelbert Ames, while not a psychologist, designed perceptual demonstrations which generated a movement called transactionalism. The Ames demonstrations included distorted rooms and the rotating trapezoidal window (Illustration 3). These produced illusions which the transactionalists explained by proposing that previous experience with the retinal patterns, produced by repeatedly encountered objects, results in hypotheses about what is out in the world. The demonstration situations used by the transactionalists produced familiar retinal patterns but were, in fact, different in structure than the objects in the world ordinarily producing the patterns; therefore, the illusions. The distorted room, for example, produced the same retinal pattern as an

Illustration 3.
Transactional Demonstrations

TRAPEZOIDAL WINDOW

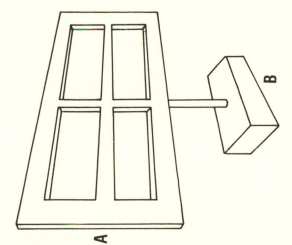

A

B

A - Actual shape is a trapezoid
B -Motor to rotate window. Window
seems to oscillate.

DISTORTED ROOM

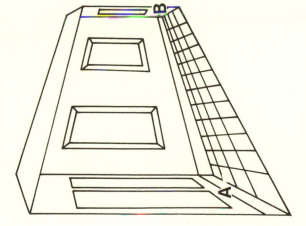

A

B

A is longer than B. The room is
constructed so that it looks like
a square room from one perspective.

undistorted room. It was only when the viewer was able to get more information about the room by means of a pointer that he or she would realize the room was distorted. This orientation was called transactionalism because perception is considered to be a product of the viewer's active interaction with the environment, a process whereby various hypotheses about the world are tried out and either accepted or rejected.

Egon Brunswick's theory of probabilistic functionalism is similar in principle to transactionalism so his theoretical ideas will not be discussed in detail. Brunwick's most significant contributions were his interrelated concepts of representative design and ecological validity. He pointed out that when designing a study, it is important to select tasks and settings that are representative of the natural activities and environments of the people or animals being studied. To the degree that a design is representative in this sense, to that extent it is said to be ecologically valid. Ecological validity refers to the extent to which the findings of a study can be generalized to the subjects involved in the context of their respective natural environments.

Donald O. Hebb, the most influential Canadian psychologist during the post-World War II period, pointed out that "the initial perceiving of figures is not so complete and organized a process as the gestaltists have claimed... [and] that perception in some of its most essential features is not an innate process; it has to be learned."[14] Hebb claimed that, while figures have a primitive unity right from the beginning, that is, before any learning takes place, it is only through experience that we can differentiate a square from a triangle. By looking at the various sides and corners of a figure, Hebb believed, a person constructs a neural circuit (cell assembly) which is activated in the future provided any part of the original stimulus class is attended to. Information from the muscles moving the eyes about becomes part of the total neural configuration associated with a figure and the perceptual process. Experience also results in organizations of cell assemblies which Hebb called "phase sequences" and which, in his opinion, account for the unity of complex experiences.

The work of some of the behaviorists, particularly Skinner, deemphasized physiological research by concentrating on behavioral and environmental events. Hebb's theory played a significant role in reminding psychologists of the relevance of research on brain processes. Hebb, because of his emphasis on past experience, is also considered a major developmental theorist (see chapter 8). His most important book is *Organization of Behavior* (1949).[15]

Bodily Tonus and Perception Heinz Werner and Seymour Wapner proposed that both sensory and muscular activities may affect the organism in identical ways and therefore bring about the same perceptual changes. This proposition was the primary assumption underlying what became known as the sensory-tonic theory.

To demonstrate the equivalency of sensory and muscular effects on perception, Werner and Wapner had subjects sitting in a dark room indicate to an experimenter when a rotating luminous rod viewed at some distance seemed to be in the vertical position under three conditions: (1) with electrical stimulation to one side of the neck; (2) with a tone sounded to one ear; or (3) with no external stimulation. In both conditions 1 and 2, the vertical setting of the rod was tilted to the side opposite that being stimulated by either electric current or sound. Werner and Wapner interpreted this to mean that both the electric stimulation (which induced a change in muscle tonus) and the tone (which was a sensory stimulus) influenced the perception of verticality in the same way.

While Hebb pointed out that information from the eye muscles apparently plays a role in visual perception, Werner and Wapner's theory proclaimed that the body as a whole was involved in perception. Regardless of the validity of the specifics of the theory, this perspective was an important contribution. It has become increasingly evident, for example, that vision involves more than the eyes, the optic nerve, and even the visual cortex of the brain. And that hearing depends not only on the ears, auditory nerves, and auditory cortex. Rather, perception is a function, to varying degrees, of all bodily activities.

Gibson's Theory of Psychophysical Correspondence Although James Gibson was influenced by Gestalt psychology and functionalism, his theory of psychophysical correspondence was inspired mostly by work he did during World War II for the Air Force on visual perception under flight conditions.[16] By psychophysical correspondence is meant that stimulus patterns impinging upon our sensory receptor systems, for example, the eyes, ears, and skin, are adequate to account for what we perceive. That is, to explain perception we do not have to infer additional factors such as cognition, associative processes or innate states.

Traditional theories tended to propose that the ability to perceive distance or three-dimensional space is either inborn without any particular stimulus pattern needing to be present or that we learn to see depth by our experiences of moving through and testing the environment. Gibson, on the other hand, said that the stimulus for distance or depth is a specific pattern characterized by a gradient of texture density. See Illustration 4. A surface receding in the distance reflects a gradient of light which is a direct cue to distance.

Gibson also clarified the difference between the visual world made up of objects in three-dimensional space and the visual field experienced as patterns, colors, areas of bright and dark, and so forth. The distinction is the same one discussed earlier concerning perception and sensation.

Finally, Gibson emphasized that visual stimuli are not static images, but that because of eye movements and movements of our heads and

Illustration 4.
Texture Gradient as a Distance Clue

bodies, stimulation consists of complex pattern-transformations. Perception, consequently, involves a dynamic searching process rather than the passive reception of information. The process, however, is not a matter of associating various bits of information, but instead entails more and more efficient use of the information present. See Gibson (1960) for an interesting discussion of the many meanings of the concept "stimulus."[17]

In summary, by the middle fifties, perception was viewed as an active, exploring process that involved past experience, the immediate state of the body and, to some degree, innate organizing tendencies. There was, however, little agreement as to the ways experience influenced perception. Most of the research concerned visual phenomena although important work was being done in audition and the other sensory modalities. The predominate outlook was functional in the sense that past experience was felt to influence perception in ways that help organisms survive.

Developments during the Second Decade (1956-1965)

During the late fifties and early sixties work in all the areas just discussed continued. Some new developments, however, also occurred. Among the most important were (a) research on sensory deprivation (the study of animals and people in relatively unchanging environments); (b) a renewed interest in the study of attentional processes; (c) new approaches to psychophysical research (the study of human and animal sensitivities to various types of stimulation); (d) promising psycholinguisitic research; (e) the publication of The Measurement of Meaning by Osgood, Suci, and Tannenbaum in 1958, a book that is concerned with the connotative meaning of concepts; (f) advances in cognitive social psychology; and (g) the appearance of new cognitive theories of personality.

This description is a potpourri of events, but the selection demonstrates the increasing diversity of interests which was manifest in American psychology by the early 1960s, a diversity which by the late 1960s had ushered in a full-fledged cognitive psychology and by the 1970s had created an atmosphere permitting the readmission to the discipline of the concepts of mind and consciousness and research based on introspection.

The increasing influence of Piaget and the emergence of infant experimental psychology were also characteristic of the 1956-1965 period; both of these developments are discussed in chapter 8 on developmental psychology. In addition, inferred processes like perceptual defense (the unconscious blocking of unpleasant or anxiety-producing information) and subliminal perception (being influenced by information unconsciously) were being studied.

Research on Sensory Deprivation According to Hebb, who was most responsible for the research on sensory deprivation,

The work that we have done at McGill University began, actually, with the problem of brainwashing. We were not permitted to say so in the first publishing. What we did say, however, was true—that we were interested in the problem of the effects of monotony on the man with a watch-keeping job, or other tasks of that sort. The chief impetus, of course, was the dismay at the kind of "confessions" being produced at the Russian Communist trials. "Brainwashing" was a term that came a little later, applied to Chinese procedures.[18]

The Chinese procedures Hebb mentioned were those allegedly used by the Chinese military on American prisoners during the Korean War (1950-1953), a conflict involving thousands of Americans as part of a United Nations force charged with defending South Korea against Communist North Korea. The Chinese entered the war in October of 1950, after American troops invaded North Korea.

The aspect of the brainwashing procedures that Hebb and later other researchers were interested in was the forced isolation of prisoners from physical and social stimulation. Prisoners were put into small barren rooms and left alone for protracted periods of time not knowing what to expect.

Sensory deprivation studies took place in a variety of settings including completely dark soundproof rooms, lighted cubicles equipped with a bed and a constant auditory background, and water tanks. In the water tank situation, the person was immersed in water and as a consequence experienced about as constant an environment as possible. Not only was the light, sound, and temperature kept constant but so was the tactile stimulation because the individual was supported mostly by water. Conditions also varied in the sense that in some studies efforts were made to reduce environmental stimulation to zero; in other investigations only patterned stimulation was eliminated; and, finally, in certain settings, by Hebb's account, subjects were exposed to "some repeated stimulus figure against a patterned but fairly constant sensory background."[19]

Investigators found that, depending on conditions and the personalities of subjects, sensory deprivation produced hallucinations and decreased efficiency in intellectual as well as perceptuo-motor functioning. There is also evidence from animal isolation studies that prolonged periods of sensory deprivation result in hypersensitivity to stimulation. Cats, for example, who have during the early months of life experienced little environmental change, withdraw fearfully from shifts in the environment for a long time (months, even years) after removal from isolation.

While we do not want to overgeneralize from the findings, sensory deprivation studies seem to indicate that living things evolve to experience a certain optimal range of environmental change. If an animal or person is isolated from his normal environment, then the guidance mechanism composed of those systems involved in sensation, perception, imaging, thinking, remembering, and feeling operates less efficiently. Animal research shows that if the isolation takes place in the early months of life, the deficiencies in functioning produced may be severe and long lasting.

Research on Wakefulness, Attention, Sleep, and Dreams People have been aware of being conscious, of attending to things, of sleeping and dreaming for a long time; however, little was known about the specific characteristics of and physiological processes underlying these states until about the last thirty years. Research had been done in these areas, but scant progress was made primarily because much of the work was based on introspection alone and also because refined electronic equipment for monitoring relevant brain processes was not available.

One of the real breakthroughs came in the late 1940s when physiologists Moruzzi and Magoun[20] showed that electrical stimulation in the reticular formation of the brain stem of an animal exhibiting an EEG sleep pattern would cause that pattern to change to that of wakefulness (illustration 5). Subsequent research supported this finding and demonstrated convincingly that the reticular formation is directly involved in determining the states of sleep and wakefulness (consciousness). Further studies indicated that the reticular formation plays a role in selective attention, that is, in determining what is attended to.

According to British psychologist Neville Moray,

The renaissance of interest in attention seems to be connected with three developments. Firstly, the use of operational definition couched in stimulus-response language has become accepted to a degree which allows us to undercut the difficulties of the appeal to introspection.... Secondly, towards the end of the Second World War a number of important problems arose for which answers were required from applied psychologists, and which were...clearly to do with attention. Communications systems in ships, planes and air-traffic control centers all produced situations in which there was a very high flow of information, and in which the human operator might be required to do two things at once.... The third important factor...has been the development of new kinds of apparatus and techniques which have made the control of experiments very much more easy.[21]

The tape recorder, which we now take so much for granted, was particularly invaluable.

The individual who did most to make the study of attention respectable was British psychologist Donald Broadbent. In 1958 Broadbent published a book entitled *Perception and Communication* in which attentional processes play a key role.[22] Broadbent's work centered on situations wherein people had to deal with two different auditory messages simultaneously.

Illustration 5.
Location of Reticular Formation

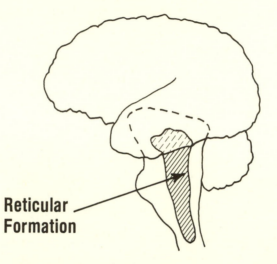

Reticular Formation

Research on attention was further stimulated by vigilance studies. Vigilance is the process of maintaining attention in the context of monotonous settings. While vigilance research apparently started in the early 1930s with the widespread introduction of boring assembly-line tasks, the real catalyst for such studies was again World War II. During the war technological developments, in particular radar and sonar, made it necessary for key personnel on ships, planes, and ground stations to monitor various electronic detection devices for long periods of time. There was naturally interest in finding out under what conditions attention was best maintained. Detection, decision, and information theories were also spinoffs of the electronic advances stimulated by the war. (See chapter 3 on the impact of World War II.)

Another development that sustained interest in consciousness and attention was the familiarization by American psychologists during the early 1960s with the research of Russian physiologist E. N. Sokolov on arousal and the orienting reflect or reaction. In describing the response, Richard Lynn reports as follows: "When an animal is presented with a new stimulus it pricks up its ears, looks in the direction of the stimulus and alerts itself to deal with possible eventualities which the stimulus may herald."[23]

Pavlov discovered the orienting response but Sokolov introduced Western scientists to the reaction in a paper he delivered in 1960 at a conference concerning the central nervous system and behavior.[24] Studies have shown that the act of orienting to a new situation is a complex process involving changes in the sensitivity of the sense organs, the skeletal muscles, EEG patterns, vasoconstriction, and the galvanic skin response.

Research on attention has also included looking-time studies, that is, investigations concerned with what it is that people and animals look at and for how long. This technique has been particularly useful in finding out what it is that infants are interested in. Psychologist Robert Fantz, for example, placed various displays in front of young infants and determined that, in general, babies look at a pattern depicting a human face longer than they look at abstract designs.[25]

As indicated earlier, interest in sleep and wakefulness was stimulated in part by the discovery that the reticular formation is involved in both states. Research on sleep was also prompted by studies on sleep deprivation done at the Walter Reed Army Institute of Research in Washington, D.C., in the middle and late 1950s.[26] Early investigators like Nathaniel Kleitman had done pioneer studies of sleep and wakefulness prior to the 1940s, but the reticular formation findings, improved equipment, and interest in sensory and sleep deprivation resulted in a surge of interest in this area during the postwar period.

Another important landmark in sleep-dream research was the finding in 1955 by Aserinsky and Kleitman that "about 74% of the awakenings [of subjects] during REM [rapid eye movement] periods resulted in detailed reports of dreams, while only 17% of non-REM awakenings did so."[27] Rapid eye movements provided the first reliable index of dreaming. There is still disagreement, however, as to the function of dreams.

Research on consciousness (wakefulness), attention, sleep, and dreams led to many significant findings and helped free psychology from the constraints of behaviorism. Not only were physiological investigations producing striking new insights but the process of self report was also seen again as a necessary approach to psychological inquiry. Furthermore, as already mentioned, productive research on these processes and states helped legitimate the concepts of mind and consciousness during the late 1960s and 1970s.

Modern Psychophysics One of the first psychological problems to be studied experimentally had to do with the sensitivity of people to various environmental changes. Gustav T. Fechner, a German physicist, tried around the middle of the nineteenth century to determine how heavy a weight held in hand had to be before a person experienced the object or how different in weight two objects had to be before the difference was detected. Fechner, in other words, attempted to identify the absolute and difference thresholds for specific, carefully measured, stimulus events. While Ernest Weber had conducted similar studies a few years before Fechner started his investigations, it was Fechner who developed a systematic research program. Because Fechner was trying to relate measurable changes in the physical world to human experience (sensation), he referred to his work as psychophysics. Psychophysics provided one of the preconditions for the emergence of experimental psychology in the late 1870s.

The central concept for Fechner's psychophysics was threshold, both absolute and difference. The inference was that the human body is characterized by fixed and specifiable sensitivities to changes in the world. There is either enough stimulation to make a person experience a change or there is too little excitation to bring about such an experience.

However, attempts to determine thresholds in nonprobablistic terms failed; and it was not until the early 1950s that an entirely new approach to psychophysics emerged. This approach, called the new or modern psychophysics, was based primarily on detection and decision theories, developed by communication engineers as mentioned previously in connection with vigilance research. Once again World War II played a role in bringing about a new development in psychology because it was during the war that psychologists and individuals who were to become psychologists came in contact with communications and electronics specialists involved in providing better radios, radar and sonar systems, and gunnery-control devices.

It is recognized by today's psychophysicists that expectancies, motivation, fatigue, and other states influence the ability of an individual to detect subtle changes in the environment. A radar operator, for example, may miss detecting a blip caused by a briefly surfacing submarine on one day because he is tired or apathetic toward his job, and yet notice a similar signal with little difficulty on a day when enemy action is expected.

Modern psychophysics represented a powerful new approach because it not only acknowledged the influence of set and motivation on signal detection but provided ways to measure the role played by such variables in psychophysical tasks. One could, in other words, manipulate expectancy and motivation and see how they influenced performance.[28] For a more detailed account of detection and decision theories see chapter 3 on the influence of World War II on psychology.

Another significant development in the area of psychophysics had to do with research designed to determine sensory thresholds of animals. While not usually classified as part of modern psychophysics because decision and detection theories are not involved, psychophysical studies of animals certainly constituted an interesting advance.

Donald S. Blough, a member of the psychology department of Brown University, is generally credited with developing psychophysical techniques appropriate for animal research. In 1958 he reported a study concerned with determining the brightness thresholds of pigeons.[29] These birds were selected because they have excellent vision. Based on operant conditioning principles, the procedures Blough used involved training a pigeon to peck one design (Key A) when it could see the light presented and to peck another (Key B) when it could not see the light. The setup was ingenious in the sense that every peck of Key A would slightly reduce the brightness of the light and every peck at Key B would increase the intensity. It was therefore possible to identify the area of absolute threshold. The Blough procedure, incidentally, is another example of how Skinnerian techniques contributed to areas of psychology other than conditioning.

The Measurement of Meaning Most of this chapter so far has been concerned with developments relating to either perception or sensation. We have largely ignored cognition (thinking, reasoning, imaging) and affect (feeling). While both of these psychological processes are discussed later in this chapter in the section on the third decade (1966-1975), there were important developments during the 1946-to-1965 period, particularly in the cognitive-linguistic area. There was strong interest, too, on the part of clinical and psychometric psychologists and some investigators of personality in anxiety which is, of course, a feeling.

In the cognitive-linguistic area, much of the work prior to 1960 concerned long-term memory; in the sixties, however, research shifted to the study of short-term memory. At various times during the 1946-1965 period interest in concept formation, concrete and abstract thought, and creativity also surfaced.

Charles Osgood's book, *The Measurement of Meaning* (1958),[30] represented an important contribution to American psychology because it was a frontal assault on the concept "meaning," one of the most abstract and difficult conceptions for any discipline to tackle. Furthermore, it was a successful effort in the sense that Osgood was able to develop a convenient way to measure the connotative meaning of concepts. The procedure he developed is called the Semantic Differential and involves "defining" concepts in terms of the following three factors: evaluative, potency, and activity. Seven-point polar scales are used to reflect the three factors. The most common scales used are, respectively, the good-bad scale, the hard-soft scale, and the fast-slow scale. Many subsequent studies, however, were based only on the good-bad dimension.

It should be made clear that the Semantic Differential measures connotative rather than denotative meaning. The procedure does not concern the dictionary definitions of terms; it provides a way of determining what words connote. The approach assumes that each concept is characterized by a unique semantic space defined in terms of the aforementioned three major factors.

Osgood's theory generated much research and has proven especially useful in cross-cultural studies. It is convenient, for example, to be able to determine the semantic space of concepts such as democracy, profit, work, men, and women for people in different countries or regions of a country.

Important Developments in Psycholinguistics As pointed out by Chaplin and Krawiec (1979), research and theory in psycholinguistics

can be categorized most simply in terms of its adherents' position on nativism and empiricism in language development during childhood. Nativistic psycho-linguists believe that human language is predicated on biologically determined neural processes, which provide every human child with a kind of species-specific ability to organize sounds into words and, further, words into sentences with a crude but highly efficient grammar. . . . The empiricists, on the other hand, be-lieve that language is primarily learned by a conditioning process.[31]

The predominate theory of language acquisition prior to the mid-1950s was based on classical conditioning principles. Words were learned, it was proposed, by being associated with specific experiences. The word "no," for example, might be learned by being associated with the nega-tive feelings accompanying a spanking.

In the late 1950s, however, two important events happened: Skinner published *Verbal Behavior* in which he argued that language was learned primarily through operant conditioning; and Chomsky[32] published *Syn-tactic Structures* in which he developed a nativistic theory of language acquisition. Interest in psycholinguistics was spurred by the Indiana Conference on the Interdisciplinary Study of Language held in 1953. Other conferences, for example, the Minnesota Conference on Asso-ciative Processes in Verbal Behavior (1957), also signaled the fact that by the mid-1950s psycholinguistics was an exciting "new" area of study in American psychology. In the 1960s Eric Lenneberg joined Chomsky in arguing for a theory of language acquisition emphasizing biological factors.[33]

Nativistic theories of language acquisition were part of a more general development referred to as modern structuralism, which includes Piaget's theory of cognitive development and Levi-Strauss's theory of myths. The basic tenet of this movement is that thinking and the ability to communicate verbally are to an important extent under the control of innate biological processes and that, as a result, the development and form of thought and language are predetermined. Piaget, for example, proposed that the emergence of cognitive skills follows a set pattern over time. Similarly Levi-Strauss claimed that the same themes can be found in the myths of all cultures. The structuralists believe that much of the structure of our conscious experiences is a function of innately con-trolled factors.

Skinner takes an almost entirely empiricist view toward language ac-quisition. People acquire language through reinforcing experiences. Those sounds which parents encourage through praise are repeated by infants, and those which are ignored by Mom and Dad and other caretaking adults or children are discontinued. The rules of grammar are, according to Skinner, learned in the same way.

Chomsky, who criticized Skinner's explanation of language acquisition, proposed that all children everywhere develop language characterized by the same basic deep structure and furthermore that they acquire language amazingly quickly. Chomsky believes, therefore, that as infants mature they develop a capacity for language; once this capacity emerges they are ready to learn the specific sounds and words used by their societies to communicate.

During the 1950s and 1960s interest in nondevelopmental aspects of verbal behavior also increased. Verbal learning, in particular, was vigorously studied. The major variables investigated were the meaningfulness of material to be learned, the nature of rehearsal or practice involved, the method used in organizing the material to be learned (for example, getting an overview or concentrating on the details), and motivation. In addition, there was considerable research on variables influencing the transfer of training from one task to another as well as on long-term memory and forgetting.

Anthropologist B. L. Whorf published his influential book *Language, Thought, and Reality* in 1956.[34] The Whorfian hypothesis, as his point of view became known, proclaims that our view of the world is determined by our language. People notice those things and events for which they have words. Zuni Indians, for example, tend to confuse yellow and orange because their language contains one term for both colors.

Advances in Cognitive Social Psychology Prior to World War II, social psychology tended to be little concerned with the perceptions, thoughts, attitudes, and beliefs of people in the context of social situations. Like most of American psychology, the predominate orientation was behavioral. Social psychologists were interested in the effects of people upon the performance of specific tasks; they were not concerned with the perspectives of people when they were taking part in group activities.

World War II changed all that. Psychologists were brought together with other social-behavioral scientists to work on problems that frequently focused on the attitudes, opinions, and feelings of participants involved in group activities. Kurt Lewin, whose work is discussed in chapter 3, was particularly effective in designing studies pertaining to real-world problems and in conceptualizing personality structure in terms of cognitive and motivational factors.

Equipped with new research procedures and concepts, social psychologists during the immediate post-world War II years were confident that a viable experimental social psychology had emerged. While progress was probably not up to that originally envisioned, social psychology has developed into a productive and diverse area of study. During the last thirty years, cognitive social psychology has produced a number of highly-researched phenomena and theories. Among these are balance theories, cognitive dissonance theory, research on attitudes and beliefs, person perception research, and attribution theory.[35]

During the 1950s and 1960s when behavioral perspectives were intense in American psychology, social psychologists, among all psychological researchers, did more to preserve a cognitive strain in the discipline than anyone else except a few personality theorists. Krech, Crutchfield, and Ballachey in their widely used social psychology text, *Individual in Society* (1962) state, "Perhaps one of the most heartening theoretical developments in American psychology in the last decade or so has been the increased acceptance of cognitive theory among psychologists—among even the most respectable and most scientific of the tribe. This has been especially true in social psychology where we have seen various attempts to apply cognitive theory toward the understanding of this or that aspect of social behavior."[36]

Personality Theories as a Catalyst for Cognitive Psychology The growth of clinical psychology during and immediately following World War II in conjunction with the increasing influence of psychoanalysis generated interest within both applied and academic-research psychology in personality theory and research. This development returned the attention of American psychologists to cognitive and affective processes because most personality theories are concerned with the ways people perceive themselves and the world around them and how they deal with their feelings and problems.

Of primary importance in helping preserve a cognitive-affective perspective within American psychology during the 1940s and 1950s were the psychoanalytic theories of Freud, Jung, Adler, Horney, Fromm, and Erikson; Lewin's field theory; the existentially-oriented theory of Carl Rogers; and George Kelly's theory of personal constructs. Psychoanalysis, Lewin's theory, and existentialism are discussed elsewhere. Kelly's basic postulate is that "A person's processes are psychologically channelized by the ways in which he anticipates events."[37] The focus is on how we perceive, think, and feel about future encounters with the world. We construct schemas or templates against which we compare new experiences. The fit between a particular anticipation and an event determines the appropriateness of a schema or template.

One derivative of psychoanalytic theory deserving mention here is ego psychology, which is concerned with the strategies people develop to deal with the real world. Ego psychology played an important role in preserving cognition within research psychology because of the work done on cognitive styles.

Cognitive-style investigators conceive of the mentalistic realm as being analyzable along various dimensions. An individual can, for example, sort things into a few general classes or many specific categories; emphasize (sharpen) or deemphasize (level) differences among stimuli; or be strongly influenced by background stimulation in making judgments (be field dependent) or very little influenced (be field independent). Research on cognitive styles had crested by the late sixties.

One of the most important developments of the early sixties was the emergence of a new field called infant experimental psychology. While this development is discussed in some detail in chapter 8, it should be pointed out that, since much of the research done in this area concerned sensation and perception, infant experimental psychology played a role in bringing about a better balance between behavioral and cognitive psychology.

The final event occurring during the 1956-1965 period to be considered, albeit briefly, is the publication in 1960 of a book entitled *Plans and the Structure of Behavior*[38] written by George Miller (Harvard University), Eugene Galanter (University of Pennsylvania), and Karl Pribram (Stanford University). The book is a landmark because it was the first detailed attempt "to discover whether the cybernetic ideas have any relevance for psychology."[39]

The central concern of the authors is what they call the "theoretical vacuum between cognition and action."[40] Cognitive theories, they felt, failed to show how a cognitive state or process influenced the behavior of organisms. Their solution to the problem is to show that both cognitive and behavioral activities are represented by temporal patterns in the brain and furthermore that the entire interrelated organismic functioning is organized into a hierarchical system of feedback mechanisms. For a more detailed discussion of cybernetics, see chapter 3.

Developments during the Third Decade (1966-1975)

The late 1960s, plagued by the Vietnam War and characterized by student rebellion against the Establishment, created an atmosphere ripe for change within the academic disciplines. Subjectivism, anti-intellectualism, interest in drug-induced states, humanism, existentialism, phenomenology, and Eastern philosophies accelerated the move within psychology away from manipulative behaviorism toward a more cognitive psychology. Even such vague processes and states as feeling, imagery, and consciousness were readmitted to the discipline as legitimate professional concerns.

However, the return to mainstream American psychology of cognition, affective processes, imagery, and consciousness was possible primarily because of developments occurring during the 1950s and early 1960s. Of special significance were the availability of new and refined electronic equipment; progress in understanding the brain and sensory systems; new conceptual models such as detection, decision, and information theories; impressive research on perceptual processes; the emergence of a vigorous cognitive social psychology; Piaget's theory of cognitive development; and promising cognitive personality theories. The mood of the late sixties facilitated the shift toward a more cognitive psychology, but the foundation for such a change had already been prepared.

Emergence of a Full-Fledged Cognitive Psychology According to Richard N. Williams, "Almost all authorities in psychology seem to agree that some type of 'cognitive revolution' has taken place. It is impossible to discover who first used the term; today it falls easily into lectures and forms the title of chapters in many texts. . . . The cognitive revolution is young; although it cannot be assigned a specific beginning, most people consider it to have started in the early part of the 1960s."[41] While cognitive psychology as a discrete field of study did not emerge until the early or at least the middle 1960s, it is clear that developments in the 1940s and 1950s and the failures of behaviorism set the stage for the cognitive revolution.

Books that signalled the move toward a more cognitive psychology during the early sixties include George Miller's *Psychology, The Science of Mental Life* (1962),[42] Silvan Tomkins's *Affect, Imagery, Consciousness* (1962),[43] George Humphrey's *Thinking: An Introduction to its Experimental Psychology* (1963),[44] and *Cognition: Theory, Research, Promise* (1964) edited by Constance Scheerer.[45] The work which best symbolizes the reemergence of a mentalistic strain in American psychology is Ulric Neisser's *Cognitive Psychology* published in 1967.[46] Neisser states: "A generation ago, a book like this one would have needed at least a chapter of self-defense against the behaviorist position. Today, happily, the climate of opinion has changed, and little or no defense is necessary. Indeed, stimulus-response theorists themselves are inventing hypothetical mechanisms with vigor and enthusiasm and only faint twinges of conscience."[47] New journals which indicated that research on cognitive processes was increasing are *Cognitive Psychology* (1970), *Cognition* (1971), and *Memory and Cognition* (1973).

During the 1962 to 1974 period many articles appearing in the *American Psychologist* analyzed or proselytised for the movement toward a more cognitive psychology. Some of the major themes expressed were that (*a*) awareness or consciousness is an essential focus of psychological inquiry (Attneave, 1974; Farber, 1963; Holt, 1964; Murphy, 1969); (*b*) behavior is guided by expectancies and feedback (Seward, 1963), or by intentionality or goal setting (Bühler, 1971), or by consciousness generally (Collier, 1964); (*c*) psychology needs a model that can account for both cognitive and behavioral processes (Dember, 1974; Hitt, 1969; Holt, 1964; Kagan, 1967; Kendler, 1971); (*d*) more emphasis must be placed on the study of perceptual and cognitive development (Bruner, 1965; Bühler, 1969; Cole and Bruner, 1971; Kagan and Klein, 1973;

Tuddenham, 1966); (e) the image is enjoying a revival in American psychology (Bugelski, 1970); (f) neobehaviorism, which was a paradigm from the 1930s through the 1950s, has declined and been replaced by a cognitive psychology legitimized by set theory, computer science, linguistic theory, philosophical analyses of science, and a questioning of the neobehavioristic data base (Segal and Lachman, 1972); (g) psychology includes all subfields concerned with the study of mind, with mind defined as the capacity for thought (Hebb, 1974); (h) introspection can be a fruitful data source for psychologists (Deese, 1969; Radford, 1974); and (i) decision and information theories may provide a conceptual bridge between behavioral and cognitive psychology (Boneau, 1974).[48]

What, specifically, is contemporary cognitive psychology about? According to Neisser, his book "follows stimulus information 'inward' from the organs of sense, through many transformations and reconstructions, through to eventual use in memory and thought."[49] Neisser's volume is divided into three main parts: visual cognition, auditory cognition, and the higher mental processes. The visual cognition section deals with iconic storage[50] and verbal coding, pattern recognition, focal attention and figural synthesis, words as visual patterns, and visual memory. The section on auditory cognition concerns speech perception, echoic memory,[51] auditory attention, active verbal memory, and sentences. The final section on higher mental processes presents a cognitive approach to memory and thought.

A more general look at cognitive psychology indicates that most research concerns memory and psycholinguistics, and centers on language acquisition, grammatical structure, and the process by which information is classified verbally. Memory research concerns types of memory and variables affecting remembering and forgetting.

The trend toward a more explicitly cognitive psychology is a potentially integrative development because it receives support from humanists, phenomenologists, psycholinguists, social psychologists, information theorists, and, of course, those long engaged directly in perceptual or cognitive research. Even some behaviorists have acceded to cognitive orientations. They talk about imaging stimuli or outcomes, imitating behavior, or reinforcing your self. Only Skinner and strict Skinnerians have refused to extend their professional language beyond stimulus and response terms.

Mind and Consciousness Return To Psychology Theoretically, psychology could have become more cognitive during the sixties and seventies without embracing the concepts of mind and consciousness which the behaviorists and operationists had worked so hard to expunge from the discipline. As the cognitive orientation returned to psychology, however, "mind" was again found by some psychologists to be a convenient term for cognitive functioning. For example, social psychologist Milton

Rokeach entitled his book on dogmatism *The Open and Closed Mind* (1960);[52] perceptualist Lloyd Kaufman named his book on visual perception *Sight and Mind: an Introduction to Visual Perception* (1974);[53] developmentalist Thomas Rowland wrote a book called *The Mind of Man: Some Views and a Theory of Cognitive Development* (1971);[54] neurophysiologist Karl Pribram, whose work has been important for psychology, edited a book with the title *Brain and Behavior: I. Mood, States and Mind: Selected Readings* (1969);[55] physiological psychologist José Delgado published a book called *Physical Control of the Mind: Toward a Psychocivilized Society* (1969);[56] and Julian Jaynes, an experimental psychologist at Princeton University, wrote a controversial book with the title *The Origin of Consciousness in the Breakdown of the Bicameral Mind* (1977).[57] In addition to appearing in titles of books written by mainstream American psychologists, "mind" was used increasingly in research and theoretical articles.

Consciousness found its way back into American psychology for some of the same reasons that the discipline became more cognitive. Tomkins explains the return of consciousness as follows:

The paradox of this second half of the twentieth century is that the return to the classical problems of attention and consciousness was not a return by psychologists who had a change of heart. It is a derivative rather of the initiative of the neurophysiologists and automata designers. The neurophysiologists boldly entered the site of consciousness with electrodes and amplifiers. They found that the stream of consciousness from the past could be turned on and off by appropriate stimulation. They found that there were amplifier structures which could be turned up and down, by drugs and by electrical stimulation, and that consciousness varied as a function of such manipulation.... The renewed interest in the problem of awareness and attention is a consequence also of the extraordinary achievements of automata creators. It appears that the regaining of consciousness is less awkward for Behaviorists if it can first be demonstrated with steel and punched cards that automata can think, can program, can pay attention to input, can consult their memory bins, all in intelligent sequences—in short, that they can mimic the designers who intended they should do so."[58]

The readmission of consciousness to psychology was also a function of (a) the drug culture of the late sixties which was interested in altering conscious experience with LSD, peyote, cylocybin, marijuana, and other chemicals; (b) the interest in Eastern thought which became prevalent in the early 1970s; and (c) the increasing influence of existentialism and phenomenology. Perhaps the most effective voice for a psychology considered as the study of conscious experience has been Robert E. Ornstein who wrote a book entitled *The Psychology of Consciousness* (1972)[59] and edited a volume of readings called *The Nature of Human Consciousness* (1973).[60] Journals concerned with states of consciousness also appeared. In 1969 the *Journal of Transpersonal Psychology* was first published, followed in 1970 by *The Journal of Phenomenological Psychology* and in 1973 by the *International Journal of Altered States of Consciousness*.

Existentialism and phenomenology played important roles in returning consciousness to psychology because both orientations are directly concerned with conscious experience. The existentialists see existence, that is, the world as actually experienced, as more important than concepts, principles, and theories that try to give order to experience. What you are aware of and what you do are the vital matters, not theoretical explanations of your feelings, perceptions, thoughts, and behavior.

Phenomenology is an approach to studying consciousness which emphasizes the complementary nature of person and world, assumes that there are nonreflective conscious experiences, that is, experiences not given form by labels or categories, and proposes that consciousness can be fruitfully studied by means of disciplined reflection. Phenomenologists are directly interested in studying conscious experience with the understanding that perceiver and perceived are two aspects of one process.

For a recent review of consciousness in post-World War II psychology, see Hilgard (1980).[61]

Research on Feelings and Emotions The study of affect has not been a highlight of American psychology during the postwar decades. The "Loyola Symposium on Feelings and Emotions" organized by Magda B. Arnold and held in 1968, however, indicated that important thinking and study in this area had occurred during the 1950s and 1960s.[62] While a few of the conference participants were psychiatrists or physiologists, the majority were psychologists. The papers had to do with theories based on biological considerations; physiological correlates of feeling and emotion; cognitive theories of feeling and emotion; psychological approaches to the study of emotion; and the role of feelings and emotions in personality. Though some attempts were made to construct a comprehensive theory of affective processes, the presentations taken as a whole demonstrate that the research involved was diverse and framed in a variety of conceptual schemas.

Aside from clinical studies of anxiety and research done by physiological investigators such as K. H. Pribram, R. Melzack, and J. V. Brady, the most important direct study of emotion has been that of Stanley Schachter. Schachter demonstrated that emotions have a cognitive component that reflects external conditions. Hunger, joy, apathy, and other states are not automatically a function of the level of a particular chemical in the bloodstream. Rather the feeling or emotion exhibited is a function of environmental conditions. Epinephrine may, for example, key you up; but the circumstances determine whether or not you experience joy or hostility.[63]

The work of Harry Harlow on monkey love was also important. However, since it was done on animals rather than people, its implications for understanding human emotions are limited. (See chapter 8 for more on Harlow.)

Although the Loyola Symposium demonstrated that there have been psychologists during the post-World War II period who were specifically interested in the study of feeling and emotion, there is even today a tendency, particularly in academic-research psychology, to avoid using these concepts. Skinner, for instance, takes the position that inferred or privately experienced states like feelings, images, and percepts have no causative function and therefore are not useful in explaining behavioral changes. Most non-Skinnerians steer away from research on feelings and emotions unless it is couched in such terms as aggressive behavior, sexual responses, affiliative tendencies, or consummatory behavior.

The fragmentation of psychology is perhaps nowhere better demonstrated than in the theory and research on the psychological processes. While there is general agreement that the overall guidance system of man and other complex organisms involves a coordination of sensory, perceptual, cognitive, and affective processes, virtually no one has attempted to study the entire mechanism. There are, instead, those who do research on visual perception, others who investigate the chemical senses, some who study short-term or long-term memory, and even a few who attempt to probe one or another emotion or feeling. Research on the guidance system as a whole is complex and foreboding; nevertheless, an adequate theory of human functioning will not be forthcoming, in my opinion, until a reasonable number of psychologists make a serious attempt to investigate the system in its entirety.

Physiological Psychology and Psychological Processes

The mind-body problem has been central to psychological inquiry since the time of the ancient Greeks. Aristotle believed that form and substance were the essential characteristics of all objects and that mind and body constituted the form and substance of a person. Many centuries later Descartes proposed that mind and body were separate but interacting realms. For Leibniz mind and body operated in parallel and did not influence each other. Some theorists have suggested that mind and body are two aspects of a transcendent reality, others that mind and consciousness emerge from the interaction between people as physical entities and their surrounds.

Most post-World War II American psychologists, while not necessarily interested in the mind-body issue in a formal sense, agree that advances in psychological inquiry are to an extent related to the degree to which we understand the functioning of the body. Even Skinner, who has urged that psychologists concentrate on the relationships between behavioral and environmental changes, acknowledges that behavioral psychology will be furthered by progress in the neurosciences.

As has been stated before, interest in psychological processes was augmented during the postwar period by advances in psychophysiological research. Much of this work, it should be pointed out, was not conducted by individuals with degrees in psychology but was done by neurophysiologists and other scientists. In that sense progress in this area was not primarily a contribution of psychologists; rather, psychology has benefitted from the findings of investigators in other disciplines.

Equipped with refined electronic hardware and techniques such as microelectrodes, oscilloscopes and computer analyses of wave forms, researchers have studied every prominent bump and fissure in the central nervous system as well as the identifiable components of the sensory systems. Some progress has been made in deciphering the functioning of all the major subsystems comprising the brain, the brain stem, and peripheral nervous system.

The findings which have had the most bearing on psychology during the postwar period are that (*a*) the memory process can be activated by electrical stimulation of the cortex (Penfield, 1958);[64] (*b*) there are centers in the brain associated in complex ways with pleasure and discomfort (Olds, 1956);[65] (*c*) the reticular formation of the brain stem is directly involved with sleep, wakefulness, and selective attention (Moruzzi and Magoun, 1949);[66] (*d*) the functional organization of the visual cortex of cats is produced to some degree by early visual experiences (Wiesel and Hubel, 1965);[67] (*e*) activity level influences gland size in rats (Levine, 1960);[68] (*f*) the brain is active even when separated from external stimulation (Burns, 1958);[69] (*g*) many of the processes of the brain involve feedback mechanisms (Pribram, 1962);[70] (*h*) the left and right hemispheres perform different functions (many of the details of this differentiation are still being worked out) (Sperry, 1968);[71] (*i*) psychological processes (for example, perception and affect) are directly a function of the chemical activities taking place in the minute spaces (synapses) separating neurons-in-sequence (Eccles, 1964);[72] and (*j*) certain drugs can relieve anxiety and depression and inhibit thinking processes that interfere with productive living. The evidence which indicates that behaviors of all types are influenced by hormone levels has also been important.

A number of general theories of brain functioning have influenced American psychology during the post-World War II years. Foremost among these have been the Gestalt theory of isomorphism,[73] Hebbs' cell assembly-phase sequence theory,[74] and Pavlov's brain excitation theory.[75] Of somewhat lesser importance has been Stellar's brain center theory.[76] More recently, Pribram's holographic theory of brain functioning[77] has been of considerable interest to psychologists. Neurophysiological considerations, of course, also underlie the Freudian personality model; and

Hans Selye's three-phase stress reaction theory (General Adaptation Syndrome)[78] is based directly on a physiological analog.

In addition to helping make the study of psychological processes, mind, and consciousness respectable within psychology, advances in the neurosciences have also demonstrated the inappropriateness of stimulus-response theories of behavior change. Equally significant has been the gradual replacement of simple input models of sensation and perception by cybernetic conceptions that recognize both the self-monitoring nature of the sensory-perceptual systems and the fact that the brain as a whole is involved in every psychological event. Much of the fragmentation which characterizes the discipline may be dissipated as an adequate theory of physiological functioning is developed. A conceptually unified psychology will be based, I strongly believe, on a model of man with four major dimensions: the behavioral, the mentalistic-affective, the physiological, and the developmental.

8

TOWARD A COMPREHENSIVE DEVELOPMENTAL PSYCHOLOGY

Nature and Scope of the Field

Developmental psychology is concerned with the study of age-related (ontogenic) changes in psychological processes and behavioral capabilities from birth to death as they are manifested in man and other life forms.[1] Developmental psychologists assume that the full meaning of a particular psychological state or behavioral act can only be discerned if the event is considered in the framework of some nontrivial segment of the life span. Developmentalists play an important role in the discipline by reminding their colleagues that life is a process and that people and living entities in general have significance within temporal as well as spatial contexts.

The main controversies of the field center around the following questions: How much of psychological development is a function of hereditary factors and how much is due to environmental influences? (This is known as the nature-nurture issue.) Are developmental changes continuous or discrete? Are all changes unidirectional or do reversals take place? And, does psychological development go through predetermined stages with each stage characterized by the emergence of new perspectives and capabilities?

While none of these questions is as yet definitively answered, the cumulative evidence indicates that human psychological development is a function of complex interactions between genetic and environmental factors which allow for considerable flexibility in the developmental process. There is no data now unequivocally supporting theories that divide all or part of the human life span into specific stages (for example, the theories of Freud, Erikson, and Piaget). Each theory appears to account for some aspects of development, but none explains every major dimension of human psychological functioning.[2]

It should be pointed out that not all psychologists who study infants, children, or some other age group are in a strict sense developmentalists, believing that unique principles need be invoked to account for human functioning at different periods of life. Skinnerians, for example, propose that the principle of reinforcement essentially explains what people do whether they are two years, fifty years, or eighty years old.[3]

Although most of the developmental research since World War II has focused on infants and children, developmental psychology encompasses the entire life span and thus includes research on adult development and aging. Since developmentalists study species other than man, there is also considerable overlap between developmental and comparative psychology. Comparative psychologists conduct research involving two or more scientifically selected species of animals.

Developmental investigations have to do with every process or event of concern to psychologists in general. In addition to studying such basic psychological processes as sensation, perception, cognition, language, and emotion, developmentalists look into the emergence of social skills, the formation of personality, the genesis of the self concept, the acquisition of roles, the etiology of psychological problems, the factors involved in generating important psychological differences among people, and the identification and explication of the major transitional stages and periods of crisis characterizing human life.

Developmental research is complex, time consuming, and challenging. Longitudinal studies, which observe and measure the behavior of the same people or animals over time, are beset with the problem that the environment does not remain constant for the duration of the project. Cross-sectional investigations, on the other hand, which involve individuals differing in age or development, must take into account the fact that the subjects do not share common past experiences. Research strategies combining longitudinal and cross-sectional features reduce, to some degree, the limitations of each approach used alone.

There are also nonexperimental ways of conducting developmental research. Biographies, autobiographies, or other writings and productions of particular individuals are frequently used as sources. In addition, the observations of child psychologists, pediatricians, educational specialists, gerontologists, psychiatrists, clinical psychologists, and psychohistorians provide useful information about the course of human life. Finally, cross-cultural studies afford valuable data and perspectives.

Investigators performing across-species comparisons (comparative studies) face special problems. To begin with, there is the question of which species to choose. While convenience, cost, and ethical factors must be considered, the most important scientific issues concern the appropriateness of the animals being considered for the processes to be investigated; the evolutionary relationships between or among species under consideration; and the question as to whether or not a meaningful across-species taxonomy of behavior is available. Species selection is, in short, not a casual matter in properly conducted comparative research. The ability to make meaningful generalizations from one animal to another or from animals to humans requires that subject choice be based on sound biological reasoning.

In 1957 University of Minnesota psychologist Wallace A. Russell wondered whether it would ever be possible for experimentalists, who by training tend to be interested in short-run studies, precisely defined variables, functional determinants of behavior, and the formulation of general behavior theories, to conduct developmental investigations. He concluded that the essentials of experimental research do not preclude the investigation of developmental processes and, in fact, predicted correctly the emergence of a strong experimental strain in developmental psychology.[4]

The major theoretical positions concerning human psychological development include preformationism, predeterminism, empiricism, and interactionism.

Robert G. Cooper has observed, "Until the 17th century all important aspects of humans (personality, values, thinking, abilities, etc.) were thought to be, like activity level, *preformed* at birth. Infants and children were viewed as being smaller and less knowledgeable than adults, but in all other respects the same."[5] Although infants are no longer viewed as miniature adults, there is increasing evidence that sensory, perceptual, and affective processes are already well-developed in the newborn. In that sense there is some support for the preformationist position.

Predeterminist theories assume that there is a regularity to human psychological development regardless of environmental and cultural variability and that this regularity is a function of a genetically-controlled program. The theories of Freud, Erikson, and Piaget, which contend that psychological development involves discrete, biologically-determined states, are contemporary predeterminist formulations.

Empiricism emphasizes the role of the environment in human development. While empiricists acknowledge the limits on psychological functioning placed by biological factors, they assume that the ways people behave, speak, think, and feel are functions of their particular experiences rather than a genetic code. Skinnerians are the leading contemporary proponents of developmental empiricism.[6]

The most comprehensive developmental orientation is probably interactionism. The interactionist proposes that development is a product of the continual interaction between genetic and environmental variables. To some degree all the major predeterministic theories (Freud, Erikson, Piaget) are interactional because all accept the proposition that psychological development, whether it be affective, cognitive, or social, is a function of both the particular experiences of the individual and genetic factors. Interactionism, which has been espoused by some psychologists for many years, is nothing more than a general orientation toward developmental processes; we know very little at this time about the nature and importance of particular interactions. However, the perspective is quite certainly an advance over preformationist, predeterminist, and empiricist doctrines, each of which ignores factors clearly important to human psychological development.

There is reason to believe that the move, since World War II, toward an interactional view of development, in conjunction with research on infancy and childhood, significant methodological advances, and increasing interest in a life-span perspective, signals the gradual emergence of a comprehensive developmental psychology.

Historical Background[7]

Child rearing, the metamorphosis of youngster to adult, questions concerning the roles of adults and the old in society, and the experience of death have been integral to human existence since the beginning of mankind. In all generations and all cultures adults have, of necessity, held certain beliefs concerning human development and the care of children. Even in the most primitive tribes some of these beliefs become formalized into guidelines for each successive set of parents and their offspring. Interestingly, Freud proposed that certain prescriptions of the Judeo-Christian tradition were originally adopted to protect children from their fathers.[8] Hunt points out that the "idea that early experience is of special importance for psychological development is [also] very old. It appears in *The Republic* (Book II) and in *The Laws* where Plato had the Athenian prescribe a course of experiences beginning even before birth."[9]

The direct roots of developmental psychology go back to the early eighteenth century when a small number of physicians and scholars produced reports of the behavior and development of "unusual" children.[10] For example, William Cheselden, a surgeon, compiled a short report in 1728 about the experiences of a boy who apparently saw clearly for the first time at the age of fourteen after a cataract operation. In 1770, Daines Barrington, a lawyer, wrote about the early musical genius of Mozart. In a theoretical vein, French-Swiss philosopher Jean-Jacques Rousseau (1712-1778) proposed that the development of a child is biologically predetermined, with the environment having little positive influence on the course of development. And finally, in 1777, J. N. Tetens, a German philosopher, published a book reviewing "the current status of thinking about development across the life span."[11] Tetens is credited with being the father of adult developmental psychology.

Interest in observing and writing about children with special talents, problems, or nurturing experiences continued throughout the nineteenth century. During the late 1800s Darwin's theory of evolution stimulated investigations of the developmental processes. By the 1890s a number of detailed "baby biographies" appeared. Adolph Quetelet, a Belgian statistician, conducted scientific research on the aging process; and Francis Galton, a British scientist and scholar, notes Merrill Elias, "established the experimental psychology of adult development in Great Britain."[12] According to John Cavanaugh, "the first major published records of child development were [apparently] William Preyer's *Die Seele des Kindes* (1882/1889) and G. Stanley Hall's *Contents of Children's Minds* (1883)."[13] Toward the end of the century William James wrote about educational applications of psychology, Edward Thorndike was systematically studying the learning process, and Lightner Witmer founded a clinic for children at the University of Pennsylvania.

During the last decade of the nineteenth century, genetic psychology, which some scholars consider the pioneer science of human development, emerged.[14] In 1893, G. Stanley Hall, then president of Clark University, offered the first course presenting this theory systematically. With its roots in evolutionary theory, genetic psychology assumed that (*a*) "the growth and development of children [is] instinctively controlled and fragilely liable to arresting social pressures," and (*b*) "the growth and development of adolescents [is] malleable and susceptible to environmental thrusts that, in contrast to their effects on children, might advance evolution."[15] The basic premise was that development is mostly under the control of genetic factors; however, during adolescence environmental events could bring about inheritable changes. The latter assumption is in compliance with Larmarck's, rather than Darwin's, theory of evolution. Furthermore, the theory also proposed that "ontogeny recapitulates phylogeny," that is, "that the order of appearance of original tendencies in the individual is more or less exactly that in which they have appeared in the race."[16] The period from conception to adolescence, in other words, is controlled by genetic factors reflecting the biological history of the species as a whole.

Early in the twentieth century (1900-1919), the events most important for developmental psychology included the founding of many child guidance clinics (though little research was conducted at these institutions);[17] mental testing of children, particularly when the Stanford-Binet intelligence test was developed in 1916; the gradual emergence of an experimental approach to developmental research, stimulated mostly by behaviorist John B. Watson and learning theorist Edward L. Thorndike; research and theorizing on schooling and the educational processes under the leadership of Edward Thorndike, G. Stanley Hall, and philosopher John Dewey; the formulation of several stage-theories of development;[18] and, finally, the establishment of a number of child study institutes, the first by Arnold Gesell at Yale in 1911.

During the 1920s more child study institutes were founded; some experimental work continued, with the influence of behaviorism increasing; Freud's ideas stimulated anthropologists to investigate child-rearing practices in a variety of cultures; and a number of long-range longitudinal studies were initiated, three at the University of California, Berkeley. (These investigations are still in progress.)[19] As noted by Don Charles, most of the research of the period concerned "tests and clinical reports, intelligence and other ability studies (especially mental deficiency), and learning, both human and animal."[20] The publication of Carl Murchison's *Handbook of Child Psychology*[21] indicated that child psychology was emerging as a separate research area.

The most significant developments in the 1930s were the increasing influence of Freudian theory on child psychology; the gradual emergence late in the decade of an interest in developmental processes by a few Hullians, in particular Robert Sears and Hobart O. Mowrer; Gestalt psychologist Kurt Lewin's demonstration that one could do empirical studies of child behavior in natural settings; and concern over the problems of the old because of the plight of many of the elderly, brought about by the Great Depression. In 1939, the U.S. Public Health Service established a National Advisory Committee on Gerontology. Also in that year Sidney L. Pressey and Raymond G. Kuhlen published one of the first textbooks concerned with development across the life span.

To summarize, while interest in human development and child rearing is integral to the survival of the species, formal developmental studies did not appear until the eighteenth century. The first real catalyst for developmental theorizing was Darwin's theory of evolution which led to genetic psychology (recapitulation theory) toward the end of the nineteenth century.

Early in the twentieth century interest in child welfare and education produced movements which eventually stimulated much descriptive (normative) research on infants and children. By the 1920s behaviorism and psychoanalysis provided important new perspectives on child development, and a few long-range longitudinal studies were initiated. In the 1930s the problems of the elderly during the depression inspired gerontological research.

Overview of the Post-World War II Period

Among the major trends and events in developmental psychology during the thirty years following World War II were replacement of descriptive, normative studies with experimental investigations; transformation of the behavioral influence from a Hullian (1940s-1950s) to a Skinnerian (1960s) and finally a cognitive orientation (late 1960s-1970s); broadening the scope of the area from one concerned almost entirely with child development (1940s-1950s) to one encompassing the entire life span; increasing animal research; a gradual change in the psychoanalytic influence away from classical Freudian theory toward neo-Freudianism and ego psychology; the emergence in the field of a vigorous cognitive and psycholinguistic strain (1960s-1970s); and the general acceptance of a multifactor, interactional view of human development.

In addition, the specialty grew substantially not so much in terms of number of developmental psychologists but in terms of the amount of research done in the area. The burgeoning of publications in the field is referred to repeatedly by the authors of the chapters on child psychology and developmental psychology in the *Annual Review of Psychology* even as early as the late 1950s. The appearance of the following new journals also reflect the growth of the field: *Merrill Palmer Quarterly of Behavior Development* (1954), *Journal of Child Psychology and Psychiatry* (1960), *Journal of Experimental Child Psychology* (1964), *Developmental Psychology* (1969), *Journal of Clinical Child Psychology* (1972), and *Journal of Abnormal Child Psychology* (1973).

Looking at the period as a whole in 1979, psychologist Sheldon H. White concludes: "Developmental psychology has had an anomalous history, standing outside the mainstream of psychology for some time and then coming into the middle of the mainstream in the last two decades."[22]

Important research took place in a wide variety of areas, in particular: child-rearing practices and parent-child interaction; the effects of early experience on human and animal behavior; IQ and the nature-nurture controversy; imprinting and critical periods; animal social behavior; experimental studies of infants; language development; perceptual learning; cognitive development; the process of dying and death; the development of individual differences in personality and sex roles; and psychological studies of the elderly.

According to a recent survey of three groups of American psychologists,[23] events and influences with direct relevance for developmental psychology which were ranked among the one hundred top occurrences in psychology as a whole were the increasing influence of cognitive theory; the impact of Piaget; Harlow's primate research; the growth of developmental psychology; social learning theory; experimental research on neonates and infants; increased interest in complex psychological processes; a changing view of the IQ concept; the influence of ethology; the *Brown* vs. *Board of Education* Supreme Court decision; the growth of psycholinguistics; research and theory on personality; the competent infant concept; deprivation (sensory, maternal) research; Jensen's views on race and IQ; Hebb's theory and research; research on monkey language; the influence of psychoanalysis; research on death and dying; the new structuralism; transformational grammar; and ego psychology.

Another survey of American psychologists, this one concerned with identifying the leading individuals insofar as post-World War II American psychology is concerned,[24] determined that the following people, who had some bearing on developmental psychology, were considered among the most important: B. F. Skinner, Sigmund Freud, Jean Piaget, Erik Erikson, Harry Harlow, Kurt Lewin, and Donald O. Hebb.

Recent citation studies[25] affirm the importance for American psychology of these individuals. Other developmentalists whose work was highly cited include Albert Bandura, Jerome Bruner, Arthur Jensen, Jerome Kagan, Roger Brown, Lawrence Kohlberg, Walter Mischel, John Bowlby, Anna Freud, R. Zajonc, G. H. Bower, Eleanor J. Gibson, Urie Bronfenbrenner, J. McV. Hunt, and J. P. Guilford.

Also having a significant influence on developmental psychology were Austrian ethologists Konrad Lorenz and Nikolas Tinbergen, who shared the Nobel Prize in 1973.

The Late 1940s and 1950s

Since many of the psychologists conducting developmental studies in the 1930s worked for the government during the war, little developmental research was done between 1940 and 1945.[26] In the late 1940s and 1950s, there was, however, increasing interest in methodological issues.[27] As Richard M. Lerner has pointed out, this was accompanied by "a progressive shift from studies involving the mere collection of data toward those concerned with more abstract psychological processes and behavioral constructs."[28] A truly experimental developmental psychology was still in the formation stage. Most of the research conducted at that time was cross-sectional in design.

The major theoretical influences were classical Freudian theory, Hull's general behavior theory, Lewin's Gestalt theory, which tried to view development as a function of the total situation, and, increasingly, Hebb's interactional theory of early development. The organismic perspective, emphasizing, in the words of Hall and Lindzey, "the unity, integration, consistency, and coherence of the normal personality,"[29] also generated some developmental studies, particularly by Heinz Werner at Clark University. Finally, ego psychology, an extension of Freudian theory concerned primarily with strategies for dealing with the demands of the environment rather than intrapsychic conflicts, was, through the work of Anna Freud (Freud's daughter) and Heinz Hartmann, becoming a significant theoretical force within developmental psychology.

During this period the focus was on child psychology,[30] with most important research being done at the child research stations of the Universities of California (Berkeley), Minnesota, and Iowa. Investigations tended to focus on personality development, parent-child relations, social behavior, childhood illnesses, intelligence, institutionalized children, and delinquency. At the same time anthropologists and sociologists were conducting numerous studies on children. British psychiatrist John Bowlby, with United Nations support, wrote an important cross-culturally oriented book on the effects on children of maternal deprivation. Roger Barker observed children in natural settings. The long-range longitudinal studies initiated during the 1920s continued; and noteworthy developmental animal research was being conducted by psychologists Hebb, Harlow, Eckhard Hess, and Frank Beach, Austrian ethologists Lorenz and Tinbergen, and a few others.

There was also considerable interest in the capabilities and problems of the elderly. In 1946, the *Journal of Gerontology* was founded; and, in 1947, Division 20, concerned with maturity and old age, was established.

The major controversies had to do with the role of theory in developmental research, methodological issues, the nature-nurture question, and two opposing views on the nature of perceptual learning.

Analysts of the period tended to be critical of the field as a whole. Roger Barker, who reviewed child psychology in 1951, wrote: "A conspicuous feature of child psychology in 1950 is the absence of a well-defined body of literature to which a reviewer can turn.... There is little evidence of the existence of a professional group of skilled child behavior specialists....Child psychology in 1950...lacks vigor....The low level of scientific output to child psychology...is in contrast with the amount of programatic, didactic, and speculative writing."[31]

Helen L. Koch, a reviewer of child psychology in 1954,[32] stated: "Too many studies, though not without some merit, have little foundation in systematic theory. Their goal seems to be rather to observe and see what 'turns up'."[33] She also believed that psychoanalytic assumptions were frequently being accepted uncritically.

Wayne Dennis in 1955 also took a negative view of the situation in child psychology: "We support science to an extent to which it has never been supported before. At the same time, there is much public concern with problems of child rearing, personality development and education. But a genuine experimental attack upon the problems in these fields is almost lacking."[34]

There were acknowledgements during the late 1950s and early 1960s by analysts of the field that more systematic research, much of it inspired by psychoanalysis, field theory, learning theory, Hebb's interactional theory, and even the Piagetian orientation, was being conducted. There was also recognition of the fact that research on the effects of early experience on development, studies concerned with perceptual learning, Harlow's surrogate mother work, and analyses of child-rearing practices in Israeli Kibbutzim were significant contributions.

Some reviewers, however, continued to take a very negative view of developmental psychology. Henrietta T. Smith and L. Joseph Stone, while expressing some optimism over the state of affairs in 1960, indicated that their dismay arose from "papers of an arid scientism; from 'theoretical' papers dealing with theory at a level of medieval disputation, insusceptible to real generalization; from clinical reports riddled with *post hoc* reasoning and dubious assumptions."[35] Smith and Stone felt that there was "a need and hunger for genuine theoretical advance and the opening of new research areas."[36] They were also distressed by the fact that the most productive hypotheses often came from outside the field of psychology.

Emergence of an Experimental Developmental Psychology Although scientific psychology came into being during the 1870s in Europe and the 1880s in the United States, modern experimental research, that is, studies involving the careful manipulation of specific variables in relatively stable settings and the statistical analyses of data, did not appear in American psychology until around 1900. Most of the early experimental work had to do with the learning processes. Virtually all the developmental research conducted prior to World War II was directed primarily toward identifying those capabilities associated with chronological age. Most of it was not truly experimental.

The roots of experimental developmental psychology, however, do extend back to the beginning of the twentieth century. Of special significance were Edward L. Thorndike's research on education and learning; the infant conditioning studies of John B. Watson; the extensive testing of children during the 1920s and 1930s; and Arnold Gesell's normative studies of infants and children. Considerable animal research was also conducted in those years.

It was the work of Lorenz on imprinting and Freud's contention that early experience is important to human development which led directly to the coming into being of experimental developmental psychology. The psychologists most responsible for the creation of an experimental psychology of development, according to Lee Cronbach, were Harlow, Hebb, and Eckhard Hess.[37] One can also make a strong case for adding Kurt Lewin, who insisted on an empirical approach to the study of human behavior, and Hullians Robert R. Sears[38] and Hobart Mowrer.

Research on the Influence of Early Experience on Development Until the nineteenth century the predominant view of human development was preformationism. During the nineteenth century predeterminism emerged, largely as a result of Darwin's theory of evolution. The predeterminist doctrine prevailed until about the 1950s, even though educational theorists going back to the eighteenth century argued for the importance of early experience in human development and the behaviorist orientation, which had become a significant force in American psychology by the 1920s, emphasized environmental rather than hereditary factors. J. McVicker

Hunt, in his 1979 review of the research on early experience and development, states, "[T]he idea that early experience is of special importance for psychological development is very old [but] this idea never . . . became educationally or socially or politically significant until after World War II."[39]

Hunt identifies four main sources for the post-World War II investigation of early experience and development: paradoxically, the denial that early experience plays a significant role in behavioral development; the work of Freud; the studies of the ethologists; and the neurophysiological theory of Hebb. He also recognizes the special importance for the early experience issue of the investigations done on maternal deprivation and maternal attachment.

Research questioning the importance of early experience on development attempts to show either that "instincts constitute unlearned patterns of behavior which emerge automatically with neuromuscular maturation," or that "the rate of behavioral development is determined by maturation which, in turn, is fixed or predetermined by heredity."[40] While some studies, particularly of animals, demonstrated that the appearance of many behavioral capabilities seems to be under the control of innate factors, little influenced by specific organism-environment interactions, subsequent research indicated that experience clearly plays a role in behavioral development. The evidence increasingly showed that, if capabilities are not used as they emerge, development is less than optimal. It was also demonstrated that the longer a young organism is deprived of the opportunity to use a system, for example, the visual system, or the longer it is prevented from interacting normally with mother or peers, the more serious is the developmental impairment.

Most early views of intelligence also tended to deny the importance of experience during infancy. As studies became more sophisticated, however, it was apparent that the type of caretaking infants and children undergo determines, in part, how well they perform in intelligence tests.

Hunt points out that "Probably no one has done more than Freud to foster a belief in a special importance of early experience."[41] The specific conceptions that contributed directly to research on early experience were, in Hunt's view: "(1) the theory of psychosexual development, (2) the theory of infantile trauma, and (3) the role of mothering as the basis for attachment."[42] While most of Freud's specific ideas concerning early development received little support from the studies his theory generated, the research did demonstrate the special significance of early experience for human development.

Ethology is a branch of biology based on the naturalistic observation of insects and animals. It was founded in the 1930s by Austrians Lorenz, Tinbergen, and Karl von Frisch. Although their primary interest was instinctive behavior, the ethologists' work also highlighted the importance of early experience. The phenomenon of imprinting and the concept of critical periods, in particular, contributed directly to the emergence of an experimentally-oriented developmental psychology.

Naturalists had for a long time observed that birds which can walk immediately after hatching follow the first object they see moving, but it was Lorenz who first named the phenomenon "imprinting." Lorenz noticed that incubator-hatched goslings followed him instead of an adult goose because he was the first moving entity they saw. The ethologists also determined that imprinting occurs only during a brief time span, a critical period, following hatching. Subsequent research has shown that there are critical periods in different species for a variety of developmental events such as the formation of specific fears, attachments, visual capabilities, and socialization.

The person most responsible for conducting laboratory research on imprinting is American psychologist Eckhard H. Hess at the University of Chicago. Hess's work, which extends back to the middle 1950s, has focused on identifying the specific variables involved in the phenomenon.[43,44] His investigations represent the first systematic or programmatic attempt to study experimentally a specific developmental event. They, therefore, comprise one of the landmarks of early experimental developmental psychology.

Hunt states, "Hebb's neuropsychological theory, Riesen's discovery that infant chimpanzees reared for their first 16 months in the dark are functionally blind, and Hebb's own finding that pet-reared rats made progressively fewer errors than cage-reared rats in learning a series of mazes set off three separate streams of investigation."[45] Hebb's most important publication was *The Organization of Behavior* (1949), a book in which he first presented his neuropsychological theory. His ideas and research have, however, continued to be influential throughout the entire post-World War II period. In addition to contributing to the emergence of an experimental developmental psychology, he was also responsible for initiating research on sensory deprivation during the late 1950s and early 1960s; stimulating interest in physiological psychology; and helping return a cognitive perspective to American psychology by the late 1960s.

The three separate streams of investigation on early experience which Hebb's and Riesen's work inspired, according to Hunt, concerned respectively (*a*) the role sensory and motor processes play in perceptual development (Hebb emphasized sensory factors, but subsequent research showed that both processes are involved.); (*b*) the effects of early sensory deprivation on neurophysiological and neuroanatomical development (Studies appear to show, for example, that deprivation of early experience does hamper neuroanatomic and neurochemical maturation relative to the visuo-motor system.); and (*c*) the question of whether or not enriched environments have positive effects on the development of problem-solving skills and intelligence (Research findings as of now have not resolved this issue.)

Almost every textbook on introductory psychology includes photographs of some of the monkeys involved in Harry Harlow's research at the University of Wisconsin Primate Center. The pictures usually show young animals relating either to peers or to cloth-and-wire mother surrogates.

Harlow's research is notable for four reasons: first, because he carefully investigated some of the neglected factors like touching that are involved in the maternal role; second, because he systematically studied the relative importance of mother and peers relative to later social and sexual development; third, because he used monkeys, rather than rats or pigeons, which made his findings appear more relevant to human behavior; and, finally, because he was a pioneer in the experimental investigation of attachment and love.

The fact that Harlow experimentally studied love, a positive affect, was particularly significant because post-World War II psychologists, strongly influenced by the doctrine that one must investigate only those phenomena which can be easily defined (operationism), ignored feelings and emotions. The small minority of psychologists who were interested in this area (mostly clinicians) tended to concentrate on negative affects such as anxiety, fear, and pain. It was only Harlow who demonstrated that it was possible, and indeed essential, for experimental psychologists to study those experiences that bring social animals together.[46]

To summarize, the influence of psychoanalysis and ethology and the work of psychologists Hebb, Hess, and Harlow during the 1940s and 1950s led to the experimental study within American psychology of the effects of early experience on behavioral and psychological development. During the 1960s and 1970s, research in this area has burgeoned. Hunt, for example, reported that by 1954 fewer than 300 studies had been reported, while during the 1968 through 1977 period over 1,500 articles were published.

Perceptual Learning and Perceptual Development In their classic article, "Perceptual Learning: Differentiation or Enrichment?" James J. Gibson and his wife Eleanor J. Gibson[47] ask: "Is perception a creative process or is it a discriminative process? Is learning a matter of enriching previously meager sensations or is it a matter of differentiating previously vague impressions?"[48] If the first hypothesis is true, then with experience perception becomes increasingly imaginary; if the second hypothesis is valid, then with experience we become more aware of the information in the stimulus—that is, we make more refined differentiations.

The Gibsons presented research findings that support the differentiation position and in the process demonstrated a procedure held in high regard by research psychologists, that is, the design of a study with the ability to test two competing hypotheses.

Joachim F. Wohlwill, in his highly cited 1960 review of developmental studies of perception, wrote: "There are . . . signs of a definite reawakening of interest in the problem of perceptual development of late, parelleling perhaps the similar revival in the area of perceptual learning."[49] He went on to state that the revival had been more extensive in Europe than in the United States. Wohlwill summarized the findings of studies on sensory thresholds; illusions; orientation and perceptual localization; depth, form, number, movement, and time perception; perceptual learning; and the perceptual constancies (Perception of size, shape, and other characteristics of the visual display remain constant even though the information received by the retina changes.). He reported three general findings: first, that "assimilation tendencies decrease with age, while contrast effects, at least of the temporal variety, increase.";[50] second, that "the younger child generally fails to relate a stimulus to the spatial framework in which it appears";[51] and third, that "compared to the adult the young child requires more redundancy in a pattern to perceive it correctly."[52]

Nature-Nurture Controversy While the nature-nurture debate has a long history, during the 1940s and 1950s the controversy centered around George E. Coghill's theory postulating a relationship between the growth of the nervous system and changes in behavioral characteristics (His most influential research involved salamanders.);[53] Arnold Gesell's contention that the development of human behavioral and psychological capabilities is largely determined by innate mechanisms;[54] the question as to whether or not IQ is fixed or influenced by experience; and the determination of the degree to which perceptual organization is innate or acquired.[55] The specific manifestations of those issues were a direct legacy of work done prior to World War II. Coghill's research, for example, extended from 1902 to the late 1930s; many of Gesell's most well-known writings appeared in the 1920s and 1930s, as did a number of important studies concerning the stability of IQ over time and the origins of perceptual structure. The Gestalt psychologists were largely responsible for rekindling the controversy in the area of perception.

During the 1940s and 1950s, research findings seemed to suggest that both Coghill's and Gesell's positions placed too much emphasis on genetic factors. There was also increasing disagreement not only about the determinants of IQ but what it was that IQ signified. Relative to the origins of perceptual organization, the controversy was a standoff, there being some support for both the nativists (those placing emphasis on innate factors) and the empiricists (those emphasizing the role of experience).

The 1960s

The amount of research done by developmental psychologists during the 1960s increased dramatically, but no unifying theory evolved. The influence of classical Freudian theory declined; however, the neo-Freudian outlook of Erik Erikson, which presents a developmental schema across the entire life span, remained significant. Within the behaviorist tradition the Skinnerian perspective replaced the Hullian by the early 1960s. Skinner's operant conditioning played a central role in making possible an experimental approach to the study of neonates and young infants.

The single most important trend was the increasing influence of Swiss psychologist Jean Piaget's theory of and research on cognitive development. Also noteworthy was the theory of language acquisition proposed by linguist Noam Chomsky, which emphasized genetic rather than environmental factors and represented a view diametrically opposed to Skinner's. Finally, toward the end of the decade, interest in the study of death and dying, inspired in part by existentially-oriented psychologists, signaled what was to develop into a vigorous new concern in the 1970s with the study of the elderly. Methodologically, progress was made both by the introduction of Piagetian research techniques and the design of procedures combining longitudinal and cross-sectional features.[56]

Other contributions of some consequence were the cross-cultural studies of child rearing conducted by Urie Bronfenbrenner, Jerome Kagan, Melford Spiro, and Albert Rabin (Spiro and Rabin investigated practices in Israeli kibbutzim.); Jerome Bruner's research on cognitive development; Roger Brown's work on language acquisition; the theory of cognitive and moral development proposed by Lawrence Kohlberg; the research and social learning theory of Albert Bandura which combined cognitive and behavioral factors and processes; the studies of childhood autism and childhood schizophrenia done by Bruno Bettelheim, a psychoanalyst, and O. Ivar Lovaas, a Skinnerian; and the work of James Birren, who did systematic gerontological investigations years before the renaissance of gerontological psychology in the 1970s.

Reviewers of the period were in general heartened by the growth of developmental psychology and the infusion of new perspectives, but discouraged by the fact that there were no signs of a unifying theory and by indications that recently fresh perspectives were beginning to rigidify.[57]

The Influence of Jean Piaget Among the most important influences on American developmental psychology during the post World War II period has been the work of Swiss psychologist Jean Piaget (1896-1980). Trained in biology with a strong interest in philosophy, particularly epistemology, Piaget set out in the 1920s to study intellectual evolution from childhood to adult life. As a consequence, he spent approximately

sixty years, most of them as director of the Jean-Jacques Rousseau Institute in Geneva, researching the thought processes of children.

His first five books, published between 1923 and 1932, concerned
language and thought, judgment and reasoning, children's conceptions
of the world, physical causality, and moral judgment. As a consequence
of this early work, he became convinced that intellectual development
involves qualitatively different stages of thought. He also proposed that
early development is primarily a function of the infant acting on the
environment rather than social reinforcement or the emergence of language.

During the rest of his career (1940s-1970s), Piaget's research on intellectual development continued to center on specific phenomena such as
the child's conception of time, movement, speed, space, geometry, and
chance. He also wrote on symbolic thought, genetic epistemology, the
growth of logical thinking, memory, structuralism, the science of education, and consciousness. In all, Piaget published over fifty books and
numerous articles.

Piaget's theory of intellectual development proposes that infants and
children construct and reconstruct reality out of their interactions with
the environment. Reality is, in other words, not a copy of sensory impressions but rather a product of particular transformational processes
involving sensory information and actions, with these processes changing across the period from birth through adolescence.[58] The world of the
infant is, therefore, qualitatively at variance from the world of the five-
year old and others of different ages.

Piaget, according to Herbert Ginsberg and Sylvia Opper, conceives of
the person as inheriting "physical structures which set broad limits on
intellectual functioning. Many of these are influenced by physical maturation. The individual also inherits a few automatic behavioral reactions
or reflexes which have their greatest influence on functioning in the first
few days of life. These reflexes are rapidly transformed into structures
which incorporate the results of experience."[59] Piaget's theory further
assumes that all species by nature have a tendency to organize their
processes and to adapt to the environment. Adaptation is, according to
Piaget, accomplished by the complementary processes of assimilation
(using available schemas to deal with the environment) and accommo-
dation (modifying existing schemas in response to environmental demands).

Piaget divides intellectual development into four stages, each depending on the cognitive skills characterizing the previous stage and, in fact,
representing an integration at a more complex level of earlier transformational processes. The stages are (a) sensory-motor (birth to two years)
during which time the infant constructs his/her world out of sensory
information and action (the action at first being entirely reflexive); (b)
preoperational (two to seven years) when mental representations and
symbols become part of the reality of the child and he or she is no longer

limited to interactions with physically present objects; (c) concrete operational (seven to eleven years) when children can operate logically with symbols which refer to concrete situations (They can, for example, understand that the weight or volume of material remains the same even if its shape changes.); and (d) formal operational (twelve years on) when children develop the ability to deal with hypothetical situations.

In summarizing Piaget's theory, Cooper states: "[D]evelopement is the result of an *interaction* between adaptation, organization, and hereditary structures, all of which are preformed; maturation of the nervous system, which is predetermined; and physical and social experience, which depend on the particular environment to which the child is exposed. Piaget's theory is truly an interactionist theory because development depends on the joint operation of all these factors."[60]

There was some interest on the part of American psychologists during the 1920s and 1930s in Piaget's work, but his influence on the discipline was rather minimal until the 1960s. By the late 1970s Piaget, Freud, and Skinner were judged by three groups of American psychologists to be the individuals most important to post-World War II psychology.[61] In 1967, by contrast, 220 department chairmen considered Piaget only the seventh most important person in psychology at that time.[62]

Piaget's theory and research were slow to influence American psychology for a variety of reasons. His writings are in French, and good translations of his publications were frequently not immediately available; early translations were sometimes inaccurate. His research is based on naturalistic and clinical observations of individual children rather than the manipulation of variables, group comparisons, and the statistical analysis of data. His theory places considerable emphasis on genetically-controlled processes, a position not very compatible with the behavioral and environmental orientation of American psychology during the 1930-1960 period. Moreover, cognitive processes were of little interest to most American researchers before the 1960s, again because of the strong behavioral slant of the discipline.

There was perhaps another more subtle reason for the relative disinterest in Piaget's work on the part of American psychologists during the 1940s and 1950s, namely the very grandiosity of the task Piaget set for himself. Even as a youth, for example, Piaget believed that it was his mission to dedicate his life to the biological explanation of knowledge. Unlike most American psychologists, he was not content to study one particular phenomenon or process, or to build a theory based on preselected laboratory techniques. Instead, his research was directed toward bringing together his knowledge of epistemology and logic with the careful observation of infants' and children's sensory, perceptual, and cognitive capabilities and strategies.

Piaget's broad conception of his work is illustrated by the following statement:

The psychology of intellectual evolution leans . . . upon the biological theories of adaptation, the psychological theories of understanding, the sociological theories of signs and norms (the rules of socialized thought), the history of science, and upon comparative logic. One can then consider this special branch of psychology as a genetic theory of knowledge, a broad theory which must borrow its elements from a great number of fields of research, thus partially synthesizing them, but withal an exact and well-defined theory, which has its own method, namely, the envisaging of intellectual realities only from the point of view of their development and genetic construction.[63]

Piaget was, in other words, anathema to most American psychologists, both because he tried to deal with a seemingly unmanageable question and because he used the techniques of naturalists and clinicians rather than experimentalists. Unlike Clark Hull, for example, who also set for himself a monumental goal, namely that of deriving a general theory of behavior, but who tied his quest to a particular experimental paradigm and methodology, Piaget's research program was generated by biological, sociological, and philosophical principles and assumptions. Using this approach, Piaget created the procedures necessary to demonstrate the developmental processes he inferred, as opposed to identifying developmental sequences utilizing an existing instrument or experimental environment. The research question generated the methodology rather than vice versa.

The influence of Piaget's work on American psychology increased dramatically by the middle sixties because the sheer volume of his work was by then difficult to ignore, books summarizing his theory and research appeared,[64] and attempts by behaviorally-oriented psychologists to explain intellectual and psycholinguistic development in terms of various conditioning paradigms were far from successful. Furthermore, Piaget's orientation was compatible with the interactional view of human psychological development which was gradually emerging.

Investigations inspired by Piaget continue unabated. In 1976, for instance, Herbert Ginsburg and Barbara Koslowski, who attempted to review the work done on cognitive development, wrote: "Research 'on Piaget' proceeds with a ferocity which makes a comprehensive review impossible."[65] These reviewers concluded that the three developments which "created a new field of cognitive development"[66] were Piaget's work; developments in psycholinguistics, particularly Noam Chomsky's theory of transformational grammar; and Eleanor J. Gibson's research on perceptual learning and development. They also pointed out that, in general, Piaget's theoretical proposals have been neither confirmed nor refuted. This is due primarily to the difficulty of adequately simulating naturally occurring events in the laboratory.

Contributing to the general resurgence of interest in cognitive and linguistic development were several American psychologists: Jerome Bruner, who unlike Piaget believed that verbal stimulation and schooling play a central role in conceptual development; Roger Brown, who carefully studied the role of parent-infant interactions in language acquisition; and Jerome Kagan, who investigated cognitive development in other cultures. In addition, the work of Russian psychologist Lev S. Vygotsky on conceptual development was increasingly appreciated by American investigators during the 1960s and 1970s.

The Experimental Study of Neonates and Young Infants The gradual move toward a more experimentally-oriented developmental psychology after the World War II included a significant increase in research on human infancy. According to psychologists L. Joseph Stone, Henrietta T. Smith, and Lois B. Murphy, who reviewed infancy research in the early 1970s, this growth was due to the following factors: (*a*) the realization that the patient observation of infants can provide useful insights; (*b*) the finding that babies are able to discriminate among a variety of stimuli; (*c*) the availability of more refined techniques for monitoring physiological changes, which in turn provide information concerning infants' responses to various stimulus presentations; (*d*) studies of attachment behavior in infant monkeys which helped legitimize research on affect and emotion; (*e*) new and innovative uses of classical and operant conditioning procedures to study sensory, perceptual, and learning processes in neonates and very young infants; and (*f*) increasing social concern during the 1960s and the 1970s over the effects of poverty, deprivation, and malnutrition on infants and children.[67]

Stone, Smith, and Murphy were particularly impressed with the work of Peter Wolff who, in the ethological tradition, observed four infants for periods up to eighteen hours, Robert L. Fantz's finding that babies would look for different lengths of time at various patterns indicating that they had the ability to make rather complex discriminations (These observations challenged Hebb's contention that pattern recognition requires a considerable learning period.), and Harry Harlow's studies of the emotional and social behavior of infant monkeys.

Other investigations which became widely known and therefore demonstrated to psychologists and other professionals that productive empirical research on human infants was possible were Eleanor Gibson and Richard D. Walk's visual cliff research that provided some evidence that young infants had the ability to use patterns of visual information in judging distance;[68] T. G. R. Bower's studies showing that young infants could recognize objects at various distances and object shapes at different orientations (In the language of perceptualists the infants demonstrated size and shape constancy.);[69] and the work of Lois Murphy, a psychoanalytic researcher, concerning the precursors in infant behavior of the coping devices and defense mechanisms developed later by children as they deal with the environment on the one hand and intrapsychic conflicts on the other.[70]

Interest in the study of infant behavior was also stimulated by the concern with the influence of early experience on both human and animal behavior generated by the theories of Freud and Hebb, the findings of ethologists, and the studies of Rene Spitz and John Bowlby on the effects of institutionalization and maternal deprivation, respectively, on psychological and emotional development.

Of all the research done on human infants, the most significant may turn out to be that done on neonates and infants no more than a few days old. It is this work that bears most directly on the question: What is the human being capable of before learning takes place (the nature-nurture issue)?

Interestingly, before it became possible during the late 1950s to study very young infants experimentally, the prevailing view was that neonates were extremely limited both behaviorally and in terms of their sensory and perceptual capabilites. Since the nervous system is not completely developed at birth, it was inferred that the "world" as experienced by the neonate was at best a sequence of rather misty transformations involving color, shadows, and unstable patterns. William James referred to it as a blooming, buzzing confusion. The highly structured world of adult consciousness was believed to be almost entirely a product of experience (the empiricist position).

Careful study of the sensory and perceptual capabilities of young infants has, however, led to a very different view of the consciousness of the newborn. It is evident now that human beings are born with the ability to make almost all judgments and discriminations that adults are capable of, though not as efficiently. Very young infants can, for example, differentiate among odors, colors, sounds, shapes, patterns, and tactile stimuli, indicating that the world as experienced at, or soon after, birth is highly structured and not an amorphous display of undulating, diffuse changes. The infant is, in short, now viewed as much more competent sensorily and perceptually than was the case before the advent of experimental infant psychology.

The "competent infant" concept [71] is without question one of the most revolutionary perspectives to come out of post-World War II American psychology. In relation to the nature-nurture controversy, this new view of the neonate gives support to the nativist position concerning the origins of the structure characterizing human consciousness. While experience allows us to make discrimination using less information, the basic organization of consciousness is apparently mostly there at birth.

The research techniques that made possible the experimental study of neonates and young infants were those involving the study of eye movements relative to various presentations (patterns, objects, colors) and those based on classical and operant conditioning and the phenomenon of habituation. Habituation is the process by which a response to a repeatedly presented stimulus gradually ceases. Eye movement (looking time) studies assume that one can make inferences about the visual capabilities and perhaps preferences of infants by first determining what it is that they look at and then finding out how long they look at various stimuli. Fantz, for example, found that infants as young as fifteen days old looked longer at a figure resembling a face than at other patterns.[72]

The use of conditioning and habituation techniques in research on neonates and young infants is illustrated by the investigations conducted at Brown University since the 1960s under the directorship of Lewis P. Lipsitt.[73] Using primarily head turning and sucking responses and operant conditioning techniques, Lipsitt and his associates have demonstrated that very young infants can be conditioned to discriminate among various odors, tastes, tactile stimuli, and sounds. Their success has been due, in part, to their recognition of the fact that, as Lipsitt notes, "those response systems of the young infant which are performed with the greatest ease, grace, or facility tend to be the ones which are probably most subject to alteration through the superimposition of environmental stimulation."[74] Head turning and sucking are easily performed even by neonates and are therefore susceptible to modification through the Skinnerian control of important contingencies like food or something to suck on.

Habituation studies of infant sensory capability tend to take the following form. An infant sucking a bottle is repeatedly presented with a particular stimulus, for example, a red light. At first the baby stops sucking when the light goes on. Eventually, however, the light fails to interrupt the sucking. The response of not sucking has habituated. Now a light of a different color (for example, orange), is substituted for the red light. If the infant identifies the orange light as different from the red, sucking should again be interrupted at least for a few presentations. If, on the other hand, the orange and red lights look identical, then the responses remains habituated when the lights are switched.

To summarize, most psychologists prior to the 1960s believed that the sensory and perceptual capabilities of young infants were virtually non-existent. During the 1960s and 1970s, as experimental approaches were developed to study neonates and infants less than a few hours old, it became apparent that the ability to discriminate among a variety of sensory and perceptual experiences was well developed at birth. The competent infant concept emerged.

The experimental study of the infant became possible because of a number of methodological advances. However, the most fruitful development, in my opinion, was the use of Skinnerian techniques to study sensory and perceptual phenomena. It may eventually be realized, paradoxically, that Skinner's primary contribution to research psychology has been to provide techniques which allow us to unravel the mysteries of infant consciousness. This would be paradoxical because it is Skinner who has most forcefully and persistently proclaimed that the concern of a scientific psychology is behavior, not mind or consciousness.

Research on Death and Dying Studies on the psychological implications of death and dying are not generally considered part of developmental psychology; nevertheless, it is clear that at least those investigations concerned with death as the inevitable termination point of the aging process are developmental in nature. As Paul B. Baltes, Hayne W. Reese, and Lewis P. Lipsitt, in their review of life-span developmental psychology, state, "When death is 'natural' rather than accidental, it is associated with a number of developmental objectives and processes. They include adaptation to finitude, adaptation to a process of physical debilitation, the continual restructuring of social environments because of the loss of significant others, the task of life review, and the phenomenon labeled predeath terminal drop...these themes of the dying process are properly identified and investigated as developmental phenomena."[75] It is interesting to note that, while a developmental perspective that deals with life as a process extending from birth to death should be concerned with the psychological aspects of death and dying, there is as yet little evidence that research in this area is finding a formal place within life-span developmental psychology.

Until the middle to late 1960s, American psychologists were not very interested in the psychological implications of death and dying. Of the just over four hundred publications (articles, books, presentations) listed by Richard A. Kalish in an annotated bibliography on death and bereavement published in 1965, only about forty are articles appearing in journals of psychology. Of these, approximately one-third were published during the 1960-1965 period.[76] A review of *Psychological Abstracts* (1927-1975) shows that psychologists did do some research on death during the 1930s, but interest decreased during the 1940s and 1950s. The most significant increase occurred during the 1965-1975 period.

It should be pointed out that, although American psychologists seem to have been relatively unconcerned with the study of death and dying before the middle sixties, work in the area was being done by psychoanalysts, psychiatrists, sociologists, and anthropologists. Psychologists were slow to become involved in research on death and dying because the phenomenon does not lend itself to experimental manipulation. In addition, there are problems in securing research subjects and the cooperation of other professionals, such as doctors and nurses in hospitals. Moreover, the subject matter can arouse strong negative feelings. Even in the early 1960s, for example, research on both death and suicide were classified as "taboo topics" along with the study of human sexual behavior, male homosexuality, parapsychology, graphology, religion, hypnosis, and international affairs.[77] These were all areas of study which psychologists for a variety of reasons tended to ignore.

The book which indicated that psychologists were becoming more interested in the study of death and dying was Herman Feifel's *The Meaning of Death* published in 1959. Feifel was at that time chief psychologist at the Veterans Administration Outpatient Clinic, Los Angeles, and Clinical Professor of Psychiatry (Psychology) at the University of Southern California School of Medicine. In the preface of the work Feifel observes, "Even after looking hard in the literature, it is surprising how slim is the systematized knowledge about death. Far too little heed has been given to assessing thoroughly the implications of the meaning of death. There is no book on the American scene which offers a multifaceted approach to its problems."[78] Although focusing on diagnosis and treatment, the work of psychologists Edwin S. Shneidman and Norman L. Farberow, who along with psychiatrist Robert E. Litman founded the Los Angeles Suicide Prevention Center in 1955, also played a prominent role in turning psychologists' attention to the study of death and dying.[79]

Interest in the topic was sustained during the 1960s primarily by the fact that helping professionals became increasingly concerned with the proper care of dying patients. In addition, books like Jessica Mitford's *The American Way of Death* (1963),[80] Jacques Choron's *Death and Western Thought* (1963),[81] and Elizabeth Kübler-Ross's *On Death and Dying* (1969)[82] helped create a far more serious concern on the part of the educated public with the problems associated with dying in our society.

In 1970 *Omega*, a journal specializing in articles on dying, was founded, as was a publication sponsored by the Foundation of Thanatology. In 1971, a journal entitled *Suicide* was established.

Psychologists became more involved with death and dying in the 1960s for several reasons. First, the growing percentage of individuals over sixty-five years of age made the care of the old more and more salient. Second, the growth of clinical psychology, which is concerned with the problems of people of all ages, including those associated with dying, brought the experience home to psychologists in general. Third, psychoanalytic thinkers, whose influence on American psychology was most profound during the 1940s and 1950s, had since the 1920s written fairly extensively about death anxiety. Finally, the influence of existential philosophers and novelists—for example, Heidegger, Sartre, and Camus—stimulated interest in questions having to do with the meaning of life and death. The existential influence was, in part, augmented by the growth of clinical psychology.

The Early 1970s

Research on the developmental aspects of cognitive processes and psycholinguistics, inspired by Piaget, Chomsky, Brown, Bruner, and eventually many others, continued during the early 1970s, as did work on the sensory and perceptual capabilities of neonates and young infants. Interest in the psychological aspects of death and dying was also sustained, not only within the discipline, but in other areas of study as well, particularly in sociology, religion, and the helping professions.

There were two major new trends within developmental psychology during the period. First, more psychologists became involved in studying the old (gerontology) largely because federal funds were made available for research in this area; and second, the need for a life-span perspective was gradually recognized. These years were also characterized by concern over the civil rights of children; research on the implications for the development of offspring of single-parent families and families wherein the father takes primary responsibility for child rearing;[83] the continuing study of the effects of TV on the young; and recognition that middle age, a period of the human life generally neglected by psychologists, was an important area of study for developmentalists.

The Surfacing of Gerontological Psychology The first prominent American psychologist to be formally concerned with the psychological aspects of aging was G. Stanley Hall who in 1922 published a book entitled *Senescence: The Second Half of Life*. Hall was, apparently, rather pessimistic about life after forty-five, believing strongly that the period between twenty-five and forty-five constituted the best years. Jarvik notes, "Regrettably, as pointed out by his psychobiographer, Dorothy Ross...Hall failed to resolve the conflicts of his own adolescence and resented every moment that moved him further away from his unlived youth. The tendency to equate old age with oblivion permeated Hall's writings."[84]

There was some interest in the study of the elderly during the 1930s because of the special burden placed on this group by the depression. The Gerontology Society was founded in 1945, which in turn sponsored the *Journal of Gerontology* in 1946. Then, in 1947, Division 20 on Maturity and Old Age (now called the Division of Adult Development and Aging) was established by the American Psychological Association.

According to Klaus Riegel, the professional literature on the psychological aspects of aging in the 1945-1970 period concerned the following areas of investigation (in descending order of frequency): intellectual deterioration, general intellectual changes, vocabulary achievements, verbal skills, psychomotor skills, short-term retention, dichotic listening, studies of adjustment, and social variables.[85] The most important gerontological psychologists during the period were James E. Birren and Jack Botwinick whose research focused on psychomotor and perceptual processes (Birren also edited an important handbook on aging in 1959.); Robert J. Havighurst and Bernice Neugarten at the University of Chicago who investigated a variety of social variables; and K. Warner Schaie and Paul B. Baltes, who by the middle 1960s created new developmental research designs that allowed investigators to study the interrelation-ships between sociohistorical and individual changes. Most of the psy-chologists who did studies using elderly subjects, however, were not gerontological psychologists. David Wechsler, for example, designer of several widely used intelligence tests, investigated the relationships be-tween age and IQ; but he was primarily a psychometrician rather than a gerontological researcher.

Evaluating the state of gerontological research in 1951, Nathan W. Shock concluded that while some progress had been made in the areas of perception and mental testing, "Far too much of our knowledge of elderly people is based on residents of institutions."[86] He also felt there was a need both for new methods capable of analyzing age trends in individuals and for more longitudinal studies.

In 1956, Irving Lorge, although acknowledging the increase in research on human aging since 1951, was concerned that too much emphasis was being placed on the problems associated with the elderly who were in need of some kind of help. Psychologists should, he felt, "recognize that not all the old are needy."[87] Like Shock, he called for more longitudinal studies; in addition, he urged that greater attention be given to theory construction.

Reviewing the work done from 1955 to 1959, James E. Birren pointed out that while there had been a significant increase in gerontological studies, "research on aging remains one of the large, relatively unex-plored areas in psychology."[88] He also mentioned that more books pre-senting a life-span developmental perspective were being published, a new journal named *Vita Humana* emphasizing life-span views had ap-peared, subjects of several longitudinal projects who were first studied as children were now middle-aged adults, some psychology departments were beginning to offer courses on gerontology, and the federal gov-ernment had called for a White House Conference on Aging to be held in January, 1961.

A decade later, Jack Botwinick looked back at the progress made from 1963 through 1968. He identified three related developments: the con-tinued growth rate of the number of publications on aging; recognition that there was a need to integrate research findings (more books were published); and increased attention to methodological issues.[89]

Despite the important research on the psychology of aging and signif-icant methodological advances occurring during the 1950s and 1960s, gerontological psychology did not surface within the discipline as an important, or at least visible, research area until the early 1970s. This change was mostly due to the "graying" of the American population. By then the group over sixty-five had become a significant segment of soci-ety and the federal government was providing generous support for psychological studies of the elderly.

Increasing interest in gerontological research within psychology was evidenced by the formation of a Task Force on Aging in 1970 by the American Psychological Association to prepare materials for a second White House Conference on Aging, which took place in 1971. This task force prepared a list of recommendations for the conference concerning: assumptions of the intellectual functioning of older people; the educational, mental health, and social needs of the elderly; and potential psychogerontological research. It also resulted in the compilation of two important books, *The Psychology of Adult Development and Aging*, published in 1973,[90] and *Aging in the 1980s*,[91] released in 1980. Further contributing to the establishment of gerontological psychology as a vigorous research area was the publication in 1977 of a three-volume set entitled, *The Handbooks of Aging*, edited by James E. Birren.[92]

The most direct evidence that gerontological psychology had emerged as a separate field of study, at least by the middle 1970s, was the fact that departments of psychology started recruiting for gerontological psychologists. While there were, and still are, few specialists of this type available, two things happened: first, more doctoral students selected gerontological thesis topics and thus gained some familiarity with the area; and second, psychologists became aware of the fact that there were graduate programs emphasizing adult development at the University of Chicago, Duke University, Pennsylvania State University, Washington University, Wayne State University, The University of West Virginia, and the Gerontology Center at the University of Southern California.

Vital to sustaining interest during the 1970s in the psychological aspects of aging were the methodologies and theories associated with cognitive development which had stimulated research on childhood during the 1960s. When it became apparent that these ideas and techniques could be applied to people of all ages, many new studies using elderly subjects were suggested.

A Life-Span Perspective Appears In 1980, Paul B. Baltes, Hayne W. Reese, and Lewis P. Lipsitt, authors of the first review of life-span developmental psychology to appear in the *Annual Review of Psychology*, wrote: "The last decade has seen a massive increase in research and theory related to life-span developmental psychology, particularly in the United States and German-speaking countries."[93] This trend, they proposed, was a function of three circumstances. First, there had for some time been programs emphasizing the life-span approach at the University of Chicago and several other American universities; second, the subjects of a number of longitudinal studies initiated prior to World War II reached adulthood during the 1960s and 1970s, stimulating research across the life span; and third, the growth of gerontological psychology, particularly in the 1960s, helped focus interest on adult development. To these factors one could certainly add Erik Erikson's theory that pertains to the entire life span.

The psychologist probably most responsible for bringing the life-span approach to the attention of American psychologists is Paul B. Baltes, now affiliated with the College of Human Development at Pennsylvania State University. In 1969, 1971, and 1972 he helped organize several conferences on life-span developmental psychology at the University of West Virginia. These conferences produced three influential, edited volumes.[94] In addition, Baltes has since 1978 edited an annual series entitled *Life-Span Development and Behavior* published by Academic Press.

The history of the life-span perspective goes back at least to J. N. Tetens, a German philosopher who published the first major work on human development from birth to death. The specific roots of a life-span perspective, however, extend back only to G. Stanley Hall's book on senescence written in the 1920s. While Baltes, Reese, and Lipsitt acknowledge that some of Swiss psychiatrist Carl Jung's writings in the 1930s helped generate an interest in a life-span framework, they identify the following three pre-World War II works as contributing most to the modest life span perspective which was sustained in American psychology during the 1950s and 1960s: Hollingworth's *Mental Growth and Development: A Survey of Developmental Psychology* (1927); Charlotte Bühler's *Der menschliche Lebenslauf als psychologisches Problem* (1933); and Pressey, Janney and Kuhlen's *Life: A Psychological Survey* (1939).

A life-span orientation is essential for developmental psychology, not only because it recognizes that organisms and people change in significant ways during the entire period from conception to death, but because this perspective offers the only comprehensive and potentially integrative theoretical framework for the field. One of the most important manifestations of the life-span view, to date, has been to highlight the systematic study of middle age. As a consequence, psychologists are only now becoming familiar with the work done on middle-aged adults by Carl Jung, Charlotte Bühler, Else Frenkel-Brunswik, Erik Erikson, Robert Havighurst, Bernice Neugarten, Lawrence Kohlberg, Jane Loevinger, Roger Gould, Daniel Levinson, Marjorie Fiske Lowenthal, George Vaillant, Ira Progoff, and, of course, Gail Sheehy, who wrote the best seller *Passages: Predictable Crises of Adult Life* (1974).[95]

Conclusion

In summary, developmental psychology has, since World War II, changed from a field devoted primarily to studies of child-rearing and the psychological capabilities of infants and children to a discipline characterized by several powerful theoretical formulations and an increasing focus on life-span perspectives. Most progress has been made in identifying the sensory and perceptual capacities of young infants; making a start toward unraveling the mysteries of cognitive and psycholinguistic development; and correcting some of the early mistaken notions concerning the relationships between aging and the diminishing of psychological functioning. There are, for example, large individual differences with regard to the ways the aging processes influence intellect and personality. Although recent interest in life-span perspectives represents real progress toward the formation of a comprehensive developmental psychology, there is at this time no theory capable of integrating and accounting for the many complex dimensions of psychological development.

Klaus F. Riegel, in analyzing the history of developmental psychology, contends that American developmentalists, at least prior to Piaget's influence in the 1960s, embraced what he calls the "capitalistic-mechanistic" model that conceives of development as "an accumulation of environmental information by essentially passive organisms."[96] Continental European developmental psychologists such as Piaget have, on the other hand, adhered to the "mercantilistic-mentalistic model," which insists that development is "the spontaneous emergence of new modes of operation for which the environment merely provides the information necessary to enable the organisms to make their own selections."[97] Riegel proposes that what is needed is a dialectic approach incorporating both these viewpoints and recognizing that development involves an active, constructive, and continuous interplay between person and world, including the sociohistoric context, which in the process changes both. Basically, Riegel is arguing for the type of interactive view of development that has, in fact, been emerging.

9

A CHALLENGE TO PSYCHIATRY: THE DRAMATIC GROWTH OF CLINICAL PSYCHOLOGY

Nature and Scope of Clinical Psychology

Clinical psychologists are concerned with the study, diagnosis, and treatment, through counseling and psychotherapy, of human psychological problems. Where possible, some practitioners also try to change or eliminate societal conditions that are psychologically disruptive.[1] Clinicians receive training in the traditional areas of academic psychology, research methodologies, testing techniques, interview procedures, abnormal psychology, personality theory, psychotherapy, and, since the middle 1960s, community psychology. Some are engaged in private practice but the majority work in hospitals, outpatient clinics, correctional agencies, and schools.

The professions most directly concerned with alleviating psychological problems are psychiatry (a medical specialty), social work, counseling, and clinical psychology. Only psychiatrists can utilize physiological or biochemical treatment procedures. The others must rely entirely on non-medical therapies. These amount primarily to listening and talking. Of all the helping professionals, clinical psychologists are generally the best trained in psychometrics (test design, administration, and interpretation) and experimental research methodologies.

The nature and scope of contemporary clinical psychology are, generally speaking, relatively clear; nevertheless, there has been unceasing controversy, since World War II, concerning the training of clinicians, the scientific credibility of the field, the efficacy of testing and the various psychotherapies, the appropriate relationship between clinical psychology and experimental psychology, and the relative competencies and responsibilities of psychiatrists and clinical psychologists.

In 1956, for example, in an article entitled "Clinical Psychology and Logic," David Bakan stated: "The considerations in this essay originate in a prevailing sense of the scientific untenability of clinical psychology among many psychologists. Frequently, clinical psychology is critically envisaged as an art; or if the critic is inclined to be more critical, it may be conceived of as an attempt to obtain knowledge mystically and effect changes magically."[2]

The following year Carlton W. Berenda proclaimed: "There are some who have said or implied that psychology as a whole is not much of a science and that clinical psychology and the theories of personality dynamics and psychoanalysis are a combination of mere practical techniques and obscure or poetic speculations."[3] Berenda goes on to say that, with the exception of psychological testing, "the rest of the field is often dismissed as vague, intuitive, metaphysical meanderings and incantations, a survival of the *Malleus Maleficarum* of the Dark Ages."[4]

Three years later in a somewhat more optimistic vein Starke R. Hathaway wrote:

Clinical psychology is now established among psychologists and to a large extent in the public culture...the clinical psychologist of today has gained some prestige. Where he has gained a foothold, he has prestige over the social worker and nurse with his research competence and his doctorate. He has succeeded in transposing from the psychiatrist a considerable standing in the eyes of the public.[5]

Analyzing clinical psychology as a clinician might diagnose a person with psychological problems, Marvin W. Kahn and Sebastian Santostefano in 1962 contended:

Clinical psychology presents itself in a state of chronic anxiety, great ambivalence, insecurity, and self-doubt. Clinical psychology states that it is a science, and then says that it is an art. It asserts that it is an independent and self-contained field, but then confesses that it is ancillary and in need of close relationships with other sciences and professions.[6]

According to Leonard Small (1963): "The immediate task confronting clinical psychology is to obtain recognition for its competence. Without such recognition clinical psychology will become a secondary, an ancillary, group in the nation's mental health effort, with a status comparable to that of the X-ray technician or the laboratory technician."[7] Small believed that competence comes with professionalism but that many tests of professionalism confront the field including "legislative decisions concerning the use of mental health funds"[8] and legal cases having to do with the rights and competencies of the various helping professions, differences of opinion concerning the proper training of clinical psychologists, and the ability of psychologists to enforce ethical practices.

The situation was further complicated, as Harvey Peskin has noted, by a serious division "between members of university clinical faculties and those in clinical practice"[9] and dramatic differences in the "psycho-diagnostic milieu" of East and West coast universities. In New York City, for example, "projective techniques [particularly the Rorschach Inkblot Test] have a nearly exclusive hold on the imagination of the clinician in his role as psychodiagnostician."[10] In the San Francisco Bay area, on the other hand, the use of objective tests, in particular the Minnesota Multiphasic Personality Inventory (MMPI), predominated. The difference was apparently due to the fact that "The Rorschach and its attendant psychoanalytic spirit were migrants from Europe and naturally took stronger hold in the East."[11] Both East and West coast clinicians, however, placed importance on carefully acquired case histories.

In 1964 David A. Rodgers proposed that the training of professional psychologists should be distinctly different from the training of experimental psychologists. He maintained that "Professional training would emphasize greater breadth of basic content and less specialization in depth than is appropriate for basic research training."[12] There would be more emphasis on physiology and sociology, more practicum experience, and an applied orientation. Such a clear separation between academic and clinical psychology would, Rodgers felt, reduce the fruitless controversies surrounding the nature of clinical psychology and the appropriate competencies of clinical psychologists.

Controversy and uncertainty, however, have continued to plague the field. In his presidential address presented at the meeting of the American Psychological Association in 1970, George W. Albee noted that: "Clinical psychology has entered a paradoxical phase in its development where its problems of identity and relevance threaten it with extinction at the same time that its opportunities seem boundless."[13] This strange state of affairs was being brought about, according to Albee, for two reasons: first, because many universities were admitting fewer students for clinical training and were in some cases even dropping clinical programs; and second, because clinicians were becoming increasingly more critical of the heavy weight placed by most university clinical graduate programs on research methodology and the traditional material of academic-research psychology.

Albee suggested that the appropriate place to train clinicians is neither in academic departments nor psychiatric settings but in separate professional schools. During the late 1960s and 1970s an increasing number of such schools were, in fact, founded. By the late seventies more clinicians were graduating from professional schools than from traditional university programs.

Background

As a helping profession, the roots of clinical psychology extend back to some ancient unknown time and are entwined with the histories and

prehistories of religion, sorcery, magic, and medicine, particularly psychiatry. As a psychometric specialty—that is, one concerned with psychological assessment, the field, along with the test movement in general,
originated in the early twentieth century. The research emphasis of the
area is of even more recent vintage, being a product primarily of the
decision by the leadership of the discipline following World War II to
adopt a scientist-practitioner model. This model left the basic training of
clinicians in the hands of academic-research psychologists in university
departments.

Writing about the history of psychiatry, Karl Menninger (1963) points
out:

Our immediate ancestors were human beings like ourselves, with nerves and
brains like ours, desires and disappointments like ours. They, too, became partially disorganized under stress and sought medical help. It is not surprising,
therefore, that scattered through ancient records one finds descriptions of behavior corresponding in an identifiable way with clinical syndromes still seen
today. Sumerian and Egyptian references to what we call melancholia and
hysteria...are found as far back as 2600 B.C....An attempt to classify mental-
illness pictures—perhaps the first and at least the oldest one now known—is to
be found in the Ayur-Veda (1400 B.C.), a system of medicine in ancient India.[14]

During the approximately 3400 years that followed, much of psychiatric history has related to attempts to classify abnormal and unusual
people or behaviors.[15] A variety of classification principles were employed
including those based on inferred causes of the problems (for example,
possession, bodily imbalances), detailed descriptions of behavior, de-
ductions from certain general assumptions concerning human psychological makeup, the course a disease followed, or types of treatment
recommended. Sometimes the classification systems included hundreds
of categories, and other times psychological deviations were condensed
to a few major types. Karl Menninger, in fact, reduced all psychological
dysfunctions to one category.

Treatments that have at various times been prescribed for psychological difficulties have included tender loving care, exorcism of demons,
confinement, punishment, abandonment, prayer, bleeding, death (for
example, witch burning), a variety of specific, usually rather extreme,
procedures like spinning people in large centrifuges or placing them in
small cages or special ovens, and, more recently, lobotomies, hypnosis,
chemotherapy, convulsive therapies, numerous psychotherapies, and
behavior therapy.

The idea that psychological problems are symptoms of diseases or
illnesses, while an ancient one, was given scientific support during the
nineteenth century by the findings that both severe malnutrition and
syphillis, in its later stages, are usually accompanied by dramatic and

maladaptive personality changes. Here, after hundreds of years of speculation, was concrete evidence that physiological deterioration is at the
root of certain serious psychological and emotional problems. These
findings seemed to imply that only those trained in medicine were qualified to diagnose and treat people burdened with psychological dysfunctions. This view, sometimes referred to as the disease or disease-medical
model of psychological abnormalities, predominates even today, though
other helping professions, including clinical psychology, social work,
and counseling psychology, all of which emphasize the role of personal
and social factors, provide other perspectives. These non-medical speci-
alities and some orientations within psychiatry itself have served to
balance, to a degree, the disease-medical concept of abnormal behaviors. Freudian theory also offered an alternative to a strictly disease view
of mental or psychological problems. Although Freud was a medical
doctor, who emphasized biological factors in personality development,
he proposed that certain psychological difficulties are due to early infantile and childhood experiences rather than to physiological deterioration
or damage. He also advocated "talking" therapy instead of medical treatment for many problems.

Clinical psychology emerged at the end of the nineteenth century
about ten or fifteen years after psychology as a research field appeared.
According to Sundberg, Tyler, and Taplin,

During the period from 1890 to 1919 clinical psychology was established and laid
claim to its basic settings, clientele, and activities. It was not on a very firm
foundation at this time and had already begun to develop the organizations and
training procedures it needed. But psychological clinics had been started in
some universities, and psychologists were working in some child service agencies and some mental hospitals. By the end of the period they had demonstrated
their abilities to carry on large-scale testing and research. Aside from military
work [during World War I], clients with whom clinicians worked were mainly
children, especially children with educational and learning problems and juvenile delinquents, but some work had been initiated with adult mental patients.
Psychologists emphasized intelligence testing, but they had given some attention to personality investigation. They conducted a great deal of educational
guidance. At the same time, some psychologists in Europe were working with
Freud to become "lay analysts."[16]

Clinical psychology has roots in psychiatry, but the genesis of the field
was due primarily to the development of psychological tests during the
first decade of the century and the increasing need in the United States
to have people tested. The children of immigrants were tested for school
placement; group intelligence tests were developed during World War I
to screen military recruits; and by the 1920s personality and interest tests
were available. It was during this period—the first quarter of the twenti-

eth century—that social work, the mental health movement, and the child welfare movement, as well as professional psychology, came into being. Though clinical psychology did not entirely preempt the task of test design and administration, clinical psychologists increasingly tended to serve the role of psychometric experts. Graduate programs in clinical psychology provided the strongest quantitative training of all the applied social-behavioral programs. The psychological test made it possible for clinical psychology to develop into a credible field independent from psychiatry and other helping professions.

In general, the period from 1890 to 1919 can be viewed as the "period of establishment"[17] for clinical psychology. Sundberg, Tyler, and Taplin have noted, "The turn of the century was a time of ferment, reform, and social creativity. Almost all the basic concepts, methods, and organizations of clinical psychology have their origins in that period—psychoanalysis, behaviorism, community efforts, intelligence testing, personality inventories, projective techniques, psychological clinics, and the professional organization of psychologists."[18] Robert I. Watson has described the era as "the period of . . . lusty, disorganized infancy."[19]

On the other hand, the two decades between World War I and World War II, the 1920s and 1930s, were a time of consolidation[20] or, in Watson's words, constituted the adolescent stage of the discipline. The Freudian influence increased; many tests were developed and psychological assessment became a major activity of psychologists. The emphasis was on the study, education, and treatment of children. Many clinical psychologists, along with other applied psychologists, left the American Psychological Association to join the American Association for Applied Psychology which was formed in 1937.

Specific developments of importance to clinical psychology prior to World War II include[21] (a) the establishment in 1896 by Lightner Witmer of the first psychological clinic; (b) Freud's published works (1895-1939); (c) development in 1905 of the first intelligence test by Alfred Binet and Theodore Simon in Paris; (d) publication in 1906 and 1907, respectively, of the *Journal of Abnormal Psychology* and the journal, *Psychological Clinic*; (e) publication in 1908 of Clifford Beers's book, *A Mind That Found Itself* and his founding of the mental hygiene movement; (f) the offering in 1908 of psychological internships at Vineland Training School in New Jersey; (g) development by Lewis M. Terman at Stanford in 1916 of an English version of the Binet intelligence test; (h) development of the Army Alpha and Beta tests during World War I (1916) to screen recruits; (i) the founding in 1917 of the Judge Baker Guidance Center in Boston; (j) the founding of the Section on Clinical Psychology by the APA (1919); (k) publication of the Rorschach inkblot test (1921); (l) the support by the Commonwealth Fund of a child guidance program in 1921; (m) in the late 1920s, the publication of Goodenough's Draw-A-Man Test and Strong's

Vocational Interest Blank, and the founding of the Harvard Psychological Clinic; (*n*) in 1931, concern by the Clinical Section of APA with training standards; (*o*) the development of the Thematic Apperception Test (TAT), an important projective technique (1935); (*p*) the use of electroconvulsive shock therapy to treat schizophrenic problems (1936); and (*q*) in the late 1930s, the use of psychosurgical procedures as treatments for chronic psychoses, the disbanding of the Clinical Section of APA and formation of a separate organization (American Association for Applied Psychology), the establishment by APA of a committee on Scientific and Professional Ethics, the publication of the *Mental Measurement Yearbook*, and the introduction of four important tests: the Bender-Gestalt (to detect brain damage), the Primary Mental Abilities Test, the Wechsler-Bellevue intelligence test, and the Kuder Preference Record.

Clinical Psychology during World War II

Of the approximately 1500 psychologists serving in the Armed Forces during World War II, Watson recounts,

almost half...used clinical and counseling procedures....Many psychologists, willy-nilly, were placed in a position where they functioned in selection and assignment, sat as members of discharge boards, worked as members of clinical teams, conducted therapeutic sessions, both group and individual, and in these and many other ways used diagnostic and treatment methods.[22]

Of most importance for clinical psychology were the use of clinicians as therapists as well as diagnosticians and the development of group intelligence, ability, and personality tests and short forms of existing instruments. The war both provided psychologists with useful new psychometric instruments and demonstrated to society that nonmedically trained individuals could be effective psychotherapists.

Test development during the war was facilitated by the appointment of a committee of psychologists chaired by Walter Bingham, a prominent industrial psychologist, to serve as an advisory group to the adjutant general. As Reisman notes, "These psychologists assisted in the development of the Army General Classification Test [and] a number of other tests...devised for use in the selection of naval officers, pilots, instructors, and candidates for assignment to training in particular skills."[23] The use of tests for military purposes was phenomenal; during 1944, for example, "It was estimated that...sixty million standardized tests were administered to twenty million persons."[24]

Also in 1944, the American Association for Applied Psychology, after only five years of existence, disbanded, and clinical psychologists returned to the American Psychological Association. This important reunification of applied and academic-research psychology contributed directly to the adoption by clinical psychologists of the scientist-practitioner model (formalized by the Boulder Conference in 1950) which, as mentioned earlier, requires that clinical graduate students be given training in the content and methods of academic-research psychology.

Overview (1946-1975)

During the thirty-year period following World War II, clinical psychology grew dramatically, was seen as increasingly relevant to more problems and institutional settings, and was transformed from a field concerned mostly with the diagnosis of psychological problems to one also engaged in psychotherapy and research. Growth brought a deeper concern with such professional issues as training guidelines, ethics, confidentiality, and relations with other disciplines. The psychoanalytic influence, which was particularly strong during the 1940s and 1950s, gradually diminished and was supplanted by Carl Rogers' client-centered theory and therapy, chemotherapy, various behavioral approaches, and, more recently, a variety of cognitive orientations. Therapies, in general, became more short-run. Group approaches flourished. The move away from a predominantly psychoanalytic perspective was brought about both by psychoanalysis being time-consuming, costly, and of questionable efficacy and by the influence of existentialism, behaviorism, and cognitive psychology.

Noteworthy is the fact that in spite of the burgeoning influence of clinical psychology within the discipline and many professional differences between clinical psychologists and their academic-research colleagues, the two groups have chosen to stay affiliated with the American Psychological Association. A new organization, "The Psychonomic Society," was formed in the early 1960s by a group of disgruntled experimentalists; but it represents no more than a supplement to the APA. What apparently holds the applied and academic branches of the discipline together is the shared belief that psychologists of all types should be well schooled in the basic areas of psychology including experimental research methodology.

The profound expansion of clinical psychology is evidenced by the fact that membership in APA divisions concerned with clinical functions increased from 1,148 in 1950 to 2,376 in 1960 and 4,016 in 1975. The growth of the field was also reflected by the number of universities offering APA-approved graduate programs in clinical psychology. According to Sol Garfield, "In the mid-1940s, for example, just over 30 universities were accredited by the APA for training in clinical psychology. By 1956, 45 universities had been so accredited; in 1962, 60 universities, and in 1979, 110 universities" (references omitted).[25] In addition, a substantial number of professional schools of psychology not associated with universities have since the early 1970s graduated increasing numbers of clinicians holding the Doctor of Psychology rather than the Ph.D. degree.

The increasing psychotherapeutic emphasis of clinical psychology was brought about initially by the need for more psychotherapists during World War II and the demonstration that psychiatrists were not the only helping professionals capable of providing effective treatment of psychological problems. During the last three decades, the shift from administering and interpreting tests to providing therapy by clinical psychologists was sustained by a gradual change in society's outlook. Garfield has observed "that psychotherapy and psychological services in general, [have] been more positively accepted by the public at large."[26] Psychotherapeutic services are now provided in "community mental health centers, hospitals, counseling centers, outpatient clinics, rehabilitation centers"[27] and, of course, in the offices of private practitioners. The move from testing to helping people through therapy was also a function, in part, of the failure to validate even those tests, like the Rorschach, TAT, and MMPI, which for a while (primarily during the 1940s and 1950s) were believed to be credible diagnostic instruments. Further contributing to the growing emphasis by clinical psychologists on treatment has been the fact that not only is diagnosis a tenuous procedure but even the standard psychiatric categories (for example, paranoia, schizophrenia, depression, and neurosis) are themselves recognized as being of questionable validity.

The professionalization of clinical psychology has involved setting guidelines for graduate training, formulating a code of ethics, and lobbying for legislation establishing the discipline as a responsible helping profession. Laws sought have related to licensing requirements, guaranteeing the confidentiality of information divulged by people involved in psychotherapy or counseling with clinical psychologists, and requiring health insurance programs to reimburse patients being helped professionally for psychological and emotional problems regardless of whether the therapist is a psychiatrist or a clinical psychologist in private practice. Considerable progress has been made on all fronts except the health insurance issue. Health insurance programs generally do not pay for services provided by a clinical psychologist unless he or she is on the staff of an agency employing at least one psychiatrist.

In addition to a more enlightened view of psychological problems, the major societal influences on clinical psychology since the 1940s were the war itself, government support for training and research, the shortage of therapists, and federal funding of community mental health centers during the middle and late 1960s. Another development that had an extraordinary impact on all the helping professions was the production of drugs capable of controlling and/or diminishing anxiety, depression, and certain thought disorders. These chemicals made it possible for many more people to receive outpatient care instead of being institutionalized and, in turn, helped generate the community mental health movement during the 1960s.

The individuals of most direct importance to post-World War II clinical psychology include Sigmund Freud (psychoanalysis); Carl Rogers (client-centered, nondirective therapy and humanist view of people); David Shakow (guidelines for the training of clinical psychologists); David Wechsler (intelligence tests); Hermann Rorschach (Rorschach inkblot test); Starke R. Hathaway (Minnesota Multiphasic Personality Inventory); Henry Murray (Thematic Apperception Test); Oscar K. Buros (*Mental Measurement Yearbooks*); Paul Meehl (careful analysis of the relative efficacy of diagnoses based on clinical judgment and actuarial data); Hans Eysenck (influential critique of psychoanalysis); Rollo May (existential approach to the human condition); John Wolpe (desensitization therapy, a behavioral approach based on classical conditioning); and B. F. Skinner (behavior modification based on the operant conditioning paradigm).

Also of considerable importance were (*a*) the neo-Freudians, in particular Erik Erikson, Karen Horney, Erich Fromm, and Harry S. Sullivan who emphasized social variables in personality organization and dysfunction; (*b*) ego psychologists, for example, Anna Freud, Lois Murphy, and Karl Menninger, who were interested in the coping mechanisms people develop to deal with the challenges of life; (*c*) Clark Hull who inspired attempts to transform Freudian concepts into behavioral terms; (*d*) Thomas Szasz, a psychiatrist who launched a strong criticism against the disease-medical model of psychological dysfunction; (*e*) social learning theorists like Albert Bandura who demonstrated the importance of modeling in human development; (*f*) Walter Mischel who, perhaps more than anyone else, has demonstrated the significance of situational rather than personality variables in determining human behavior; and (*g*) individuals with various orientations, for example, Viktor E. Frankl (logotherapy), George A. Kelly (cognitive personality theory), Fritz Heider (attribution theory), Jean Piaget (cognitive development) and Israel Goldiamond (operant conditioning), to name but a few who contributed to the return of a cognitive perspective to clinical psychology as well as to the discipline as a whole.[28]

1946-1959

Clinical psychology grew rapidly during the immediate postwar years for four reasons: first, there was a pressing need for more psychotherapists, in part to service the many veterans with psychological problems; second, clinical psychologists had, during the war, demonstrated their proficiency as psychotherapists; third, the federal government provided both direct support for the training of clinicians and jobs in the veterans hospitals; and, finally, university psychology departments were able almost immediately to design and implement rigorous graduate programs in clinical psychology.

While all these elements were essential for the growth of the field, the true catalyst for expansion was federal support for training and the employment of clinical psychologists by Veterans Administration (V.A.) hospitals. More specifically, in 1946, the Veterans Administration established four-year training programs for clinicians, declaring that clinical psychology had to do with treatment and research as well as diagnosis. Furthermore, the V.A. stipulated that, insofar as their facilities were concerned, clinical psychologists were individuals trained to the Ph.D. degree.[29] In 1947, the U.S. Public Health Service also started providing training funds. Eventually, the generally high level of interest in mental health programs during the 1940s and 1950s brought state and community support to clinical psychology as well as the other helping professions.

Although clinical and other applied psychologists have been concerned with training guidelines, ethical standards, and professional respectability ever since World War I, clinical psychology did not really become a distinct profession until after World War II when graduate programs in the field were established in the context of a well-defined and generally accepted training model. The professionalization of clinical psychology, in other words, is essentially a post-World War II phenomenon.

Standards for the training of clinical psychologists were established by the 1947 report "Recommended Graduate Training Program in Clinical Psychology" compiled by the Committee on Training in Clinical Psychology of the APA. The document is known as the "Shakow Report" after David Shakow who was the chairman of the committee and primary author. Shakow had been concerned with the training of clinical psychologists since the early 1930s.[30]

The report proposed that the clinician must be primarily a psychologist with traditional and rigorous training in research as well as professional competencies. To accomplish this, graduate programs were to provide for the study of general psychology, psychodynamics, diagnostic techniques, research methods, related disciplines, and therapy. Programs were to focus on principles, provide contact with clinical material, develop a sense of responsibility to patients, and make students aware of the social implications of their work as clinicians. Graduate training was to take at least four years with the third year constituting an internship.

The impact of the Shakow Report on clinical psychology was substantial, not only because its recommendations were, in general, compatible with the professional *Zeitgeist* of the discipline as a whole, but because it was followed in 1948 and 1949 by two studies evaluating existing graduate programs. Also in 1949, the first of a series of conferences on clinical training took place at Boulder, Colorado, thus establishing a process whereby the monitoring of graduate programs was insured.

The Boulder model as described by Shakow "set up university and practicum programs to implement the scientist/professional concept in courses but placed responsibility for acquiring professional competence, beyond bare entry-level skills, on the student in his or her post-doctoral years."[31] The recommendations of the Boulder Conference were published in 1950 in a book entitled *Training in Clinical Psychology*, edited and compiled by Victor C. Raimy.[32]

Two other major conferences focusing on clinical training were held during the 1946-1959 period, at Stanford in 1955 and Miami in 1958. Both reaffirmed the Boulder model. The only serious challenge to the scientist/professional training concept was to come in 1973 at the Vail Conference[33] which recommended that accreditation standards be changed to allow for programs emphasizing professional rather than research competencies.

In 1978, an American Psychological Association committee, however, concluded that the clinical curriculum "should include core content of the biological, cognitive-affective, and social bases of behavior, and of individual differences, as well as content in research design and methodology, statistics, and psychometrics."[34] Amazingly, while there has been an almost constant and sometimes agonizing reappraisal of the nature of clinical psychology during the past thirty years, the general consensus remains that professional competency requires both a solid foundation in academic, research-oriented psychology and firsthand experience in applied settings. The Boulder Conference view continues to prevail.

Other indications that clinical psychology was evolving into a distinct profession were the creation in 1946 of the American Board of Examiners in Professional Psychology (ABEPP), the licensing of psychologists by some states starting with Kentucky in 1948, and the publication in 1953 of a formal code of ethics by APA. According to Misiak and Sexton, ABEPP "was authorized to certify candidates who hold the Ph.D. degree; who have had five years of experience; and who after completing the educational and experience requirements, passed oral and written examinations in their professional specialty. . . . ABEPP filled an immediate postwar need to identify qualified psychologists to a public which made heavy demands for psychological services."[35]

The predominant personality theory and therapeutic orientation within both clinical psychology and psychiatry during the 1946-1959 period was clearly psychoanalysis. The primary assessment tools were the Stanford Binet and Wechsler intelligence tests; the Rorschach inkblot technique and Thematic Apperception Test (TAT), both projective personality instruments;[36] and the Minnesota Multiphasic Personality Inventory (MMPI), a so-called paper-and-pencil test of personality.[37] Much of the research being done involved the factor-analytic[38] study of various test batteries. There was concern over the reliability and validity of all psychometric instruments and clinical judgment in addition to the efficacy of the various psychotherapies.

The most important specific developments within clinical psychology, beyond the growth and professionalization of the field and its transformation into a discipline concerned with treatment and research as well as diagnosis, were Carl Rogers' client-centered therapy, clinical research innovations, and humanist-existentialist personality theory; Paul Meehl's demonstration that diagnosis based on actuarial tables is frequently superior to diagnosis based on clinical judgment;[39] and Hans Eysenck's strong critique of psychotherapy.[40]

The most substantive general development was probably the emergence of clinical psychology as the watchdog of all the professions engaged in psychological diagnosis and psychotherapy. Because clinical psychologists have intensive training in both psychometrics and research methodologies, they, along with other academic psychologists, have tended to be more involved in testing the reliability of clinical psychology and validity of diagnostic techniques and psychotherapies than psychiatrists, social workers, or counselors. This is a role many clinical psychologists have continued to play throughout the entire post-World War II era.

Other important developments in clinical psychology and related disciplines include psychiatric studies of veterans; the increasing use of various group therapies; refinements in psychosurgery; criticism of the disease-medical model of psychological abnormalities; much interest in, research on, and theorizing about schizophrenia, multiple personalities, psychosomatic problems, and juvenile delinquency; considerable cross-cultural research; epidemiological studies of mental illness; and the discovery of drugs (tranquilizers, antidepressants, and antipsychotic agents) which made it possible by the 1960s for many persons to receive outpatient treatment rather than enter a mental hospital. Also significant were a variety of theories (other than Freud's and Rogers') concerning personality and therapy, in particular those of Anna Freud, Erik Erikson, Karen Horney, Erich Fromm, Harry S. Sullivan, Abraham Maslow, Viktor Frankl, and Dollard and Miller; Hans Selye's theory of adaptation to stress; the concept of manifest anxiety and Janet Taylor's Manifest Anxiety Scale; Rollo May's writings on existential psychology; development of a new psychiatric classification system (1952); research on the effects of sensory deprivation; much concern with the question "What is psychological abnormality?"; and the beginning of behavior therapy.

Carl Rogers' Contributions In an autobiographical essay published in 1967, Carl Rogers described himself as follows:

I am a psychologist; a clinical psychologist I believe, a humanistically oriented psychologist certainly; a psychotherapist, deeply interested in the dynamics of personality change; a scientist, to the limit of my ability investigating such change; an educator, challenged by the possibility of facilitating learning; a philosopher in a limited way, especially in relation to the philosophy of science and the philosophy and psychology of human values....I see myself as...somewhat of a lone wolf in my professional activities.[41]

It is interesting to note that Rogers considers himself both a psychologist and a "lone wolf" professionally. This is not too surprising since as an undergraduate at the University of Wisconsin he first set out to study agriculture but then majored in history, taking only one course in psychology by correspondence. He later went to Union Theological Seminary in New York to study for the ministry but transferred to Teachers College, Columbia, after two years in order to work in clinical and educational psychology. His first job after completion of his Ph.D. work in 1928 was with the Rochester Society for Prevention of Cruelty to Children where he stayed for twelve years. His initial professional identification was with social work rather than psychology.

Rogers apparently did not view himself as a psychologist until 1940 when he was offered a position at Ohio State University mostly because of the publication in 1939 of his first book *The Clinical Treatment of the Problem Child*.[42] He accepted the offer and stayed at Ohio State until 1945 when he took on the task of establishing a counseling center at the University of Chicago.

During his tenure at Chicago (1945-1957), he wrote one of his most influential books, *Client Centered Therapy*,[43] and published numerous papers. He also contributed a long chapter to Sigmund Koch's series, *Psychology: A Study of a Science*,[44] which represents Rogers' most detailed account of his personality theory and therapy.

Rogers was then lured to the University of Wisconsin by the offer of a joint appointment in psychology and psychiatry that allowed him to work with psychotic as well as less disturbed individuals. He remained in Madison for seven years, but the position did not work out very well because the psychology department there placed so much emphasis on rigorous examinations that some of the students whom Rogers considered to have the most potential as therapists either failed or left the program in disgust.

In 1964 he joined the staff of the Western Behavioral Sciences Institute, described by Rogers as "a nonprofit organization devoted to humanistically oriented research in interpersonal relationships, with a particular focus on the manner in which constructive change in interpersonal relationships comes about."[45] Shortly thereafter he helped found the Center for Studies of the Person, an organization he is still associated with as a Resident Fellow.

Rogers is a humanist in the sense that he has a positive outlook on life and believes that "the individual has within himself vast resources for self-understanding, for altering his self-concept, his attitudes, and his self-directed behavior."[46] He has faith that people, if provided with a threat-free social environment by a counselor or therapist, have the ability to actualize themselves—that is, to maximize their potentialities. This represented a view of both the person and the therapeutic process radically different from the predominantly psychoanalytic perspective of the 1940s and 1950s.

Rogers is an existentialist in the sense that he believes it essential for the therapist to focus on and try to empathize with the client's experiences and perceptions of the world. The immediate conscious state of the person seeking help, as opposed to a set of theoretical assumptions and labels, is of primary concern. Theoretical constructs, according to Rogers, tend to interfere with the therapeutic process. Rogers apparently adopted an existentially-oriented perspective as a result of his own professional experiences rather than from a familiarity with existential philosophy.

The client-centered, or Rogerian, therapist attempts to create an atmosphere within which the client can grow psychologically by accepting the client unconditionally, that is, without reservations; demonstrating an understanding of and empathy with the client's perspective on the world; and by showing care for the client. According to Rogers, this requires that the therapist learn to be a good listener and a skilled communicator. If the therapist is successful, the client eventually learns to eliminate distorted symbolizations of personal experiences and to accept feelings as well as experiences that may have been denied. The basic process is one of gradual self-understanding and self-acceptance which results in a reduction of anxiety, guilt, and shame.

One of Rogers' main strengths within the context of the discipline of psychology has been his insistence that the therapeutic process be monitored and the effects of therapy measured. Rogers pioneered in the use of tape recorders during therapy sessions. This provided feedback to the therapists involved as well as to students and other staff members. He also employed techniques, particularly Q-sorts, to determine clients' perspectives of themselves before, during, and following therapy.[47] The recording of therapy sessions and the attempt to measure change brought about by professional intervention were substantive contributions because both innovations were designed to de-mystify psychotherapy and make therapists more accountable. While many therapists, especially psychiatrists, had little confidence in the procedures Rogers introduced, Rogers reinforced an already strong interest on the part of many psychologists in studying and determining the outcomes of the various psychotherapies.

A noteworthy event in American psychology during the middle 1950s was the Rogers-Skinner debate that took place in 1956.[48] Skinner, representing a behavioral point of view, argued that in the final analysis everything we do is determined by the environment. Rogers, on the other hand, vigorously defended the idea that man can make choices and "is to some degree the architect of himself."[49] The debate was important because it inspired thought on the part of both clinical and academic-research psychologists and demonstrated that behavioristic psychology would not go unchallenged. Without most psychologists being aware of it, Rogers' orientation was also exposing them to humanist, phenomenological, and existential ideas which during the 1946-1959 period had little currency within mainstream psychology.

The importance of Rogers for American psychology is apparently recognized by the majority of contemporary psychologists in this country. Survey studies indicate that he is generally included among the ten most important psychologists during the post-World War II years.[50] It is also clear that Rogers had his greatest impact on the discipline during the 1950s and early 1960s.[51]

Since the late '60s, Rogers' interest has moved away from individual therapy to group processes, such as encounter groups, and educational issues. By the early 1970s the humanist, existential, and phenomenological orientations, which only Rogers and a few others championed during the 1950s and 1960s, emerged as a full-fledged movement under the leadership of individuals who explicitly identified with one or more of these person-centered philosophies.

The major criticisms of Rogers' theories of personality and therapy include: (a) the assumption that people have a built-in predisposition to actualize themselves is unproven; (b) the concept of self-actualization is ambiguous; (c) client-centered therapy is appropriate only for certain not-too-disturbed individuals; (d) the approach tends to appeal to counselors who have or want little formal training in personality theory, abnormal psychology, and indeed psychology in general; and (e) there is too much emphasis on making yourself feel good rather than recognizing the importance of commitment to others.

Hans Eysenck's Evaluation of Psychotherapy Examining the evidence concerning the effectiveness of psychotherapy with neurotic individuals, Hans Eysenck, one of the most influential and controversial British psychologists during the postwar era,[52] reported in 1952:

Patients treated by means of psychoanalysis improve to the extent of 44 percent; patients treated eclectically improve to the extent of 64 percent; patients treated only custodially or by general practitioners improve to the extent of 72 percent. There thus appears to be an inverse correlation between recovery and psychotherapy; the more psychotherapy, the smaller the recovery rate.[53]

This was a startling set of findings that generated heated professional controversy.

Eysenck's article was a landmark for several reasons: first, it brought together information from nineteen psychotherapeutic follow-up studies and provided for comparison a reasoned estimate of the percentage of individuals whose neurotic symptoms are relieved in the absence of any formal therapy; second, it appeared at a time when American psychologists were very much concerned with the effectiveness of the various psychotherapies; and third, Eysenck, who published prolifically, became one of the most ardent critics of both psychoanalysis and American graduate programs in clinical psychology. Most of these programs, he felt, placed excessive emphasis on teaching psychotherapeutic techniques to students.[54]

In addition to casting considerable doubt on the usefulness of the then predominant psychoanalytic therapies, Eysenck's report generated interest in outcome research, that is, research designed to determine the value of the various professional approaches to helping people with psychological problems.

Eysenck's study was criticized on the grounds that he incorrectly assumed that the control subjects received no professional help; cure as defined by therapists is only one way of identifying the effects of therapy; and the apparent ineffectiveness of some of the therapeutic attempts may have resulted from inappropriate diagnosis, deficiencies in the method of treatment, inexperienced therapists, events in the lives of the patients or therapists which interfered with the therapy, and other variables.[55]

The criticisms leveled at Eysenck's report highlighted many of the problems faced by anyone trying to determine the effects of a particular psychotherapy. It quickly became evident that the outcome of any therapeutic relationship is a function of the complex interactions among personal, social, situational, and professional factors.

One of the appeals of behavior therapy, which became increasingly popular during the 1960s and early 1970s, was that specific behavioral changes were the goals of therapy as opposed to transformations of personality, attitude, self-image, or motivation that are more difficult to define. This made it possible to determine whether or not a particular therapeutic procedure worked.

Eysenck, incidentally, was an early advocate of behavior therapy. In addition, he also made contributions to personality theory and assessment. He is generally classified as a trait theorist whose primary dimensions of personality are extraversion-introversion and degree of neuroticism. His theoretical explanation of personality dynamics is based on a Pavlovian model of brain functioning.

Paul Meehl's Study of Clinical Versus Statistical Prediction In Meehl's opinion, "One of the major methodological problems of clinical psychology concerns the relation between the 'clinical' and 'statistical' (or 'actuarial') methods of prediction.... The problem is to predict how a person is going to behave."[56] The clinical method involves using information from interviews, case histories, and possibly tests to formulate, in Meehl's words, "some psychological hypothesis regarding the structure and the dynamics of this particular individual.... [and] [o]n the basis of this hypothesis and certain reasonable expectations as to the course of outer events,... arrive at a prediction of what is going to happen."[57] The statistical, or actuarial method, in contrast, involves classifying people on the basis of a predetermined and mechanical combining of information from life histories, test performance, behavior ratings, and interviews and then entering "a statistical or actuarial table which gives the statistical frequencies of behavior of various sorts for persons belonging to the class."[58] The formulas for combining information from whatever sources used are based on knowledge gleaned from previous research concerning the predictive power of each source of information. In theory, actuarial prediction can be done by a clerk while only a professional psychologist or psychiatrist has the necessary background to use the clinical method.

Psychologists, psychiatrists, and other social scientists had discussed and argued about the relative merits of the clinical and actuarial approaches to prediction prior to World War II. However, it was Paul Meehl's book *Clinical versus Statistical Prediction* published in 1954 which first offered a systematic treatment of the problem in the context of relevant empirical research findings.

On the basis of twenty separate studies involving the predictions of a wide range of outcomes, for example, academic performance, prognosis of schizophrenics and manic-depressives, success of naval trainees in a school for electrician's mates, and recidivism among parolees, Meehl demonstrated that almost without exception the actuarial approach gave better predictions than the clinical method. He urged, therefore, that clinical psychologists spend most of their time doing psychotherapy and leave the task of prognosticating to assistants trained to use the appropriate statistical tables and techniques.

Meehl's report in no way signaled the demise of the clinical approach to prediction. Nevertheless, the implications of the study were profound. It highlighted the need for more systematic research on the problem and cast doubt on the advisability of making predictions from elaborate theories of personality and psychopathology. Moreover, it affirmed what was basically a pragmatic and inductive approach to test design, an approach which, by the way, characterized psychometric research at the University of Minnesota, where Meehl was a faculty member.[59]

The study also had relevance for the design of graduate programs in clinical psychology. More specifically, the findings reinforced the scientist/professional model which required that students be trained in statistics, psychometrics, and research methodology. Ironically, Meehl urged that clinical psychologists spend most of their time doing psychotherapy instead of sitting in diagnostic conferences, at the same time that Eysenck, on the basis of his research, doubted the value of training psychologists to be therapists, since he found no evidence that therapy had any positive effects.

A potential weakness of the actuarial approach is that it tends to build on existing systems of classifying people and may therefore sometimes give an unjustified credibility to categories and labels, to the detriment of the therapeutic process. In a more general sense, the approach assumes that classification is an integral part of clinical work, an assumption that humanistically and existentially oriented psychologists seriously question.

1960-1975

Psychotherapies During the 1960s and early 1970s the psychoanalytic influence on clinical psychology was gradually displaced by behavior theories and therapies. In 1960, for example, Julian B. Rotter reviewed contributions to the theory and practice of psychotherapy, concluding: "It is still abundantly clear that the center of the stage is being held by writers who attach to themselves the label psychoanalytic, psychoanalytically-oriented, or modified psychoanalytic in describing their method of treatment."[60] In their review of psychotherapy seven years later, however, Donald Ford and Hugh Urban stated: "Changes in psychoanalytic approaches seem to be groping and tentative....By contrast, there is an optimistic, vigorous, and inventive group of behavior therapists, who are working excitedly and industriously along quite different, and in many ways promising, lines."[61] And in 1970, Eugene Gendlin and Joseph Rychlak observed: "It seemed clear that the behavior therapies were again the dominant preoccupation of the psychotherapeutic profession, and (as in the last 2 or 3 years) these techniques are now clearly the primary stimulus for publications in our area."[62] While certain behavioral intervention strategies were strongly criticized during the early 1970s, sometimes unfairly, behavior therapy in a variety of forms remains a significant influence within clinical psychology. There are also those who believe that the psychoanalytic influence within the field is far from dead.[63]

Behavior therapy includes a variety of approaches based on learning principles designed to change specific maladaptive reactions or feelings. Krasner has identified

some of the elements of the belief system common to behavior therapy [as]: (a) the statement of concepts so that they can be tested experimentally; (b) the notion of 'laboratory' as ranging from the animal mazes or shuttle boxes through basic human learning studies to hospitals, schoolrooms, homes, and the community; (c) research as treatment—and treatment as research; (d) an explicit strategy of therapy; (e) demonstration that the particular environmental manipulation was indeed responsible for producing the specified behavior change; [and] (f) the goals of the modification procedure are usually determined by an initial functional analysis or assessment of the problem behaviors.[64]

The theoretical underpinnings of the behaviorally oriented therapies of the 1950s were Pavlovian and Hullian principles and procedures. The work of John Dollard, Neal Miller, O. Hobart Mowrer, and John Wolpe was most influential. Wolpe's desensitization and reciprocal inhibition techniques were the predominate applications. The goal of these procedures was to substitute a positive feeling like relaxation for the fear or anxiety elicited irrationally by a particular stimulus or to develop a negative feeling like revulsion or nausea either for a socially taboo stimulus arousing lust or desire or for alcohol, drugs, and food in cases of alcoholism, drug addiction, and obesity.

By the middle 1960s when Skinnerianism emerged as the major force within American psychology, therapies based on operant conditioning principles represented an exciting new direction within behavior therapy.[65] The basic assumption underlying the operant approach is that the consequences of behavior control behavior. The therapist, therefore, by manipulating the outcome of responses which are targeted for modification, helps individuals either reduce the frequency of undesirable actions or increase the frequency of desired behavior.

During the 1970s these therapies, while still incorporating Pavlovian, Hullian, and/or Skinnerian assumptions, became more sophisticated. The complex role of the therapist as social reinforcer, the utility of modeling (social learning theory) in bringing about behavior change, and the importance of self-reinforcement through cognitive strategies were increasingly acknowledged as integral to all therapies including those with a behavioral orientation. The most significant development within behavior therapy during the 1970s was probably the formal recognition of the importance of cognitive processes, particularly imagination, in the therapeutic process. Contemporary behavior therapy is, in fact, an amalgamation of behavioral, social, and cognitive perspectives.

A well-publicized innovation during the 1960s and 1970s was the use of biofeedback procedures to treat such disorders as hypertension, migraine headaches, irregular heartbeat, and anxiety conditions. Biofeedback is a cognitive-behavioral procedure whereby a person controls his own heart rate, blood pressure, brain waves, and galvanic skin responses, or other autonomic reactions. The procedure involves providing visual or auditory feedback about the physiological activity being monitored so that the individual knows when the desired effect is being achieved.[66]

Some of the initial enthusiasm concerning the technique has, however, diminished because there is no convincing evidence that biofeedback has any more than very limited clinical applications.

Behaviorism waxed as psychoanalysis waned; but the situation was complicated by the simultaneous rise of humanism, existentialism, and phenomenology, introduced by Rogers in the 1950s and organized into a movement about the middle sixties. Proponents of both behaviorism and the humanist-existential-phenomenological outlook were critical of the complex and mostly unverified theoretical structure of psychoanalysis and its emphasis in therapy on past events. Both groups also recognized the danger of psychiatric labeling. Behaviorists, though, advocated a concentration on observable behavioral events, environmental causality, measurable outcomes, and experimental research. In contrast, those within the humanist, existential, and phenomenological traditions saw people as being free to make choices and believed that psychotherapy should focus on the world as experienced by those seeking help and the therapeutic relationship, with the goal of therapy being self-actualization.

Behaviorists have tended to criticize humanists, existentialists, and phenomenologists for being too subjective, irrational, mystical, and nonscientific. Humanistic, existential, and phenomenologically oriented psychologists, on the other hand, have accused behavioral therapists of being overly concerned with symptoms and short-run, trivial, and measurable changes and with ignoring the therapist-client relationship. One of the intriguing byproducts of the criticism leveled at each other by members of the two camps has been a renewed interest in that persistent controversy, the free will-determinism issue.[67]

The success of behavioral clinicians in eliminating specific symptoms and modifying behavior also raised another very important question, namely: Does short-run therapeutic efficiency generally result in desirable long-range changes in human life styles or are the conditions required to attain short-run results counterproductive in the long run? Although there is currently no definitive answer to this question, evidence from biology suggests that conditions that induce quick changes in the activities of life forms have a negative influence in the long run. In discussing an efficiency principle in nature, Anthony Wilden (1975) states that "no such principle can be discovered operating in living systems. On the contrary, in natural ecosystems, and I suspect in human ones also, it is redundancy and enormous 'waste' of effort that are the concomitants of long-range stability. Efficiency tends to be disastrously destabilizing in the long run."[68]

As a movement, humanist-existential-phenomenological psychology started in 1958 with the publication of a book entitled *Existence* edited by Rollo May, Ernest Angel, and Henri F. Ellenberger.[69] Julian Rotter in his 1960 review of psychotherapy characterized the publication of the book as follows: "Perhaps the greatest stir in this field of the past year has been created by a group of writers who ally themselves with a movement which they call 'existential analysis'. It is not easy to conceptualize briefly this orientation, but the point of view has been extensively explicated in a recent book edited by May, Angel, & Ellenberger."[70] The movement, particularly the humanistic strain, flourished during the late sixties (the Vietnam era) and early seventies. At that time, many in the academic community and society generally became disillusioned with science, technology, established theory, measurement, and rational thought.

The phenomenological dimension of the movement was in some ways the last of the three components to surface formally within clinical psychology. Rogers referred to the phenomenological approach; and the Gestalt psychologists, who had influenced academic-research psychology since the 1920s, were said to use the phenomenological method. Nevertheless, the influence of phenomenology on the field has always remained obscure. At best one can say that the phenomenological orientation reminded psychologists of the importance of studying conscious experience; warned of the dangers involved for the therapeutic process in labels, categories, theories, and cognitive structures in general; and made clinicians aware of the complementary nature of observer and observed and therapist and client.

Individuals who did the most to create the humanist-existential-phenomenological movement in clinical psychology during the 1960s and 1970s were Carl Rogers, Rollo May, Ludwig Binswanger (Swiss psychiatrist), Viktor Frankl (Austrian psychiatrist and founder of logotherapy), Abraham Maslow, Gordon Allport, Adrian van Kaam, Anthony Sutich, J. F. T. Bugental, R. D. Laing (British psychiatrist), and Fritz Perls.

Next to Rogers' client-centered therapy, Perls' Gestalt therapy is probably the most important phenomenologically-oriented procedure. Perls, according to Douglas Bernstein and Michael Nietzel, proposed that the purpose of therapy is to help people "become aware of those feelings, desires, and impulses which they have *disowned* but which are actually part of them, and...recognize those feelings, ideas, and values which they *think* are a genuine part of themselves but which, in fact, are borrowed or adopted from other people."[71] Gestalt therapy is phenomenologically oriented because the emphasis is on here-and-now experiences. Participants are asked to role play each essential element of their dreams and troublesome waking thoughts in order to explore and become aware of the full meaning of these frequently only vaguely defined dimensions of their psychological identities.

Other existential-phenomenological approaches of note are Viktor Frankl's logotherapy, which seeks to help people identify the meaning of life's experiences, and R. D. Laing's orientation which, like Rogers' client-centered therapy, emphasizes the importance of empathizing with the people who come for help. George Kelly's personal construct theory also has a phenomenological dimension but at the same time recognizes the importance for therapy of information obtained from more objective sources such as case histories and tests.

Group therapies flourished, too, during the 1960s and 1970s, in part because the group milieu was seen by some as more therapeutic than one-on-one therapist-client sessions. Another reason for their greater utilization was that, by meeting with more than one person at a time, psychotherapists could potentially help a greater number of people. Therapists of all persuasions, including the psychoanalytic, experimented with group techniques. Gestalt therapy and, increasingly, client-centered therapy took place in group settings.

Most group approaches emphasize present experience rather than analyses of the past or future. In that sense they reflect or are compatible with the existential-phenomenological perspective. At the same time there has been tremendous diversity insofar as the size of groups, activities involved, role of the therapist, meeting places, and other specifics are concerned and in terms of the goals sought and the particular experiences felt to be therapeutic. Activities, for example, range from talking to embracing and from sitting to doing a variety of exercises. In some groups aggressive encounters are emphasized, in others quiet support and mutual understanding. In most approaches participants are fully clothed but in others they are sometimes nude. Some meet wherever convenient, others in secluded retreats.[72] The most well-known formal organizations to emerge from the group movement are probably Esalen and Synanon.

The psychologist who provided the initial catalyst for group intervention strategies was Kurt Lewin. In the early 1950s he developed the T group and sensitivity training techniques designed to bring about mutual understanding between managers and employees.[73]

Working with more than one person at a time creates the potential for special problems, particularly with regard to the issue of confidentiality. Therefore, the APA in 1973 formulated a set of guidelines for psychologists conducting growth groups.[74]

In conclusion, one of the major developments during the post-World War II era, especially throughout the 1960s and 1970s, was the proliferation of new psychotherapies, both individual and group. Some were modifications of existing psychoanalytic approaches; others, the so-called behavioral therapies, were derived from learning and conditioning theories; and some reflected existential, humanistic, and phenomenological perspectives. Most of the new techniques tended to focus on the present behavior, symptoms, feelings, or thoughts of clients, and the majority were designed to bring about relatively quick results. While the cognitive-behavioral techniques probably represent the most significant specific advance within psychotherapy, the real importance of the work of all those psychologists and psychiatrists who developed new ways of dealing with human problems may lie in the fact that many of the complex variables relevant to the therapy process were identified and investigated.

The proliferation of therapies has, however, made it difficult for a person who seeks help to decide on a therapist. In 1975 Ralph Nader's Health Research Group published a consumer guide to psychotherapists in the Washington, D.C., area entitled *Through the Mental Health Maze*.[75] This was apparently the only attempt by a consumer group to help the layman select a therapist.

Although it is clearly the case that the influence of psychoanalysis has diminished sharply within American clinical psychology since World War II, the psychoanalytic orientation still predominates within psychiatry. During this period there has also been a gradual move within psychiatry away from all psychological theories and treatments of mental and emotional dysfunction toward biological perspectives and therapies. The change has been brought about by evidence which seems to link some psychological problems with genetic factors and by the tremendous increase in pharmacological preparations that appear to help some people with mental and emotional difficulties.[76] One hopes, of course, that even if more convincing biological treatments are discovered, psychiatrists will not forget the psychological factors that are integral to successful medical practice in general.

Psychometrics At the same time that psychotherapy became an important function of clinical psychology during the post-World War II years, clinicians continued to spend a good deal of time administering, interpreting, and evaluating tests. The most consequential developments within psychodiagnostics were probably the diminishing credibility of projective techniques, particularly the Rorschach, as indices of personality, and a lessening reliance on tests in general as research failed to establish the validity of even the most carefully designed and standardized instruments. Interest shifted toward modifying specific behaviors.

Norman Sundberg reported that the tests receiving most attention by psychologists from 1948 through 1951 were, in order, the Rorschach, Wechsler-Bellevue Intelligence Scale, Minnesota Multiphasic Personality Inventory (MMPI), Thematic Apperception Test (TAT), and the Kuder Preference Record.[77] In his 1950 review of psychodiagnostic instruments, Howard Hunt concluded: "The recent publications in the area of psychodiagnostics emphasize quite overwhelmingly the importance and potential scope and richness of projective techniques."[78] Even during the early 1950s, however, some psychologists expressed disillusionment with general tests of personality. In 1953, for instance, Julian Rotter wrote that "when so-called global tests of personality are put to some specific

predictive test, they fair much more poorly than tests designed for specific purposes."[79]

The first time a separate chapter was devoted to projective techniques
in the *Annual Review of Psychology* was in 1963. This is ironic since almost
all the many studies conducted during the 1950s designed to validate
projective methodologies had clearly failed. Goldine Gleser, the author
of the review, concluded that the only reasons for optimism about the
future were to be found in the "evidence of increased awareness of the
limitations of traditional techniques and the need to modify and improve them . . . [and] . . . the increased use of a combination of experimental techniques and measures of individual differences."[80] Gleser also
noted that some critics, such as Eysenck, questioned whether or not
projective tests had any value whatsoever.

In his 1967 review Seymour Fisher pointed out that: "The term 'projective test' has become overloaded with connotations that automatically,
with little regard for the facts, elicit positive or negative responses."[81]
Decrying the irrationality of this situation, Fisher contended that the
underlying causes of the problem are that experimenter bias frequently
determines the outcome of validation research, that very different instruments are lumped under the projective label, and that the tests
involved are used for a variety of divergent purposes. With regard to the
last point, Rorschach responses are, for example, used as measures of
personality, specific motives, the impact of subliminal stimuli, deviancy,
and intelligence. Fisher also made this interesting observation:

It is doubtful whether in the long run there will be much profit in assuming that
the problems facing the development of projective tests are fundamentally different from those encountered in fashioning any class of techniques for measuring personality traits and sets. The apparently simpler and less complicated
conditions of measurement obtaining for 'objective tests' have proven to be largely
illusory.[82]

From the perspective of 1972, H. Barry Molish wrote: "It is of significance that whereas these classical issues [normative data, reliability,
validity] still are relevant in any contemporary review, in the relatively
short period of almost a decade, one of the core issues is now that of the
continuing decline in the importance and application of projective methodologies."[83] Molish noted that the decline was viewed by a variety of
contemporary psychologists as being due to several factors including
disillusionment with the instruments, decreasing emphasis by clinical
psychologists on psychodiagnostics in general, less attention to projective tests in clinical graduate programs, and the increasing influence of
behavior modification with its focus on behavior change rather than
diagnosis.

Perhaps the most telling comments about the state of personality test-ing during the middle sixties came from Oscar Buros, editor of the *Mental Measurement Yearbook*, when he wondered why 2,274 studies of the MMPI had not led to an improved version of the test and why 3,747 investigations of the Rorschach had not produced a validating body of information.[84]

The diminished role of psychodiagnostics in clinical psychology by the 1970s is documented by a study published in 1976 by Sol Garfield and Richard Kurtz.[85] Analyzing a sample of one-third of the membership of Division 12, the Division of Clinical Psychology (response rate 69%), they found that clinicians spent only about 10% of their professional time on diagnosis and assessment. Approximately 30% of their time, on the other hand, was devoted to psychotherapy.

During the 1960s and early 1970s, when psychological assessment became a secondary task of most clinicians and psychometric instru-ments came under close scrutiny within psychology as a whole, testing also came under fire by various segments of society, the news media, and special committees of the federal government.

In 1961, for example, Eron and Walder published an article entitled "Test Burning: II" in which they reported encountering irrational resis-tance to a survey study of aggression in children conducted in the small New York State town of Hudson. Although the investigators had em-ployed extremely thorough pre-study procedures obtaining permission from school administrators and parents, an attack on the study was eventually launched "by a few members of the Hudson Post of the American Legion opposing the organized 'mental health movement.' A series of articles was published in the Hudson newspaper linking men-tal health with 'world citizenship, one worldism, internationalism, com-munism, and socialism'."[86] The overriding fear of the Legionnaires was that the Eron-Walder study was part of a conspiracy on the part of the mental health enterprise "to bring about conformity to the Marxist ideology."[87]

Disturbed by the rising tide of criticism of testing, the American Psy-chological Association organized a major program for the 1964 meeting of the organization entitled Psychological Tests and Public Responsibil-ity. The five papers presented in this program were published the follow-ing year.[88] Launor F. Carter observed that the public had become increasingly concerned with testing because "individuals' educational programs, ca-reers, marriages, emotional adjustments, indeed their lives, may well be affected by testing programs."[89] It was also noted that much of the out-cry against tests originated from individuals, for example, newspaper columnists and politicians, with little or no background in psychomet-rics or test administration. Serious criticisms of testing, according to Orville G. Brim, Jr., have to do with the "inaccessibility of test data, invasion of privacy, rigidity in use of test scores, types of talent selected by tests, [and] fairness of tests to minority groups."[90]

The basic sources of criticism derive from concerns on the part of certain individuals over testing having to do with personality, values, and intelligence, and opportunities lost as a function of poor performance. Samuel Messick stressed that

(a) tests dictate permanent status and hence undermine self-esteem and limit motivation; (b) tests decrease diversity of talent by focusing attention on narrowly conceived, easily measurable attainments; (c) the widespread use of tests gives the tester potential control over educational and industrial practice, as well as over the destinies of individuals; and (d) tests foster impersonal and mechanistic evaluations and decisions at the expense of individual freedom of choice.[91]

In the November, 1965, issue of the *American Psychologist*, which was devoted entirely to "Testing and Public Policy," Michael Amrine in the lead article stated: "The attacks upon psychological testing and upon psychologist-guided selection methods reached a new height in 1965, climaxing in Congressional investigations by Senate and House Committees, accompanied by directives from the Executive side of the Government banning and restricting the uses of psychological instruments.

"Many observers feel this 1965 barrage is the most serious attack that has ever been launched by citizen groups or by Government against any part of psychological research or services."[92]

Amrine pointed out that while the House and Senate hearings took place in June of 1965, "Congressional and press criticisms of tests and of psychological testing methods had been going on for years."[93] For example, William H. Whyte, author of the widely read book, *The Organization Man*,[94] published in 1956, claimed that the personality tests used by many businesses in making personnel decisions could easily be faked by knowledgeable individuals. And books like *The Tyranny of Testing* (1962),[95] *They Shall Not Pass* (1963),[96] and *The Brain Watchers* (1962)[97] represented direct, but rather sensationalistic, attacks on psychological testing. Tests and testing were also criticized during the early 1960s by right-wing newspapers and pamphlets.

The congressional hearings were precipitated by Senator Sam J. Ervin's concern over the reported misuse of psychological tests by the State Department and other federal agencies in selecting and evaluating their employees. The senator was particularly disturbed by some of the items on the Minnesota Multiphasic Personality Inventory (MMPI) which he felt represented an invasion of the privacy of those required to take the test. While the hearings centered around the invasion of privacy issue, the question of test validity was also discussed.

The House Special Subcommittee on the Invasion of Privacy met in September, 1965, to discuss the use of personality tests and questionnaires in federally financed research activities. The committee was investigating the matter because "such tests have been given to hundreds of thousands of school children and college students across the country as part of research projects sponsored by the Federal Government,"[98] and in some instances it was not clear that informed consent had been obtained from the subjects involved or their parents. The committee was also troubled by the fact that some studies required individuals to answer questions about their families, sexual behavior, and religion.

Social science research also came under fire in 1965 because of Project Camelot, sponsored by the U.S. Army. The project was designed to measure and forecast the causes of revolutions and insurgency in underdeveloped areas of the world.[99] The Dominican Republic, which was experiencing an intense political crisis at the time, was of particular interest to the United States. When word of the project leaked out, Chilean and other Latin American newspapers published outraged attacks against the project. As a consequence, the proposed study was terminated by Defense Secretary Robert McNamara in July, 1965.

The subcommittee hearings on Project Camelot which followed and those held earlier on psychological testing revealed both the far-reaching influence of psychology on the operations of the federal government and the fact that there had emerged during the early 1960s increasing skepticism over the validity and propriety of psychological testing and research. While some of the criticism of psychological instruments and procedures was irrational and ill-informed, much of it was substantive and constructive. Testing and the ethical issues involved in research had, after all, been under scrutiny within the discipline throughout the post-World War II period.

Because of the reliance of psychologists on federal research funds, the influence of the government on the discipline increased during the 1960s and 1970s. As a result, the federal government now essentially sets the standards for psychological research. Overall the government guidelines serve to protect human and animal subjects from abuse and in that respect represent a positive development. On the other hand, some of the requirements intrude unnecessarily into the research process and may, therefore, impede progress.

By the end of the 1960s, as the civil rights movement intensified, the main criticism of tests and testing came mostly from minority groups, particularly blacks. College and professional entry examinations were viewed as discriminatory against individuals with substandard elementary and secondary level education; and tests used by employers to screen job applicants were seen as unrelated to job performance.[100] These

complaints were ironic because tests were originally considered to be
instruments for enhancing civil and human rights in the sense that
performance and not sex, race, age, and other irrelevant factors determined who was admitted to college or hired for a job. In 1969 the
American Psychological Association created a task force to examine the
problems involved in employment testing of minorities.[101]

In the 1970s institutions of higher learning did change their admissions policies, placing less emphasis on test performance, to enhance
the chances of minority group students being admitted; and businesses
were requested to discontinue using tests that appeared to have little
validity insofar as job performance is concerned. Within the discipline
interest turned increasingly to producing criterion-based tests—that is,
instruments designed, in the words of R. Glaser and A. J. Nitko, "to
yield measurements that are directly interpretable in terms of specified
performance standards,"[102] rather than norm-referenced tests, such as
the MMPI, "designed to measure a person in relation to a normative
group."[103]

Also in the early 1970s, intense controversy was generated by the
publication in the winter of 1969 of an article by psychologist Arthur R.
Jensen in the prestigious *Harvard Educational Review* entitled "How Much
Can We Boost IQ and Scholastic Achievement?"[104] Jensen, noting that
special programs for disadvantaged children had failed because they did
not permanently improve their IQ scores argued that IQ differences
both within and among racial groups were a function of genetic as well
as environmental factors. He suggested that rote learning rather than
the manipulation of abstractions be emphasized in teaching children
with low IQs.

The implication that differences in the average IQ score among various American racial groups, especially blacks and whites, were due in
part to genetic factors was, of course, the most controversial aspect of
Jensen's position. The old nature-nurture issue concerning intelligence
had been rekindled.[105]

Throughout the seventies criticisms of Jensen's work concentrated on
the limitations of intelligence tests, problems associated with defining
intelligence, and weaknesses of particular studies. The basic argument is
whether or not tests are biased against blacks. In 1980, Jensen published
Bias in Mental Testing wherein he contends:

My exhaustive review of the empirical research bearing on [the bias] issue leads
me to the conclusion that the currently most widely used standardized tests of
mental ability—IQ, scholastic aptitude, and achievement tests—are, by and large,
not biased against any of the native-born English-speaking minority groups on
which the amount of research evidence is sufficient for an objective determination of bias, if the tests were in fact biased.[106]

Counter arguments to this book focus mostly on sophisticated psycho-metric issues.

In general, the intense scrutiny and critical analyses to which tests have been exposed since World War II have helped us understand the strengths and limitations of psychometric instruments. Although global measures of personality and, to some degree, of intelligence have fallen into disfavor, particularly among clinical psychologists, the use of tests to measure special abilities, brain damage, interests, values, and achieve-ment has, if anything, increased throughout the 1946-1975 period. Col-leges and universities still require special examinations of candidates being considered for admission to undergraduate and graduate programs and professional schools. What has changed in some instances is the weight placed on test scores in determining who is to be admitted and who is to be rejected.

Community Psychology Between 1946 and 1955 the number of resident patients in state and local government mental hospitals in the United States increased from 462,000 to 558,900.[107] Had the mental hospital popu-lation continued to increase at the same rate, there would have been approximately 750,000 residents by 1971. Instead, however, the number of institutionalized patients decreased steadily after 1956 so that by 1970 there were only 338,600 residents.

The emptying of the mental hospitals was a function not of fewer admissions but of shorter periods of hospitalization. In 1955, for exam-ple, the average stay was six months; in 1966, by contrast, the period was down to two months. According to Oakley Ray, "Parallel with this increasing discharge rate from hospitals has been an increase in aftercare facilities. In 1970 there were 185 operating community mental health centers and almost 200 more approved and/or under construction."[108]

While the therapeutic value of large mental hospitals had long been doubted, it was the introduction of new psychoactive agents during the early 1950s which brought about the decline in mental hospital popula-tions after 1956. Particularly effective was isocarboxazid, an antidepres-sant; reserpine, a tranquilizer; and chlorpromozine, an antipsychotic drug. Chlorpromozine was the first of a series of phenothiazine drugs that have been used since the 1950s in the treatment of schizophrenic patients. In addition, a variety of new tranquilizers (for example, Lib-rium and Valium), antidepressants (for example, Sinequan), and drugs to control mania (for example, Lithium) were developed during the 1960s and 1970s. Concurrently, LSD was used with limited success to treat alcoholics, and mega-vitamin therapy was advocated by some psychiatrists as a treatment for schizophrenia. The biochemical treat-ment of psychological problems has been, without question, one of the most significant developments within the mental health area since World War II.

As psychoactive drugs and the availability of more helping professionals led to fewer individuals with psychological difficulties being institutionalized, the need for community-based outpatient facilities grew
rapidly. This need, in fact, was the most important factor underlying the
community mental health movement that started in earnest during the
middle 1960s.

As M. Brewster Smith and Nicholas Hobbs have noted, "The community-
based approach to mental illness and health attracted national attention
as a result of the findings of the Joint Commission on Mental Illness and
Health that was established by Congress under the Mental Health Study
Act of 1955."[109] After five years of study, the commission recommended
that no more large mental hospitals be constructed and that "a flexible
array of services be provided for the mentally ill in settings that disrupt
as little as possible the patient's social relations in his community."[110]

In 1962 the federal government appropriated funds for the states to
study their needs and derive comprehensive mental health programs.
The following year Congress authorized funds to help states build community mental health centers. Federal and state funding of the centers
continued during the late 1960s and early 1970s, with hundreds of facilities being constructed.

By the middle 1970s, most of the enthusiasm for the movement had
been lost. Assessing the situation in 1976, David Snow and Peter Newton wrote: "The fantasy of radical change that enlivened the CMHC
[Community Mental Health Center] movement in the 1960s has given
way to a sense of rudderless drift and even stagnation."[111] Psychiatry,
Snow and Newton observed, appeared to be "moving back to its biological roots in medicine."[112] However, they considered biological remedies
to be "of limited value for the socially generated psychological anguish
of whole communities."[113] They urged that psychologists adopt a
sociopsychological approach to the problems of people served by the
mental health centers.

The funding of community mental health centers during the 1963-1975
period challenged and created opportunities for all the helping professions. Psychiatrists tended to assume the leadership roles in the emerging new facilities; nevertheless, clinical psychologists and social workers
also exerted influence on the movement.

Ira Iscoe recalls: "The term *community psychology* was coined at the
Boston (Swampscott) Conference on the Education of Psychologists for
Community Mental Health in 1965."[114] Although the conference was
called to examine the education of clinical psychologists for community
service, discussion centered around "the need for American psychology
to develop a wider arena for preventive mental health measures and...the
necessity to study and deal with persons and communities in their natural habitats."[115] In 1966 the Division of Community Psychology was formed.

By the late sixties, a number of psychology departments were offering graduate programs in community psychology; more followed suit in the 1970s.

As has been true of clinical psychology in general during the post-World War II period, there has been incessant controversy over the nature and function of community psychology since its inception in the middle sixties. Most disagreement has concentrated on the issue of whether community psychologists should serve primarily as counselors and psychotherapists and perhaps consultants or whether they should also try to be agents of change working actively to improve societal conditions.[116]

In addition, there has been concern over the appropriateness of the medical model brought to the community mental health movement by psychiatry. Most psychologists have, as might be expected, taken the position that psychological problems which are to a large degree a function of poverty, discrimination, unemployment, unstable families, second-rate schools, and so forth are not diseases but rather problems in living. Right from the beginning, therefore, a majority of community psychologists urged that their work not be conceptualized within a medical framework.[117] Some have even proposed that community psychology be an area distinct from clinical psychology.

There have been differences, moreover, on the issue of the proper training of community psychologists. Disagreement has focused on the relative importance of traditional psychology, the scientific method, sociology, organizational theory, law, political science, and experience in the field. At the Boston Conference in 1965, there was consensus that the Ph.D. was the appropriate degree for community psychology and that there should be a strong emphasis on research competence and appropriate field experience. There was also a good deal of sentiment for interdisciplinary programs.

However, Seymour Sarason (1976), who conceived of the community psychologist as neither a clinical psychologist nor a mental health professional, advocated that community psychologists be trained to understand "how resources are defined and used so as to maximize the psychological sense of community."[118] To do this Sarason proposed that community psychologists must have some understanding of the groups involved, the economics of the community, and the politics of family relationships as well as psychological theory and fact. Leonard Goodstein and Irwin Sandler (1978) also considered community psychology as a distinct field with practitioners being trained in systems analysis, organizational theory, planned change strategies, social planning, environmental assessment, and stress theory.[119]

To date, community psychology has failed to evolve into a clearly defined specialty. There is some sense that it never will because the problems encompassed are too complex and the goals too idealistic. The field is primarily a product of the late 1960s, the Vietnam and civil rights era, when hopes ran high that the evils of our society could be corrected with love and the proper government programs. It has now become evident that for professionals of any kind to change even a single community for the better is an awesome task. Faith in community psychology has waned. There is even a possibility that it will with time disappear as a distinct area of concentration within the discipline.

Problems Conceptualizing Psychological Functioning and Malfunctioning In 1960 psychiatrist Thomas S. Szasz wrote a landmark paper entitled "The Myth of Mental Illness"[120] in which he argued that there is no such thing as mental illness. While he acknowledged that some psychological problems are a function of physiological factors, he pointed out that the term "mental illness" generally refers to "deviance in behavior from certain psychosocial, ethical, or legal norms."[121] Since the deviance is relative to behavioral rather than somatic norms, Szasz contended that medical conceptions and treatments are not appropriate. A person with psychological difficulties does not have a diseased personality, but rather has a problem living according to certain norms and expectancies of society. Although Szasz was not the first psychological professional to criticize the medical or disease-medical model of psychological malfunctioning, his paper and subsequent publications were influential because they constituted a systematic and well-reasoned attack by a psychiatrist on some of the basic principles and assumptions underlying contemporary psychiatry.

Szasz became known as one of the chief rebels within psychiatry during the 1960s and 1970s, not only because of his position toward mental illness but because he has been a strong critic of the institutionalization of and subsequent denial of basic freedoms to so-called mental patients.

With regard to the definition of psychological normality and abnormality, several models have been proposed. George W. Kisker, for example, in his abnormal psychology textbook, *The Disorganized Personality*,[122] mentions five perspectives: the subjective model where you set yourself up as the standard of comparison; the normative model wherein the standard for comparison is a set of ideals; the cultural model based on the assumption that "normality is the standard approved by the greatest number of people";[123] the statistical model where the average is considered normal; and the clinical model which defines normality in terms of the absence of disabling symptoms. The clinical model can, of course, be couched in either medical or social terms, although the final referent is always behavioral.

To the related question of what constitutes mental health there are almost as many answers as there are theorists. Central to Freud's conception of adaptive psychological functioning is the ability to love and work and not spend too much time and energy warding off potential anxiety; for Carl Rogers self-actualization is the key to a productive and happy life; for Viktor Frankl a person is on the right track psychologically when he/she realizes that all human experience has meaning; essential to Erik Erikson's view of normal psychological development is identity formation, and so forth. For most behaviorists the concept of mental health is irrelevant; what is important is the elimination of undesirable behavior and the acquisition of desirable responses.

In addition to general concern over the concepts of mental health and illness and psychological normality and abnormality, there has throughout the history of psychiatry and clinical psychology been continual debate over the classification system used to categorize people with psychological problems.[124] Since World War II there has also been an increasing awareness, largely inspired by existential and phenomenological influences, of the counterproductive aspects, therapeutically speaking, of the very act of classifying and labeling people.[125] Criticisms of existing psychiatric nosologies include the contentions that the taxonomies are based on more than one classificatory principle, for example, symptoms and predicted outcome; placing a human being in a particular category tends to obscure the unique characteristics of that individual; the reliability of classification is frequently poor; classifying often tells us little about the prognosis of a problem; and categorizing people may give a superficial scientific credibility to the work of the psychiatrist or psychologist, but it does little to insure successful treatment.

Every profession requires standardized systems of classification; unfortunately, however, such formulations by their nature tend to rigidify the inquiry process. Furthermore, in disciplines like psychiatry and clinical psychology that deal with human problems, the very act of labeling both obscures the individuality of a man or woman and stigmatizes him or her. The label schizophrenic, for example, tends to reduce the complex nature of a human being to a particular set of symptoms, both in the perspective of the person so labeled and in the eyes of relatives, friends, and therapists.

Most of the conceptual problems besetting psychiatry and clinical psychology are a function of conceiving psychological problems within a medical framework and of the general attempt to derive scientifically useful systems of classification. The result has been to create categories of human psychological malfunctioning which both overemphasize physiological causes and cures and depersonalize people. Offsetting this situation to some degree in recent years has been an increased awareness on the part of psychological professionals of the limitations of the disease-medical model and the intrusion into the therapy process of any attempt to put labels on people.

Professional Issues As indicated earlier, clinical psychologists have been concerned with the professionalization of the field throughout the entire post-World War II period. Of particular importance have been the design of appropriate training programs, the establishment of ethical guidelines for research and practice, the formation of a clear professional identity, the certification and licensure of practitioners, and the achievement of credibility and respectability relative to other disciplines and society as a whole.

While the field has attained many of its professional goals, psychiatry maintains a position of prominence among the helping professions both because psychiatrists continue to control the leadership structure of the primary work settings, for example, mental hospitals and mental health clinics, and because the services of clinical psychologists are not covered by the insurance plans issued by Blue Cross/Blue Shield, the nation's largest health insurer.

In 1973 both Virginia and Maryland passed freedom of choice laws that require commercial insurance companies to pay for services provided by independent clinical psychologists. Since then many other states have followed suit. However, Blue Cross/Blue Shield, or "the Blues," as the company is sometimes called, has from the beginning refused to comply with such legislation claiming that as a nonprofit organization it is exempt. In 1976, in fact, the Blues formally challenged the Virginia statute. A district court upheld the company's position in 1979, but in the following year the Fourth U.S. Circuit Court of Appeals overturned the lower court's decision.[126] Although this was a victory for clinical psychologists, the implications of the ruling are as yet unclear.

The struggle by psychologists for freedom of choice statutes got underway in earnest during the early 1970s when it appeared that national health insurance was a possibility. There was even an unsuccessful attempt to pass national freedom of choice legislation. In addition, the Council for the Advancement of the Psychological Profession and Sciences (CAPPS), a formal advocacy group, brought a class action suit against Blue Cross/Blue Shield in connection with the Federal Employees Health Benefits Plan "in order to establish judicial precedent on the issues involved, including the terms of coverage for psychological services."[127] The complaint was that Blue Cross/Blue Shield was inflating the cost of health care, as well as interfering with subscriber freedom of choice relative to psychological services. This suit did lead eventually to many federal employees having free choice of psychological treatment.

The civil rights movement of the late sixties and seventies generated increased concern over the rights of mental patients and persons seeking psychological or psychiatric help on an outpatient basis. The result was a number of legal decisions that impacted importantly on the professional responsibilities of clinicians and other helping professionals.

Several cases (*Rouse* v. *Cameron*, 1966; *Wyatt* v. *Stickney*, 1972; *Wyatt* v. *Aderholt*, 1974) upheld the principle that individuals committed to psychiatric hospitals have the right to be treated. In *Donaldson* v. *O'Connor* (1975), as Bernstein and Nietzel note, "the Supreme Court concluded that a state cannot confine without treatment nondangerous individuals who can survive by themselves or with the help of others outside the institution."[128] Conversely, a number of cases give institutionalized persons the right to refuse treatment that violates their privacy, is considered drastic, or is really a form of punishment. On the other hand, a patient may not refuse all rehabilitative efforts.

Many states have also passed laws, again according to Bernstein and Nietzel, "that establish a general psychotherapist-client *privilege*. Privilege is a legal right imposed to protect the client from public disclosure of confidences by the therapist without the client's permission."[129] Privilege and confidentiality are related concepts; however, the former is a legal requirement and the latter an ethical prescription of a profession. The usual exceptions to privilege have to do with situations where commitment is recommended, insanity is used as an argument against criminal conviction, or a client tells a therapist that he plans to commit an unlawful or harmful act (*Tarasoff* v. *Regents of University of California*).

Overall, legislation protecting the human rights of individuals with psychological problems reflects an increasingly enlightened viewpoint, even though some of the laws complicate the work of helping professionals. The "right to treatment" laws, for example, may clash with "the right to refuse treatment" regulations. And the right to confidentiality sometimes comes into conflict with society's right to protect itself against dangerous individuals.

Conclusion The growth and transformation of clinical psychology into a full-fledged helping profession was in many ways the most important development within post-World War II American psychology.[130] Not only did this development stimulate research in numerous areas of concern to the discipline such as cognition, human learning, abnormal psychology, personality theory and assessment, psychometrics, and social processes, but it contributed directly to the growth of university departments of psychology since it fell to them to provide the academic training of clinicians.

The major contributions of clinical psychology include bringing a strong research tradition to the helping professions, stressing the importance of accountability for those who claim to be providing psychotherapy, examining (more so than most psychiatrists) the role of cognitive, environmental, and social variables in psychological functioning and malfunctioning, and, along with some psychiatrists and other helping professionals, providing new ways of conceptualizing human psychological problems. Clinical psychology now affords a viable and credible alternative to psychiatry.

APPENDIX A

The Most Important People in American Psychology During the Post-World War II Period

	RANKS		
	GROUP 1	*GROUP 2*	*GROUP 3*
Skinner, B. F.	1	1	2
Freud, S.	2	2	1
Piaget, J.	3	3	3.5
Rogers, C.	4	5	7
Erikson, E.	5	21	3.5
Wechsler, D.	6	28	22.5
Harlow, H.	7	16	14
Lewin, K.	8	6	11
Jung, C.	9	29	8.5
Hull, C.	10	4	5.5
Thorndike, E.	11	8	18.5
Maslow, A.	12	22	31.5
Hebb, D. O.	13	12	18.5
Fisher, R. A.	14	9	22.5
Allport, G.	15	18	20.5
Miller, N. E.	16	14	14
Bandura, A.	17	25	54
Thurstone, L.	18	13	16.5
Terman, L.	19	17	20.5
Boring, E.	20	7	14
Adler, A.	21	50	37
Fromm, E.	22	54	85.5
Bruner, J.	23	20	48
Gesell, A.	24	57	69.5
Tolman, E.	25	10	5.5
Selye, H.	26	32.5	44.5
Eysenck, H.	27	37	54
Sullivan, H.	28	51	85.5
Guilford, J.	29	40	69.5

Masters, W. H. and Johnson, V. E.	30	102	159
Lorenz, K.	31	23	27
Cronbach, L.	32	53	51.5
Cattell, R.	33	63	107
Chomsky, N.	34	58	48
Wolpe, J.	35	62	75.5
Köhler, W.	36.5	15	3.5
Bekesy, G. von	36.5	19	37
Lashley, K.	38	11	11
Guthrie, E.	39	45	42
Hilgard, E.	40	32.5	44.5
Festinger, L.	41	48	31.5
Kinsey, A.	42	56	85.5
Bettelheim, B.	43	134	136.5
Luria, A. R.	44	36	48
Hall, C. S.	45	111	193
Murray, H.	46	39	16.5
Hubel, D.	47	72	72.5
McClelland, D.	48	68	27
Anastasi, A.	49.5	79	122.5
Menninger, K.	49.5	99	159
May, R.	51	89.5	40
Stevens, S. S.	52	27	24.5
Hunt,. J. McV.	53	41	75.5
Freud, A.	54	89.5	69.5
Horney, K.	55	82.5	119
Hartmann, H.	56	105	255
Yerkes, R.	57	46	11
Kuhn, T.	58.5	55	146
Sperry, R.	58.5	30.5	34.5
Spence, K.	60	24	37
Bronfenbrenner, U.	61	76	85.5
Campbell, D.	62	77	65
Kagan, J.	63	91	126.5
Brown, R.	64	64	72.5
Woodworth, R.	65	26	8.5
Tinbergen, N.	66	35	24.5
Azrin, N.	67	152	85.5
Simon, H.	68	52	29
Dollard, J.	69	80	149.5
Eccles, J. C.	70.5	60	85.5
Meehl, P.	70.5	82.5	75.5
Heider, F.	72	68	54

Asch, S.	73	69	69.5
Beach, F.	74	59	31.5
Bridgman, P.	75.5	44	60
Olds, J.	75.5	42	44.5
Bertalanffy, L. von	77	132	188.5
Miller, G. A.	78.5	43	40
Szasz, T.	78.5	96	219.5
Mowrer, O. H.	80.5	65	102.5
Carmichael, L.	80.5	86	196.5
Milgram, S.	82	116	65
Bayley, N.	83	103	136.5
Allport, F.	84	94.5	93
Kohlberg, L.	85	123	97
Neumann, J. von	86	70	212
Brunswik, E.	87	38	131
Perls, F.	88	193.5	168
Gibson, J.	89	30.5	51.5
Osgood, C.	90	61	50
Broadbent, D.	91	34	63
Wiesel, T.	92	84	101
Kelley, H.	93	117	145
Estes, W.	94.5	47	44.5
Lindquist, E.	94.5	126	241.5
Lacey, J.	96	163	136.5
Pribram, K.	97	81	56.6
Bower, G. H.	98	49	62
Atkinson, R. C.	99	106	147.5
Werner, H.	100	98	97
Premack, D.	101	147	85.5
Kelly, G. A.	103	75	116
Gibson, E.	104	78	67
Barker, R.	107	67	99.5
Frisch, K. von	110	73	60
Berlyne, D.	113	71	40
Wiener, N.	114	74	136.5
Dement, W.	115.5	114.4	58
Polanyi, M.	118.5	88	181
Lindzey, G.	121	129.5	65
Heidbreder, E.	122.5	144	85.5
Neisser, U.	124	92	34.5
Granit, R. A.	129	155	85.5
Krech, D.	130	113	27
Jensen, A.	134.5	153	75.5
Sears, R.	139.5	97	85.5

Hovland, C.	142	85	56.6
Shakow, D.	143	94.5	107
Delgado, J.	146	160	97
Newcomb, T. M.	147.5	87	136.5
Sherif, M.	150	118	85.5
Postman, L.	153	109	94.5
Pfaffman, C.	161	148	85.5
Helson, H.	169.5	93	60
Spence, J. T.	183.5	121	94.5
Barron, F.	214	229	99.5
Orne, M. T.	215	221	85.5
Liberman, A. M.	216	178.5	85.5
Teitelbaum, P.	257.5	157.5	85.5

[a]Based on a study by the author entitled "Important People in Post-World War II American Psychology: A Survey Study" published by the Journal Supplement Abstract Service (JSAS) of the American Psychological Association, Ms. 2171. See *Catalog of Selected Documents in Psychology* 11 (February, 1981). The study involved: 679 repondents from a random sampling of 4,000 members of the American Psychological Association (Group 1); 93 respondents from a random sampling of 250 members of the Division 26 (History of Psychology) (Group 2); and 13 recognized experts on the history of psychology (Group 3). Respondents were asked to rate 286 individuals selected on the basis of a variety of criteria using a 5-point scale of importance. Only those people ranked in the top 100 by any of the three groups are included in this table. Copyright (1981) by the American Psychological Association. Adapted by permission of the publisher and author.

APPENDIX B

The Most Important Events and Influences in Post-World War II American Psychology[a]

	RANKS		
	GROUP 1	GROUP 2	GROUP 3
Skinner's contributions	1	1	2.5
Behavior modification	2	6	10
Growth of applied psychology	3	13	16.5
Growth of behavioral psychology	4	9	27.5
Govt. funding of psychology	5	3	6
General growth of psychology	6	5	1
Impact of World War II	7	2	23.5
Growth of clinical psychology	8	7	4
Impact of Piaget	9	14	9
Information explosion	10	8	30
Federal support of mental health	11	45.5	82.5
Popularization of psychology	12	32	47.5
Reduction of federal support (1970s)	13	21	75
Computer applications	14	11	14
Licensing of professional psychologists	15	30	32
Flight of European intellectuals and professionals to the U.S. (1930s-1940s)	16	15	12
Increasing accountability of psychologists	17	18	97
Harlow's primate research	18	20	7.5
Increasing influence of cognitive theory	19	4	2.5
Community mental health movement	20	41	61.5
Research and theory on stress	21	25	55
Split brain research	22	24	18.5
New information retrieval systems	23	33	97

Biofeedback	24	27	55
Growth of higher education	25	23	34
Growth of developmental psychology	26	16.5	27.5
New openness toward mental illness	27	61	116
Experimental research on newborn and infants	28	28	42
Research in physiological psychology	29	16.5	11
Research on neurotransmitters	30	29	47.5
Influence of operationism	31	12	16.5
Social learning theory	32.5	19	27.5
Criticisms of tests (1960s-1970s)	32.5	45.5	42
Rise of chemotherapy	34	26	35
Increased interest in complex psychological processes	35	10	55
Development of a multitude of therapies	36.5	51	61.5
Emptying the mental hospitals	36.5	67	82.5
Changing views of the IQ concept	38	40	58
Research on sexual behavior	39	37	97
Brown vs. *Board of Education* (1954)	40	42	66.5
New views of abnormality	41	38	80
NSF support of social-behavioral research	42	35	89.5
Move toward more real-world psychology	43	72	79
Research on violence and aggression	44	31	47.5
Changing roles of clinical psychology	45	52	38
Audio and visual recording techniques	46	44	47.5
Testing in general	47	55	112.5
Advocacy activities (AAPS/CAPPS)	48	143.5	97
VA support of psychology	49	59	116
Govt. regs. protecting human subjects	50	48	97
Human potential movement	51	92	97
Emergence of behavior genetics	52	39	15
Competent infant concept	53	85	82.5
Research on death and dying	54	86	118
Boulder Conference	55	58	22
Szasz's attack on the medical model	56	81	69.5
Concern over the psychology of women	57	101	141

Disillusionment over science and technology	58	62	69.5
Influence of civil rights movement	59	96	131
Growth of social psychology	60	36	42
Mind and consciousness return to psychology	61	22	7.5
Information theory	62	77	75
Growth of humanistic psychology	63	95	20
Biological theories of schizophrenia	64	66	25
Growth of group therapies	65	108	61.5
Motivational theory and research	66	53	55
Factor analytic research	67	128	112.5
Micro-electrode techniques	68	56	75
Self-concept theories	69	104	86.5
Research on group dynamics	70	102	122
Increasing power of APA	71	98.5	133
Cybernetics, feedback models	72	110.5	136
Women's movement	73	115	133
Growth of psycholinguistics	74	73	5
Experimenter bias research	75	90	75
Research and theory on personality	76.5	80	42
Research on sex differences	76.5	74.5	66.5
Research on emotions	78	121	97
Deprivation (sensory, maternal) research	79	79	66.5
Cognitive social psychology	80	49.5	82.5
Influence of ethology	81	43	18.5
Computer models of cognition	82	60	66.5
Reticular formation studies	83	76	13
Increasing use of ANOVA	84	69	32
Recent criticisms of behavior modification (1970s)	85	88	137.5
Territorial hassles among professions	86	118	124
Advent of professional schools	87	84	108.5
APA's ethical guidelines	88.5	87	89.5
Rogerian client-centered therapy	88.5	126	61.5
Call for relevant research (1970s)	90	100	103.5
Research on monkey language	91	83	75
Research on pleasure centers of the brain	92	54	42
Modified admissions standards for grad. programs	93	70	97

Epidemiological studies	94	114	52
Competency-based instruction	95.5	139	126
Studies of helping behavior	95.5	103	139
Dollard and Miller's theory	97	116	120
Memory research	98	34	47.5
Hormonal studies	99	105	105.5
Decisions of the Warren Court	100	109	147.5
Research on attention and arousal	101	93	59
Ego psychology	102	127	71
Duplicating machines	103	82	51
Influence of psychoanalysis	104	89	36
Lewin's influence	106	117	27.5
Advances in visual perception research	108	47	97
Probabilistic thinking	110	78	107
Hebb's theory and research	113	74.5	55
New structuralism (1960s-1970s)	115	71	86.5
Attribution theory	117	64.5	21
Signal detection and decision theories	118	68	38
Cognitive dissonance research and theory	119	112	75
Functional theory	120	57	108.5
Controversy over models of abnormality	121	98.5	103.5
Non-parametric statistics	124	97	75
Jensen's views of race and IQ	125	63	38
Transformational grammar	127	120	32
Publication of many new journals	128.5	49.5	86.5
Concern over paradigms	128.5	64.5	97
Influence of phenomenology	135	133	91
Balance theories	136	124	100
Dream research	137.5	91	23.5
Neo-Freudianism	139	134	86.5
Mathematical modeling	143	107	97
Decline of Hullian psychology	150	94	47.5

[a]Based on a study by the author entitled "Important Events and Influences in Post-World War II American Psychology: A Survey Study" published by the Journal Supplement Abstract Service (JSAS) of the American Psychological Association, Ms. 2144. See *Catalog of Selected Documents in Psychology* 10 (November 1980). The study involved 223 respondents from a random sampling of 1,000 members of the American Psychological Association (Group 1), 77 respondents from a random sampling of 250 members of Division 26 (History of Psychology) (Group 2), and 13 recognized experts on the history of psychology (Group 3). Respondents were asked to rate 157 events and influences selected on the basis of several criteria using a 5-point scale of importance. Only those items ranked in the top 100 by any of the three groups are included in this table. Copyright (1980) by the American Psychological Association. Adapted by permission of the publisher and author.

NOTES

Chapter 1

1. Martin L. Gross, *The Psychological Society: A Critical Analysis of Psychiatry, Psychotherapy, Psychoanalysis and the Psychological Revolution* (New York: Random House, 1978).

2. James M. Perry and Albert R. Hunt, "After Cleaning House, Carter Will Attempt to Deal with 'Crisis of Confidence' by Stressing Leadership," *The Wall Street Journal*, August 23, 1979, p. 3.

3. American Psychological Association, *Biographical Directory of the American Psychological Association* (1975), p. 9.

4. *Ulrich's International Periodical Directory*, 17th ed. (New York: R. R. Bowker, 1977).

5. Julian Jaynes, *The Origin of Consciousness in the Breakdown of the Bicameral Mind* (Boston: Houghton Mifflin, 1977).

6. Thomas M. Canfield, "The Professionalization of American Psychology, 1870-1917," *Journal of the History of the Behavioral Sciences* 9 (January 1973): 66-75.

7. See chapter 9 for a brief discussion of the roots of clinical psychology.

8. John B. Watson, "Psychology as the Behaviorist Views It," *Psychological Review* 20 (1913): 158-77.

9. Maurice Davie et al., *Refugees in America: Report of the Committee for the Study of Recent Immigration from Europe* (New York: Harper, 1947).

10. See chapter 3 for a more detailed discussion of the intellectual migration.

Chapter 2

1. The developments mentioned in this section of the chapter were selected in part on the basis of the findings of the following studies conducted by the author: (*a*) Albert R. Gilgen and Stevan K. Hultman, "Authorities and Subject Matter Areas Emphasized, in *Annual Review of Psychology, 1950-1974*," *Psychological Reports* 44 (1979): 1255-62; (*b*) Albert R. Gilgen, "Important Events and Influences in Post-World War II American Psychology: a Survey Study," *JSAS Catalog of Selected Documents in Psychology* 10 (November 1980), Ms. 2144; (*c*) Albert R. Gilgen, "Important People in Post-World War II American Psychology: A Survey

Study," *JSAS Catalog of Selected Documents in Psychology* 11 (February 1981), Ms. 2171. Appendices A and B include information from these studies.

2. See chapter 3 for a detailed discussion of the influence of World War II on American psychology.

3. *Historical Statistics of the United States, Colonial Times to 1970*, Bicentennial Edition. (Washington: Government Printing Office, 1975), 1: 387.

4. Ibid., p. 1116.

5. Ibid., p. 965.

6. Robert C. Tryon, "Psychology in Flux: the Academic-Professional Bipolarity," *American Psychologist* 18 (March 1963): 134-43.

7. *Historical Statistics of the United States*, p. 808.

8. Lee J. Cronbach, Paul R. Farnsworth, and Lorraine Bouthilet, "The APA Publications Program: Status and Prospects, 1955," *American Psychologist* 10 (March 1955): 110-20.

9. Ibid., p. 113.

10. Albert R. Gilgen and Kristin Tolvstad, "Major Recipients of National Science Foundation Funds for Psychological Research," *JSAS Catalog of Selected Documents in Psychology* 11 (August 1981), Ms. 2278. Albert R. Gilgen, "Major Recipients of National Institute of Mental Health Funds: The Million Dollar Club," *JSAS Catalog of Selected Documents in Psychology* 11 (February 1981), Ms. 2170.

11. These guidelines were formulated by the American Psychological Association "Committee on Training in Clinical Psychology" and upheld at the Boulder Conference (1949) which evaluated graduate education in clinical psychology (see chapter 9).

12. Harold Borko, "History and Development of Computers," in *Computer Applications in the Behavioral Sciences*, ed. Harold Borko (Englewood Cliffs, N.J.: Prentice-Hall, 1962), p. 24.

13. Ibid., p. 39.

14. Ibid., p. 42.

15. Binary number systems are based on two digits, for example, 0 and 1. All quantities are expressed in terms of combinations of these two numbers.

16. See (*a*) Charles Wrigley, "The University Computing Center," in Borko (1962); (*b*) Charles Wrigley, "Electronic Computers and Psychological Research," *American Psychologist* 12 (August 1957): 501-8.

17. Allen Newell and Herbert Simon, "GPS, a program that Simulates Human Thought," in *Computers and Thought*, eds. Edward A. Feigenbaum and Julian Feldman (New York: McGraw-Hill, 1963).

18. Richard D. James, "Group Therapy's Help in Coping with Stress is Minor, Studies Show," *The Wall Street Journal*, April 16, 1979, p. 1.

19. John B. Watson, *Psychological Care of Infant and Child* (New York: W. W. Norton, 1928).

20. Benjamin Spock, *The Pocket Book of Baby and Child Care* (New York: Pocket Books, 1946).

21. John Kenneth Galbraith, *The Affluent Society* (Boston: Houghton Mifflin, 1958).

22. Walter D. Scott, *The Theory of Advertising* (Boston: Small, Maynard & Co., 1903).

23. Vance Packard, *The Hidden Persuaders* (New York: D. McKay, 1957).

Chapter 3

1. John C. Flanagan et al., *Current Trends: Psychology in the World Emergency* (Pittsburgh: University of Pittsburgh Press, 1952), p. 2.

2. Steuart Henderson Britt and Jane D. Morgan, "Military Psychologists in World War II," *American Psychologist* 1 (1946): 423-37.

3. Paul M.A. Linebarger, *Psychological Warfare* (Washington, D.C.: Combat Forces Press, 1948, 1952), p. 93.

4. For interesting examples of psychological warfare projects, see William E. Daugherty and Morris Janowitz, *A Psychological Warfare Casebook* (Baltimore: The Johns Hopkins Press, 1958).

5. James J. Gibson, *The Perception of the Visual World* (Boston: Houghton Mifflin, 1950), p. viii.

6. B.F. Skinner, "Pigeons in a Pelican," *American Psychologist* 15 (January 1960): 31.

7. J.P. Guilford, "Some Lessons from Aviation Psychology," *American Psychologist* 3 (January 1948): 3.

8. Ibid., p. 3.

9. See Flanagan et al., 1952, for details on these references plus listings of relevant journal articles. The 1946-1949 issues of the *American Psychologist* also contain numerous articles on military psychology.

10. Donald Fleming and Bernard Bailyn, eds., *The Intellectual Migration: Europe and America, 1930-1960* (Cambridge, Mass.: Harvard University Press, 1969), pp. 11-12.

11. Laura Fermi, *Illustrious Immigrants: The Intellectual Migration from Europe, 1930-41* (Chicago: University of Chicago Press, 1968, 1971), p. 17.

12. Ibid., p. 151.

13. Ibid., p. 170.

14. Ibid., p. 170.

15. Ibid., p. 7.

16. Fleming and Bailyn, p. 9.

17. Fermi, p. 7.

18. Ibid., p. 150.

19. *Statistical Abstracts of the United States* (Bureau of the Census, 1974), p. 82.

20. George W. Albee and Marguerite Dickey, "Manpower Trends in Three Mental Health Professions," *American Psychologist* 12 (February 1957): 60.

21. Henryk Misiak and Virginia Staudt Sexton, *History of Psychology: An Overview* (New York: Grune & Stratton, 1966), p. 215.

22. Dael Wolfle, "Comparisons Between Psychologists and Other Professional Groups," *American Psychologist* 10 (June 1955): 231-7.

23. Flanagan et al., pp. 194-5.

24. Ibid., p. 7.

25. Abram L. Sachar, *A History of the Jews*, 3rd ed. (New York: Knopf, 1930, 1940, 1948), p. 414.

26. "Torture as Policy: The Network of Evil," *Time*, August 16, 1976, pp. 31-4.

27. Wolf Wolfensberger, "Ethical Issues in Research with Human Subjects," *Science* 155 (January 6, 1967): 47-51. See also Irwin A. Berg, "The Use of Human Subjects in Psychological Research," *American Psychologist* 9 (March 1954): 108-11.

28. Ibid., p. 47.

29. A.L. Otten, "Ethical Quandaries," *The Wall Street Journal*, September 18, 1975, p. 22. Otten reviews a book entitled *The Ethical and Legal Implications of Social Experimentation* (Brookings Institute).

30. Theodor W. Adorno et al., *The Authoritarian Personality* (New York: Harper, 1950).

31. See Paul F. Lazarsfeld, "An Episode in the History of Social Research," in Fleming and Bailyn, pp. 285-337, for an interesting discussion of the early development in the United States of university research centers funded by outside funds.

32. See Theodor W. Adorno, "Scientific Experiences of a European Scholar in America," in Fleming and Bailyn, p. 358.

33. Ibid.

34. This research is also briefly discussed in chapter 4.

35. Bernard Berelson and Gary A. Steiner, *Human Behavior: An Inventory of Scientific Findings* (New York: Harcourt, Brace & World, 1964), p. 259.

36. For a detailed critique see Richard Christie and Marie Jahoda, eds., *Studies in the Scope and Method of "The Authoritarian Personality"* (Glencoe, Ill.: Free Press, 1954).

37. Berelson and Steiner, p. 259. Also Leonard Berkowitz, "Theoretical and Research Approaches in Experimental Social Psychology," in *Contemporary Scientific Psychology*, ed. Albert R. Gilgen (New York: Academic Press, 1970).

38. Rokeach continues to do research on belief systems. Two of his most well-known books are *The Open and Closed Mind* (New York: Basic Books, 1960) and *The Three Christs of Ypsilanti* (New York: Knopf, 1964). See Richard I. Evans, *The Making of Psychology* (New York: Knopf, 1976), pp. 334-45.

39. Holt, Rinehart and Winston, 1951, 1959, 1966.

40. Gordon W. Allport, *The Nature of Prejudice* (Cambridge, Mass.: Addison-Wesley, 1954). Gordon W. Allport and Leo J. Postman, "The Basic Psychology of Rumor," in *Readings in Social Psychology* 3rd ed., eds. Eleanor E. Maccoby, Theodore M. Newcomb, and Eugene L. Hartley (New York: Holt, 1958).

41. *Research Methods in Social Relations*, preface, p. vii.

42. See E.L. Gaier, "Social Psychology," in *Present-Day Psychology*, ed. Abraham Roback (New York: Philosophical Library, 1955), pp. 387-91, for a discussion of research on prejudice during the post-World War II decade.

43. See Alfred J. Marrow, *The Practical Theorist: The Life and Work of Kurt Lewin* (New York: Basic Books, 1969), pp. 160-5, 173-7, and 191-218.

44. William L. Shirer, *The Rise and Fall of the Third Reich: A History of Nazi Germany* (New York: Simon and Schuster, 1960).

45. Bruno Bettelheim, "Individual and Mass Behavior in Extreme Situations," *Journal of Abnormal and Social Psychology* 38 (1943): 417-52. A shorter version of the paper is in Maccoby, Newcomb, and Hartley, 1947, 1952, 1958.

46. Viktor Frankl, *Man's Search for Meaning: An Introduction to Logotherapy* (Boston: Beacon Press, 1962). Paperback edition (New York: Washington Square Press, 1963).

47. Charles Osgood, "The Psychologist in International Affairs," in *Taboo Topics*, ed. Norman L. Farberow (New York: Atherton Press, 1963), p. 106.

48. Herbert Kelman, ed., *International Behavior: A Social-Psychological Analysis* (New York: Holt, Rinehart and Winston, 1965).

49. Herbert Kelman, "Reducing Conflict to a Science" *APA Monitor* 12 (January 1981): 5, 55.

50. Hadley Cantril, ed., *Tensions that Cause Wars* (Urbana: University of Illinois Press, 1950).

51. Gardner Murphy, *In the Minds of Men* (New York: Basic Books, 1953).

52. John Bowlby, *Maternal Care and Mental Health* (New York: Schoken Books, 1951).

53. See James C. Coleman, *Abnormal Psychology and Modern Life*, 4th ed. (Glenview, Ill.: Scott Foresman, 1972), pp. 716-18, for more details on research projects done for UNESCO and WHO.

54. Otto Klineberg, "Historical Perspectives: Cross-Cultural Psychology before 1960," in *Handbook of Cross-Cultural Psychology*, Vol. 1, eds. Harry C. Triandis and William W. Lambert (Boston: Allyn and Bacon, 1980), p. 42.

55. Harry C. Triandis and William W. Lambert, *Handbook of Cross-Cultural Psychology*, 6 vols. (Boston: Allyn and Bacon, 1980).

56. Clarence Leuba and Henry Federighi, "A Course in the Life Sciences," *American Psychologist* 3 (January 1948): 30-4.

57. Donald W. Fiske, "Must Psychologists Be Experimental Isolationists?" *American Psychologist* 2 (January 1947): 23.

58. Donald G. Marquis, "Research Planning at the Frontiers of Science," *American Psychologist* 3 (October 1948): 430-8.

59. Clyde Kluckhohn, "An Anthropologist Looks at Psychology," *American Psychologist* 3 (October 1948): 442.

60. James G. Miller, "Toward a General Theory for the Behavioral Sciences," *American Psychologist* 10 (September 1955): 513.

61. John T. Dailey, "A Plan for Integrated Programs of Personnel Research and Development," *American Psychologist* 9 (October 1954): 629-31.

62. Frederic G. Worden, Judith P. Swazey and George Adelman, eds., *The Neurosciences, Paths of Discovery* (Cambridge, Mass.: MIT Press, 1975).

63. The National Science Foundation established a socio-physical sciences program in 1954 for interdisciplinary research. See Harry Alpert, "Social Science, Social Psychology, and the National Science Foundation," *American Psychologist* 12 (February 1957): 95-8.

64. Claude E. Shannon, and Warren Weaver, *The Mathematical Theory of Communication* (Urbana, Ill.: University of Illinois Press, 1949, 1963). This book includes Shannon's original 1948 paper and an important article by Weaver that simplifies information theory.

65. See footnote 64.

66. Fred Attnave, *Applications of Information Theory to Psychology: A Summary of Basic Concepts, Methods, and Results* (New York: Holt, 1959).

67. Norbert Wiener, *I Am a Mathematician* (New York: Doubleday, 1956), p. 240.

68. Ibid., pp. 24-5.

69. Ibid., pp. 241-7.

70. Ibid., p. 323.

71. Ibid., p. 325.

72. James G. Miller, *Living Systems* (New York: McGraw-Hill, 1978). See also Albert R. Gilgen, "The Exchange Model: Missing Link Between Physiobehavioral Psychology and Phenomenological Inquiry?" *Irish Journal of Psychology* 2 (1971): 75-86.

73. George A. Miller, Eugene Galanter, and Karl H. Pribram, *Plans and the Structure of Behavior* (New York: Holt, Rinehart, and Winston, 1960).

74. James J. Gibson, *The Perception of the Visual World* (Boston: Houghton Mifflin, 1950).

75. Franklin V. Taylor, "Psychology and the Design of Machines," *American Psychologist* 12 (May 1957): 249-58.

76. Taylor (1957). Also John G. Darley, "Psychology and the Office of Naval Research: A Decade of Development," *American Psychologist* 12 (June 1957): 305-23.

77. For more detailed accounts of human engineering psychology, see (*a*) Harry Helson and William Bevan, eds., *Contemporary Approaches to Psychology* (Princeton, N.J.: D. van Nostrand, 1967); (*b*) Melvin H. Marx and William A. Hillix, *Systems and Theories in Psychology* (New York: McGraw-Hill, 1963).

78. To determine whether or not tests measure what they claim to measure.

79. See William A. Hunt and I. Stevenson, "Psychological Testing in Military Clinical Psychology: I. Intelligence Testing," pp. 25-35; and "Psychological Testing in Military Clinical Psychology: II. Personality Testing," pp. 107-15, *Psychological Review* 53 (1946).

80. Albert Ellis and Herbert S. Conrad, "The Validity of Personality Inventories in Military Practice," *Psychological Bulletin* 45 (1948): 385-426. The authors point out that personality inventories were apparently used more successfully in military than civilian settings in part because of the specialized applications of the tests in the former situation.

81. Projective tests or techniques consist of ambiguous stimuli or presentations such as inkblots, pictures, and drawings that are by design capable of being perceived many different ways. Whatever a person reports is considered more a function of personality rather than stimulus factors.

82. Hunt and Stevenson, p. 110.

83. See (*a*) Daniel J. Levinson, "A Note on the Similarities and Differences between Projective Tests and Ability Tests," *Psychological Review* 53 (1946): 189-94; (*b*) Leopold Bellack, "Projective Techniques in Contemporary Psychology," in *Present-Day Psychology*, ed. Abraham A. Roback (New York: Philosophical Library, 1955), pp. 547-58.

84. Reliability concerns the degree to which a measuring device is consistent in its measurements.

85. Quinn McNemar, "Opinion-Attitude Methodology," *Psychological Bulletin* 43 (1946): 369.

86. Ibid., p. 369.

87. Marrow, p. 129.

88. His mother died in a concentration camp.

89. Ronald Lippitt and Ralph K. White, "An Experimental Study of Leadership and Group Life," in Maccoby, Newcomb, and Hartley, 1947, 1952, 1958.

90. Marrow, p. ix. From Edward Tolman's Presidential Address, APA Convention, 1947.

91. Dael Wolfle, "Diversity of Talent," *American Psychologist* 15 (August 1960):

535-46. (The Walter Van Dyke Bingham Memorial Lecture presented at Columbia University, May 10, 1960).

92. See J.P. Guilford, "Some Theoretical Views of Creativity," in Helson and Bevan, 1967.

93. Albee and Dickey, pp. 57-70.

94. Dael Wolfle, *America's Resources of Specialized Talent* (New York: Harper, 1954).

Chapter 4

1. Vincent Brome, *Freud and His Early Circle: The Struggles of Psychoanalysis* (London: Heinemann, 1967), p. x. (prologue).

2. Ibid., p. xi.

3. Marie Jahoda, "The Migration of Psychoanalysis: Its Impact on American Psychology," in *The Intellectual Migration: Europe and America, 1930-1960*, eds. Donald Fleming and Bernard Bailyn (Cambridge, Mass.: Harvard University Press, 1969), p. 423.

4. Norman D. Sundberg, Leona E. Tyler, and Julian R. Taplin, *Clinical Psychology: Expanding Horizons* (Englewood Cliffs, N.J.: Prentice-Hall, 1973), p. 75.

5. Alfred Kazin, "The Freudian Revolution Analyzed," in *Freud and the 20th Century*, ed. Benjamin N. Nelson (Cleveland: World Publishing, 1957), pp. 14-15.

6. Gardner Murphy, "The Current Impact of Freud on American Psychology," in Nelson, p. 103.

7. Jerome S. Bruner, "Freud and the Image of Man," in Nelson, p. 281.

8. Frederick J. Hacker, "Freud, Marx, and Kierkegaard," in Nelson, p. 128.

9. The publisher of the paperback edition was Pocket Books, Inc. (New York). A hard cover copy entitled *Common Sense Book of Baby and Child Care* was published simultaneously by Duell, Sloan, and Pearce (New York).

10. Lynn Z. Bloom, *Doctor Spock: Biography of a Conservative Radical* (Indianapolis: Bobbs-Merrill, 1972), p. 116.

11. The availability of inexpensive paperback editions of books was itself an important development. Spock's book sold for twenty-five cents in 1946.

12. A.M. Sulman did a content analysis of 455 articles written for parents of preschool-age children published in fifteen popular magazines from 1919 to 1939 to determine the degree to which psychoanalytic ideas on child rearing were popularized before the 1940s. He concluded that no such popularization took place and that "only after the Second World War when [Spock's book] achieves and retains best-seller status, does psychoanalysis become part of America's mass media." A.M. Sulman, "The Humanization of the American Child: Benjamin Spock as a Popularizer of Psychoanalytic Thought," *Journal of the History of the Behavioral Sciences* 9 (1973): 265.

13. Spock was also influenced by John Dewey's educational philosophy (see Bloom, pp. 86-7).

14. See Sulman for a more detailed content analysis of the psychoanalytic ideas in Spock's book.

15. The revolutionary nature of Spock's prescriptions can only be appreciated in the context of most previously offered professional advice on child rear-

ing which advocated rigid feeding schedules, early toilet training, and the prevention of genital touching.

16. The superego is similar to conscience but is in part a function of unconscious factors.

17. Freud eventually proposed a second instinct, the death instinct, but the original one-instinct theory was accepted by most psychoanalysts.

18. The emergence of both psychoanalysis and experimental psychology were influenced by the deterministic philosophy of Hermann von Helmholtz, one of the most productive and creative German scientists of the nineteenth century.

19. See David Shakow and David Rapaport, "The Influence of Freud on American Psychology," *Psychological Issues* 13 (1964): 78-95 for an interesting discussion of the lack of systematization of Freud's theory prior to the 1950s.

20. The lay analysts, that is, those who were not medical doctors, who helped introduce the psychoanalytic perspectives to American psychology, are not listed here.

21. The war also brought professionals from many different disciplines and orientations together to work on war-related projects. Some of these interdisciplinary projects helped spread the psychoanalytic influence.

22. Norman S. Endler, J. Philippe Rushton, and Henry L. Roediger III, "Productivity and Scholarly Impact (Citations) of British, Canadian, and U.S. Departments of Psychology," *American Psychologist* 33 (December 1978): 1064-82.

23. Not all authorities consider Sullivan within the psychoanalytic tradition.

24. Hartmann was the key figure insofar as theoretical contributions are concerned.

25. Frieda Fromm-Reichmann, "Psychotherapy of Schizophrenia," *American Journal of Psychiatry* III (December 1954): 410-19.

26. John B. Watson, *The Psychological Care of Infant and Child* (New York: Norton, 1928).

27. Arnold L. Gesell, *Studies in Child Development* (New York: Harpers & Brothers, 1948).

28. See chapter 8 for a discussion of the roots of developmental and child psychologies.

29. Lewis P. Lipsitt, "Developmental Psychology," in *Contemporary Scientific Psychology*, ed. Albert R. Gilgen (New York: Academic Press, 1970), p. 149.

30. Richard I. Evans, *The Making of Psychology* (New York: Knopf, 1976), p. 244.

31. Fritz Redl and David Wineman, *Children Who Hate: The Disorganization and Breakdown of Behavior Controls* (Glencoe, Ill.: Free Press, 1951).

32. See Laura Fermi, *Illustrious Immigrants: The Intellectual Migration from Europe, 1930-41*, 2nd ed. (Chicago: University of Chicago Press, 1968, 1971) for an interesting discussion of child analysts, many of whom were women.

33. Edwin G. Boring, *A History of Experimental Psychology*, 2nd ed. (New York: Appleton-Century-Crofts, 1957), p. 692.

34. Ibid., p. 693.

35. Ibid., p. 715.

36. David C. McClelland, ed., *Studies in Motivation* (New York: Appleton-Century-Crofts, 1955), p. v.

37. Floyd H. Allport, *Theories of Perception and the Concept of Structure* (New York: John Wiley & Sons, 1955), p. 309.

38. Ibid., p. 310.

39. Ibid., p. 311.

40. Ibid., p. 312.

41. Ibid., p. 315.

42. Ibid., pp. 317-18.

43. See (a) Robert R. Blake and Glenn V. Ramsey, *Perception, An Approach to Personality* (New York: Ronald Press, 1951), preface; (b) Paul Bakan, "Current Theoretical Approaches to Perception," in *Present-Day Psychology*, ed. Abraham A. Roback (New York: Philosophical Library, 1955), pp. 68-70.

44. David Krech, "Notes Toward a Psychological Theory," in *Perception and Personality: A Symposium*, eds. Jerome S. Bruner and David Krech (New York: Greenwood Press, 1950, 1968), pp. 73-4.

45. Gardner Murphy, "Introduction," in *Personality Through Perception, an Experimental and Clinical Study*, Herman A. Witkin et al. (New York: Harper, 1954), p. xvii.

46. James G. Miller, "Toward a General Theory for the Behavioral Sciences," *American Psychologist* 10 (September 1955): 513-31.

47. Bronfenbrenner has become well-known for his comparative research on Soviet and American child-rearing practices.

48. Bronfenbrenner, in Blake and Ramsey, p. 256.

49. "During the twenties, there appeared 38 titles having to do with the Rorschach Test. This rose to about 230 during the thirties and after that there were thousands." W.G. Klopfer, "The Short History of Projective Techniques," *Journal of the History of the Behavioral Sciences* 9 (1973): 60. See also Norman D. Sundberg, "The Practice of Psychological Testing in Clinical Services in the United States, *American Psychologist* 16 (February 1961): 79-83.

50. See J.E. Exner, "Projective Techniques," in *Clinical Methods in Psychology*, ed. Irving B. Weiner (New York: Wiley, 1976), pp. 61-122.

51. Roback, p. 356. See also the chapter by P.L. Harriman for a history of abnormal psychology.

52. Robert W. White, *The Abnormal Personality* (New York: Ronald Press, 1948, 1956).

53. James C. Coleman, *Abnormal Psychology and Modern Life*, 4th ed. (Chicago: Scott, Foresman, 1972). This book, first published in 1950, remains one of the most widely used texts.

54. Adolph Meyer was largely responsible for the emergence of holism in psychiatry. He was much influenced by Freud and played an instrumental role in the importation of the psychoanalytic perspective into American psychiatry during the early part of this century.

55. See Karl Menninger, *The Vital Balance* (New York: Viking, 1963), pp. 469-70. Menninger's book includes an extensive and useful appendix that lists and briefly discusses the major systems of classifying psychological problems since about 1500 B.C. The Menningers, as indicated before, have given strong support to psychoanalytic views of personality and psychological disorders for over forty years.

56. Emil Kraepelin (1856-1926) was a German psychiatrist who developed a system of classification based on clinical description, organic states, and the predicted course of the problems. Psychological disorders were viewed as dis-

ease states, and cures were assumed to depend on medical treatment. See Menninger (1963), pp. 457-65, for a discussion of Kraepelin's influence.

57. Menninger, p. 27.

58. There were earlier attempts by behaviorists to "master and 'domesticate' psychoanalysis to the exact science program." (Shakow and Rapaport, p. 134.) Holt tried to do so in 1915, Kempf in 1917, Humphrey in the early twenties, Troland from 1920 to 1932, and, to some degree, Watson from 1916 to 1919. None of these efforts, however, was as influential as the work done by the Yale Group.

59. The seminars were also attended at times by psychoanalysts, for example, Erikson, Zinn, Sapir, and Sullivan. (See Shakow and Rapaport, p. 138.)

60. As has been mentioned before, there was a strong feeling within psychology during the 1940s that efforts should be made to integrate the social-behavioral sciences.

61. Shakow and Rapaport, p. 141.

62. For a comparison of Freud and Hull, see David McClelland, "Freud and Hull: Pioneers in Scientific Psychology," *American Scientist* 45 (1957): 101-13.

63. Some of the interest in psychoanalysis during the 1920s-1930s was generated by the nature-nurture controversy. Watson emphasized nurture and McDougall nature with most psychologists embracing one or the other emphasis or taking compromise positions. Both nurturists and naturists, however, found some support for their respective views in Freud's ideas.

64. John Dollard and Neal E. Miller, *Personality and Psychotherapy* (New York: McGraw-Hill, 1950).

65. Ibid., p. 3.

66. Ibid., p. 3.

67. Ibid., p. 3.

68. Ibid., p. 5.

69. Ibid., p. 10.

70. Shakow and Rapaport (p. 133) believe that Lewinian approaches to the testing of Freudian concepts are more appropriate than most such efforts structured by conditioning theories.

Chapter 5

1. Norman Guttman, "On Skinner and Hull: A Reminiscence and Projection," *American Psychologist* 32 (May 1977): 321-2.

2. Melvin H. Marx, *Learning: Theories* (New York: Macmillan, 1970), p. 4.

3. Clark L. Hull, et al., *Mathematico-Deductive Theory of Rote Learning; a Study in Scientific Methodology* (New Haven: Yale University, 1940).

4. Clark L. Hull, *Principles of Behavior* (New York: Appleton-Century-Crofts, 1943).

5. Clark L. Hull, *Essentials of Behavior* (New Haven: Yale University Press, 1951).

6. Clark L. Hull, *A Behavior System* (New Haven: Yale University Press, 1952).

7. Clark L. Hull, in *A History of Psychology in Autobiography*, Edwin G. Boring et al. (Worcester, Mass: Clark University Press, 1952), 4: 155.

8. Ivan P. Pavlov, *Lectures on Conditioned Reflexes*, trans. S. Belsky (Moscow: Foreign Languages Publishing House, 1955), pp. 151-63.

9. Burrhus Skinner, in *Psychologists on Psychology* David Cohen (New York: Taplinger, 1977), p. 275.

10. Hull et al. (1940), preface.

11. Edward L. Thorndike, *Animal Intelligence; Experimental Studies* (New York: Macmillan, 1911), pp. 244-46

12. Hull (1943), p. 72.

13. Ibid, p. 71.

14. Ernest R. Hilgard and Gordon H. Bower, *Theories of Learning*, 3rd ed. (New York: Appleton-Century-Crofts, 1966), p. 147.

15. Boring et al., p. 156.

16. John Dollard and Neal E. Miller, *Personality and Psychotherapy* (New York: McGraw-Hill, 1950).

17. Howard H. Kendler, "Kenneth W. Spence (1907-1967)," in *Essays in Neobehaviorism; A Memorial Volume to Kenneth W. Spence*, eds. Howard H. Kendler and Janet T. Spence (New York: Appleton-Century-Crofts, 1971), p. 2.

18. "The fractional anticipatory goal response is a form of antedating response, or a response which occurs earlier in a sequence of events than it originally occurred, particularly a response which occurs prior to the appearance of the stimulus which originally evoked it." James P. Chaplin and T. S. Krawiec, *Systems and Theories of Psychology*, 2nd ed. (New York: Holt, Rinehart, and Winston, 1968), p. 293. In terms of a cognitive-behavioral theory such as Edward Tolman's, the fractional anticipatory goal response is similar to the concept of expectancy.

19. Sigmund Koch, "Clark L. Hull," in *Modern Learning Theory*, William K. Estes et al. (New York: Appleton-Century-Crofts, 1954).

20. See Estes et al.

21. Hilgard and Bower, p. 192.

22. Edwin R. Guthrie, *The Psychology of Learning* (New York: Harper & Row, 1935), p. 26.

23. Edwin R. Guthrie, "Conditioning: A Theory of Learning in Terms of Stimulus, Response, and Association," in *The Psychology of Learning*, National Society for the Study of Education (Yearbook, 1942), 91: 30.

24. Operationism, a derivative of logical positivism, was originally introduced into American psychology by Tolman. Physicist Percy W. Bridgman's book *The Logic of Modern Physics* (New York: Macmillan, 1927) helped popularize operationism.

Chapter 6

1. *Time* (September 1971).

2. D. B. Robinson, *The 100 Most Important People in the World Today* (New York; Putnam, 1970).

3. What Makes a Researcher "Good Copy?" *APA Monitor* (August 1975): 1, 8.

4. See Appendices A and B based on survey studies by the author.

5. Norman Guttman, "On Skinner and Hull: A Reminiscence and Projection," *American Psychologist* 32 (May 1977): 322.

6. David Cohen, *Psychologists on Psychology* (New York: Taplinger, 1977), p. 262.

7. Guttman, pp. 321-28.

8. B.F. Skinner, *Walden Two* (New York: Crowell-Collier-Macmillan, 1948). The book was released as a paperback in 1962 facilitating its use as a supplementary reading in college courses. For an interesting review of *Walden Two*, see A. E. Freedman, *The Planned Society: An Analysis of Skinner's Proposals* (Kalamazoo, Mich.: Behaviordelia, 1972).

9. B.F. Skinner, *Beyond Freedom and Dignity* (New York: Knopf, 1971). Published as a paperback in 1972.

10. B.F. Skinner, *About Behaviorism* (New York: Knopf, 1974).

11. B.F. Skinner, *Particulars of My Life* (New York: Knopf, 1976), 1, *The Shaping of a Behaviorist* (New York: Knopf, 1979): 2.

12. B.F. Skinner, in *A History of Psychology in Autobiography*, eds. Edwin G. Boring and Gardner Lindzey (New York: Appleton-Century-Crofts, 1967) 5: 387.

13. Discussed later in this chapter.

14. B.F. Skinner, *The Behavior of Organisms* (New York: Appleton-Century-Crofts, 1938).

15. B.F. Skinner, *Science and Human Behavior* (New York: MacMillan, 1953); *Verbal Behavior* (New York: Appleton-Century-Crofts, 1957); *Schedules of Reinforcement* (New York: Appleton-Century-Crofts, 1957) with C.B. Ferster; *Cumulative Record* (New York: Appleton-Century-Crofts, 1959); *The Analysis of Behavior* (New York: McGraw-Hill, 1961) with James G. Holland; *The Technology of Teaching* (New York: Appleton-Century-Crofts, 1968); *Contingencies of Reinforcement: A Theoretical Analysis* (New York: Appleton-Century-Crofts, 1969).

16. Howard H. Kendler and Janet T. Spence, "Tenets in Neobehaviorism," In *Essays in Neobehaviorism*, eds. Howard H. Kendler and Janet T. Spence (New York: Appleton-Century-Crofts, 1971), p. 37.

17. Francis Bacon was a seventeenth century British philosopher who stressed careful observation and inductive reasoning rather than appeal to authorities and deduction as far as the inquiry process is concerned.

18. B.F. Skinner, in Boring and Lindzey, p.379.

19. Burrhus Skinner, in Cohen, p. 284.

20. B.F. Skinner, "Two Types of Conditioned Reflex: A Reply to Konorski and Miller," *Journal of General Psychology* 16 (1937) : 272-79.

21. B.F. Skinner, in Boring and Lindzey, p. 400.

22. Skinner, *Behavior of Organisms*, p. 21.

23. Noam Chomsky, review of *Verbal Behavior*, by B.F. Skinner, *Language* 35 (1959): 26-58.

24. Ibid., p. 30.

25. Ibid., p. 54.

26. Ibid., p. 57.

27. B.F. Skinner,*Reflections on Behaviorism and Society* (Englewood Cliffs, N.J.: Prentice-Hall, 1978), p. 10.

28. Stephanie B. Stolz and Associates, *Ethical Issues in Behavior Modification* (San Francisco: Jossey-Bass, 1978), p. 4.

29. See Stephen J. Sansweet, *The Punishment Cure* (New York: Mason/Charter, 1975), review by Barry Kramer, *The Wall Street Journal*, May 10, 1976, p. 12.

30. William J. DeRisi and George Butz, *Writing Behavioral Contracts* (Champaign, Ill.: Research Press, 1975), p. 1-2.

31. Skinner, *Reflections on Behaviorism and Society*, p. 121.

32. James G. Holland and B.F. Skinner, *The Analysis of Behavior* (New York: McGraw-Hill, 1961).

33. See Appendix A which is based on survey research conducted by the author.

34. Noam Chomsky, "The Case Against B.F. Skinner," *The New York Review of Books* (December 1971), pp. 18-24.

35. Carl Rogers, the American clinical psychologist who developed client-centered therapy, takes this point a step further. People, Rogers believes, are basically good and have within them the potential to maximize their capabilities (to self-actualize). Rather than being molded by the environment, they are primarily guided from within. See "Some Issues Concerning the Control of Human Behavior" which presents the famous Rogers-Skinner debate in *Science* 124 (November 30, 1956): 1057-65. See also chapter 9 which discusses Rogers in some detail.

36. Gordon M. Harrington, "Responses to the Skinner Stimulus," *The North American Review* 257 (Summer 1972): 62.

Chapter 7

1. Perceiving something which upon further inspection from a different perspective does not check out; for example, seeing a wet highway ahead as we drive along, which turns out to be nothing but a dry road when we get there.

2. Being aware of something for which there is no apparent external referent; for example, hearing voices when there is neither another person nor an electronic device in the area.

3. Residual means a manifestation of psychological processes which is not directly associated with guiding human activity. When we are asleep, we do not need directional control, but the guidance system does not completely shut down. The nervous system is active during periods of both wakefulness and sleep.

4. For more detailed presentations of the author's views on consciousness, see (a) Albert R. Gilgen, "Life-Sustaining Systems and Consciousness," in *Imagery: Concepts, Results, and Applications,* ed. Eric Klinger (New York: Plenum Press, 1981); (b) Albert R. Gilgen, "The Nature, Function, and Description of Sensation, Perception, Feeling, and Imagery." Presented at the Third Annual Conference of the American Association for the Study of Mental Imagery, Yale University, June 20, 1981.

5. Floyd Allport, *Theories of Perception and the Concept of Structure* (New York: Wiley, 1955), p. 113.

6. Karl S. Lashley, K.L. Chow, and J. Semmes, "An Examination of the Electrical Field Theory of Cerebral Integration," *Psychological Review* 58 (1951): 123-36.

7. Wolfgang Köhler, *The Mentality of Apes* (New York: Harcourt, Brace, 1925).

8. Max Wertheimer, *Productive Thinking* (New York: Harper & Row, 1959).

9. Karl Duncker, "On Problem Solving," *Psychological Monograph* 58 (1945), No. 270.

10. Bluma Zeigarnik, Das Behalten Erledigter und Unerledigter Handlungen, III, The Memory of Completed and Uncompleted Actions, *Psychologische Forschung* 9 (1927): 1-85.

11. Jerome S. Bruner and C.C. Goodman, "Value and Need as Organizing Factors in Perception," *Journal of Abnormal & Social Psychology* 42 (1947): 33-44.

12. James J. Gibson and Eleanor J. Gibson, "Perceptual Learning: Differentiation or Enrichment?" *Psychological Review* 62 (1955): 32-41.

13. Harry Helson, "Adaptation-Level as a Basis for a Quantitative Theory of Frames of Reference," *Psychological Review* 55 (1948): 297-313.

14. Allport (1955), p. 165.

15. Donald O. Hebb, *Organization of Behavior* (New York: Wiley, 1949).

16. James J. Gibson, *The Perception of the Visual World*, (Boston: Houghton Mifflin, 1950).

17. James J. Gibson, "The Concept of the Stimulus in Psychology," *American Psychologist* 15 (1960): 694-703.

18. Philip Solomon et al., eds., *Sensory Deprivation* (Cambridge, Mass.: Harvard University Press, 1961), p. 6.

19. Solomon, et al., p. 27.

20. G. Moruzzi and H.W. Magoun, "Brain Stem Reticular Formation and Activation of the EEG," *Electroencephalography and Clinical Neurophysiology* 1 (1949): 455-73.

21. Neville Moray, *Attention: Selective Processes in Vision and Hearing* (New York: Academic Press, 1970), pp. 4-5.

22. Donald E. Broadbent, *Perception and Communication* (New York: Pergamon Press, 1958).

23. Richard Lynn, *Attention, Arousal, and the Orienting Reaction* (Oxford: Pergamon Press, 1966), p. 1.

24. E.N. Sokolov, "Neuronal Models of the Orienting Reflex," in *The Central Nervous System and Behavior*, ed. Mary Agnes Burniston Brazier (New York: Josiah Macy, Jr. Foundation, 1960), pp. 187-276.

25. Robert L. Fantz, "Pattern Vision in Young Infants," *Psychological Record* 8 (1958): 43-7.

26. Edward J. Murray, *Sleep, Dreams, and Arousal* (New York: Appleton-Century-Crofts, 1965).

27. Ibid., p. 66.

28. W.D. Tanner and J.A. Swets, "A Decision Making Theory of Visual Detection," *Psychological Review* 61 (1954): 401-9.

29. Donald S. Blough, "A Method for Obtaining Psychophysical Thresholds From the Pigeon," *Journal of the Experimental Analysis of Behavior* 1 (1958): 31-48.

30. Charles E. Osgood et al. *The Measurement of Meaning* (Urbana: University of Illinois Press, 1958).

31. James P. Chaplin and T.S. Krawiec, *Systems and Theories of Psychology*, 4th ed. (New York: Holt, Rinehart, and Winston, 1979), p. 368.

32. Noam Chomsky, *Syntactic Structures* (The Hague: Mouton, 1957).

33. Eric H. Lenneberg, *Biological Foundations of Language* (New York: Wiley, 1967).

34. Benjamin L. Whorf, *Language, Thought, and Reality* (Cambridge, Mass.: MIT, 1956).

35. Cognitive dissonance concerns the tensions that result from discrepancies in our cognitive structure. If, for instance, a person likes two products, for example, cars made by Ford and General Motors, and he buys a Chevrolet, then he must deal with the fact that a desired thing has been rejected, namely a Ford. Attribution theory, on the other hand, has to do with the causes we ascribe to events brought about by ourselves and others. Such causes include luck, planning, work, intelligence, and talent.

36. David Krech, Richard S. Crutchfield, and Egerton L. Ballachey, *Individual in Society* (New York: McGraw-Hill, 1962), preface.

37. George A. Kelly, *A Theory of Personality: The Psychology of Personal Constructs* (New York: W.W. Norton, 1955, 1963), p. 46.

38. George A. Miller, Eugene Galanter, and Karl H. Pribram, *Plans and the Structure of Behavior* (New York: Holt, Rinehart and Winston, 1960).

39. Ibid., p. 3.

40. Ibid., p. 11.

41. Richard N. Williams, "Structuralism and the Cognitive Revolution," *Philosophical Psychologist* 12 (1978): 18.

42. George A. Miller, *Psychology: The Science of Mental Life* (New York: Harper & Row, 1962).

43. Silvan S. Tomkins, *Affect, Imagery, Consciousness* (New York: Springer, 1962), 1.

44. George Humphrey, *Thinking: An Introduction to its Experimental Psychology* (New York: Wiley, 1963).

45. Constance Scheerer, ed. *Cognition: Theory, Research, Promise* (New York: Harper & Row, 1964).

46. Ulric Neisser, *Cognitive Psychology* (New York: Appleton-Century-Crofts, 1967).

47. Ibid., p. 5.

48. Albert R. Gilgen, "Converging Trends in Psychology." (Paper presented at the Meeting of the American Psychological Association, New Orleans, 1974.)

49. Neisser, preface, p. vii.

50. Iconic storage refers to the brief (a fraction of a second) retention by the nervous system of visual information.

51. Echoic memory refers to the fleeting retention of any part of an auditory stimulus.

52. Milton Rokeach, *The Open and Closed Mind* (New York: Basic Books, 1960).

53. Lloyd Kaufman, *Sight and Mind: An Introduction to Visual Perception* (New York: Oxford University Press, 1974).

54. G. Thomas Rowland, *The Mind of Man: Some Views and a Theory of Cognitive Development* (Englewood Cliffs, N.J.: Prentice-Hall, 1971).

55. Karl H. Pribram, ed., *Brain and Behavior: I. Mood, States and Mind: Selected Readings* (Harmondsworth: Penguin, 1969).

56. José Manuel Delgado, *Physical Control of the Mind: Toward a Psychocivilized Society* (New York: Harper & Row, 1969).

57. Julian Jaynes, *The Origin of Consciousness in the Breakdown of the Bicameral Mind* (Boston: Houghton Mifflin, 1977).

58. Tomkins, p. 5.

59. Robert E. Ornstein, *The Psychology of Consciousness* (San Francisco: W.H. Freeman, 1972).

60. Robert E. Ornstein, ed., *The Nature of Human Consciousness* (San Francisco: W.H. Freeman; New York: Viking Press, 1973).

61. Ernest R. Hilgard, "Consciousness in Contemporary Psychology," in *Annual Review of Psychology* (Palo Alto: Annual Reviews, Inc., 1980), 31: 1-26.

62. The papers presented at the symposium were published in a book entitled *Feelings and Emotions: The Loyola Symposium*, ed. Magda B. Arnold (New York: Academic Press, 1970).

63. Stanley Schachter and Jerome E. Singer, "Cognitive, Social, and Psychological Determinants of Emotional State," *Psychological Review* 69 (1962): 379-99.

64. Wilder Penfield, *The Excitable Cortex in Conscious Man* (Springfield, Ill.: Thomas, 1958).

65. James Olds, "Pleasure Centers in the Brain," *Scientific American* (October 1956): 105-16.

66. G. Moruzzi & H.W. Magoun, "Brain Stem Reticular Formation and Activation of the EEG," *Electroencaphalography and Clinical Neurophysiology* 1 (1949): 455-73.

67. T.N. Wiesel and D.H. Hubel, "Comparison of the Effects of Uniltateral and Bilateral Eye Closure on Cortical Unit Responses in Kittens," *Journal of Neurophysiology* 28 (1965): 1029-40.

68. Seymour Levine, "Stimulation in Infancy," *Scientific American* (May 1960): 80-98.

69. B.D. Burns, *The Mammalian Cerebral Cortex* (London: Edward Arnold, 1958).

70. Karl H. Pribram, "A Review of Theory in Physiological Psychology," in *Annual Review of Psychology*, vol. 2 (Palo Alto: Annual Reviews, Inc., 1960), pp. 1-40.

71. R.W. Sperry, "Hemisphere Deconnection and Unity in Conscious Awareness," *American Psychologist* 23 (1968): 723-33.

72. John C. Eccles, *The Physiology of Synapses* (New York: Academic Press, 1964).

73. Wolfgang Köhler, *Gestalt Psychology* (New York: Liveright, 1929).

74. Donald O. Hebb, *The Organization of Behavior* (New York: Wiley, 1949).

75. Ivan P. Pavlov, *Conditioned Reflexes: An Investigation of the Physiological Activity of the Cerebral Cortex* (New York: Dover, 1960; London: Oxford University Press, 1927).

76. Eliot Stellar, "The Physiology of Motivation," *Psychological Review* 61 (1954): 5-22.

77. Karl H. Pribram, "Some Dimensions of Remembering: Steps Toward a Neurophysiological Model of Memory," in *Macromolecules and Behavior*, ed. J. Gaito (New York: Academic Press, 1966), pp. 165-87.

78. Hans Selye, *The Stress of Life* (New York: McGraw-Hill, 1956).

Chapter 8

1. L.R. Goulet and Paul B. Baltes, eds., *Life-Span Developmental Psychology: Research and Theory* (New York: Academic Press, 1970), p. 3.

2. See Bernard Berelson and Gary A. Steiner, *Human Behavior: An Inventory of Scientific Findings* (New York: Harcourt, Brace & World, 1964), pp. 37-85, for a discussion of what the authors consider to be the major findings in developmental psychology. Discussing evidence for an interactional view of development are: (*a*) Helen L. Koch, "Child Psychology," in *Annual Review of Psychology* (Stanford: Annual Reviews, Inc., 1954), 5: 1-26; (*b*) J. McVicker Hunt, "Psychological Development: Early Experience," in *Annual Review of Psychology* (Palo Alto: Annual Reviews, Inc., 1979), 30: 103-43.

3. Donald M. Baer and John C. Wright, "Developmental Psychology," in *Annual Review of Psychology*," (Palo Alto: Annual Reviews, Inc., 1974), 25: 1-82.

4. Wallace A. Russell, "An Experimental Psychology: Pipe Dream or Possibility," in *The Concept of Development: An Issue in the Study of Human Behavior*, ed. Dale B. Harris (Minneapolis: University of Minnesota Press, 1957), pp. 162-74.

5. Robert G. Cooper, *Principles of Development* (Westwood, Mass.: The PaperBook Press, 1977), p. 1.

6. See Hunt (1979), pp. 103-43, for an interesting discussion of preformationism, predeterminism, and empiricism.

7. For a detailed account of the roots of American developmental psychology, see Don C. Charles, "Historical Antecedents of Life-Span Developmental Psychology," in Goulet and Baltes (1970), pp. 23-52.

8. David Bakan, *Sigmund Freud and the Jewish Mystical Tradition* (Princeton, N.J.: Van Nostrand, 1958).

9. Hunt (1979), p. 104.

10. Wayne Dennis, ed. *Historical Readings in Developmental Psychology* (New York: Appleton-Century-Crofts, 1972).

11. Merrill F. Elias, Penelope K. Elias, and Jeffrey W. Elias, *Basic Processes in Adult Development Psychology* (St. Louis: Mosby, 1977), p. 4.

12. Elias, et al., p. 6.

13. John C. Cavanaugh, "Early Developmental Theories: A Brief Review of Attempts to Organize Developmental Data Prior to 1925," *Journal of the History of the Behavioral Sciences* 17 (1981): 38.

14. Robert E. Grinder, *A History of Genetic Psychology: The First Science of Human Development* (New York: Wiley, 1967).

15. Ibid., preface, p. vii.

16. Ibid., p. 238. Selected from Edward L. Thorndike, *Educational Psychology: the Original Nature of Man* (New York: Columbia University Press, 1920).

17. Dorothy McLean, "Child Development: A Generation of Research" *Child Development* 25 (1954): 3-8.

18. Cavanaugh, p. 1.

19. Nancy Bayley, "Behavioral Correlates of Mental Growth: Birth to Thirty-Six Years," *American Psychologist* 23 (January 1968): 1-17.

20. Charles, in Goulet and Baltes (1970), p. 38.

21. Carl Murchison, ed., *Handbook of Child Psychology* (Worcester, Mass.: Clark University Press, 1931).

22. Sheldon H. White, "Children in Perspective," *American Psychologist* 34 (October 1979): 812.

23. Albert R. Gilgen, "Important Events and Influences in Post-World War II

American Psychology: A Survey Study," *JSAS Catalog of Selected Documents in Psychology* 10 (November 1980), Ms. 2144. (See Appendix B for selected information from this study.)

24. Albert R. Gilgen, "Important People in Post-World War II Americn Psychology: A Survey Study," *JSAS Catalog of Selected Documents in Psychology* 11 (February 1981), Ms. 2171. (See Appendix A for selected information from this study.)

25. (*a*) Norman S. Endler, J. Philippe Rushton, and Henry L. Roediger III, "Productivity and Scholarly Impact (Citations) of British, Canadian, and U.S. Departments of Psychology (1975)," *American Psychologist* 33 (December 1978): 1074; (*b*) Albert R. Gilgen and Stevan K. Hultman, "Authorities and Subject Matter Areas Emphasized, in *Annual Review of Psychology, 1950-1974*," *Psychological Reports* 44 (1979): 1255-62; (*c*) Eugene Garfield, "The 100 Most-Cited Social Sciences Citation Index Authors." 2. A Catalog of Their Awards and Academy Memberships, *Current Contents* 45 (1978): 5-15.

26. Some research on children was done by women psychologists. See Philip C. Kronk, "Role of Women Psychologists During the Second World War," *Psychological Reports* 45 (1979): 111-16.

27. Leonard Carmichael, ed., *Manual of Child Psychology*, 2nd ed. (New York: Wiley, 1946, 1954).

28. Richard M. Lerner, *Concepts and Theories of Human Development* (Reading, Mass.: Addison-Wesley, 1976), p. 5.

29. Calvin S. Hall and Gardner Lindzey, *Theories of Personality* (New York: Wiley, 1957), p. 298.

30. The first review of developmental psychology in the *Annual Review of Psychology* appeared in the 1957 volume. Previous reviews were about child psychology.

31. Roger G. Barker, "Child Psychology," in *Annual Review of Psychology* (1951), 2: 1, 3.

32. *Annual Review of Psychology* (1954), 5: 1-26.

33. Ibid., p. 1.

34. Wayne Dennis quoted by Bärbel Inhelder in her review of developmental psychology, *Annual Review of Psychology* (1957), 8: 139.

35. Henrietta T. Smith and L. Joseph Stone, "Developmental Psychology," in *Annual Review of Psychology* (1961), 12: 1.

36. Ibid., p. 1.

37. Lee J. Cronbach, "The Two Disciplines of Scientific Psychology," *American Psychologist* 12 (November 1957): 671-84.

38. Henry W. Maier, *Three Theories of Child Development: The Contributions of Erik H. Erikson, Jean Piaget, and Robert R. Sears and Their Applications* (New York: Harper and Row, 1965, 1969).

39. Hunt (1979), p. 104.

40. Ibid., p. 105.

41. Ibid., p. 112.

42. Ibid., p. 112.

43. Eckhard H. Hess, " 'Imprinting' in Animals," *Scientific America* 198 (1958): 81-90.

44. Eckhard H. Hess, *Imprinting: Early Experience and Developmental Psychobiology of Attachment* (New York: Van Nostrand, 1973).

45. Hunt (1979), p. 128.

46. Harry F. Harlow, "The Nature of Love," *American Psychologist* 13 (December 1958): 673-85.

47. James J. Gibson and Eleanor J. Gibson, "Perceptual Learning: Differentiation or Enrichment?" *Psychological Review* 62 (1955): 32-41.

48. Ibid., p. 34.

49. Joachim F. Wohlwill, "Developmental Studies of Perception," *Psychological Bulletin* 57 (1960): 249.

50. Ibid., p. 280.

51. Ibid., p. 280.

52. Ibid., p. 281.

53. Helen L. Koch, "Child Psychology," in *Annual Review of Psychology* (1954), p. 2.

54. See Theta H. Wolf, "Gesell-Senn 'Controversy' " *American Psychologist* 12 (October 1957): 648-50.

55. See Julian E. Hochberg, "Nativism and Empiricism in Perception," in *Psychology in the Making: Histories of Selected Research Problems*, ed. Leo Postman (New York: Knopf, 1962).

56. K. Warner Schaie, "A General Model for the Study of Developmental Problems," *Psychological Bulletin* 64 (1965): 92-107.

57. Based primarily on reviews of developmental psychology in the *Annual Review of Psychology* (1960-1970).

58. David Elkind, "Piaget," *Human Behavior* (August 1975): 115-21.

59. Herbert Ginsberg and Sylvia Opper, *Piaget's Theory of Intellectual Development* (Englewood Cliffs, N.J.: Prentice-Hall, 1979), p. 24.

60. Robert G. Cooper, *Principles of Development* (Westwood, Mass.: The PaperBook Press, 1977), p. 3.

61. Gilgen, (1981), Ms. 2171. See Appendix A for selected information from this study.

62. C. Roger Myers, "Journal Citations and Scientific Eminence in Contemporary Psychology," *American Psychologist* 25 (November 1970): 1041-48.

63. Jean Piaget, "Principle Factors Determining Intellectual Evolution from Childhood to Adult Life," in *Factors Determining Human Behavior*, ed. Edward D. Adrian et al. (Cambridge, Mass.: Harvard University Press, 1937), p. 33.

64. For example, (a) John H. Flavell, *The Developmental Psychology of Jean Piaget* (Princeton, N.J.: Van Nostrand, 1963); and (b) J. McVicker Hunt, *Intelligence and Experience* (New York: Ronald Press, 1961).

65. Herbert Ginsberg and Barbara Koslowski, "Cognitive Development," in *Annual Review of Psychology* (1976), 27: 36.

66. Ibid., p. 30.

67. J. Joseph Stone, Henrietta T. Smith, and Lois B. Murphy, eds., *The Competent Infant: Research and Commentary* (New York: Basic Books, 1973), p. 5.

68. Eleanor J. Gibson and Richard D. Walk, "The Visual Cliff," *Scientific American* 202 (1960): 64-71.

69. T.G.R. Bower, "The Visual World of Infants," *Scientific American* 215 (1966): 80-92.

70. Lois Murphy, "Coping Devices and Defense Mechanisms in Relation to Autonomous Ego Functions," *Bulletin of the Menninger Clinic* 24 (1960): 144-53.

71. See Stone, Smith, and Murphy (1973).

72. Robert L. Fantz, "The Origin of Form Perception," *Scientific American* 204 (1961): 66-72.

73. Lewis P. Lipsitt, "Developmental Psychology," in *Contemporary Scientific Psychology*, ed. Albert R. Gilgen (New York: Academic Press, 1970), pp. 148-82.

74. Ibid., p. 168.

75. Paul B. Baltes, Hayne W. Reese, and Lewis P. Lipsitt, "Life-Span Developmental Psychology," in *Annual Review of Psychology* (1980), 31: 70.

76. Richard A. Kalish, "Death and Bereavement: An Annotated Social Science Bibliography (with Supplement)," xeroxed by author (1965).

77. Norman L. Farberow, ed. *Taboo Topics* (New York: Atherton Press, 1963). This book is based in part on a symposium presented at the American Psychological Association Meeting in New York City in 1961.

78. Herman Feifel, ed., *The Meaning of Death* (New York: McGraw-Hill, 1959), preface, p. v.

79. See Edwin S. Shneidman, Norman L. Farberow, and Robert E. Litman, *The Psychology of Suicide* (New York: Science House, 1970) for a systematic treatment of much of the work done by these three clinicians from 1955 through 1966.

80. Jessica Mitford, *The American Way of Death* (New York: Simon and Schuster, 1978).

81. Jacques Choron, *Death and Western Thought* (New York: Collier Books, 1963).

82. Elizabeth Kübler-Ross, *On Death and Dying* (New York: Macmillan, 1969).

83. See Michael E. Lamb, "Paternal Influences and the Father's Role: A Personal Perspective," *American Psychologist* 34 (October 1979): 938-43. This entire issue of the *American Psychologist* is concerned with psychology and children.

84. Lissy F. Jarvik, "Thoughts on the Psychobiology of Aging," *American Psychologist* 30 (May 1975): 576.

85. Klaus F. Riegel, "On the History of Psychological Gerontology," in *The Psychology of Adult Development and Aging*, ed. Carl Eisdorfer and M. Powell Lawton (Washington, D.C.: American Psychological Association, 1973). Klaus's perspective is also discussed by Leonard W. Poon and Alan T. Welford, "Prologue: A Historical Perspective," in *Aging in the 1980s: Psychological Issues*, ed. Leonard W. Poon (Washington, D.C.: American Psychological Association, 1980).

86. Nathan W. Shock, "Gerontology (Later Maturity)," in *Annual Review of Psychology* (1951), 2: 366.

87. Irving Lorge, "Gerontology (Later Maturity)," in *Annual Review of Psychology* (1956), 7: 359.

88. James E. Birren, "Psychological Aspects of Aging," in *Annual Review of Psychology* (1960), 11: 161.

89. Jack Botwinick, "Geropsychology," in *Annual Review of Psychology* (1970), 21.

90. Eisdorfer and Lawton (1973).

91. Poon (1980).

92. James E. Birren, eds., *The Handbooks of Aging* (New York: Van Nostrand Reinhold, 1977).

93. Baltes, Reese, and Lipsitt (1980), p. 67.

94. (*a*) Goulet and Baltes (1970). (*b*) John R. Nesselroade and Hayne W.

Reese, eds., *Life-Span Developmental Psychology: Methodological Issues* (New York: Academic Press, 1973); (c) Paul B. Baltes and K. Warner Schaie, eds., *Life-Span Developmental Psychology: Personality and Socialization* (New York: Academic Press, 1973).

95. A useful sampling of the literature on the adult life cycle, particularly middle age, is offered by *The Adult Life Cycle; Training Manual and Reader* prepared by Vivian R. McCoy, Colleen Ryan, and James W. Lichtenberg. (Lawrence, Kansas: Adult Life Resource Center, University of Kansas, 1978).

96. Klaus F. Riegel, "Three Paradigms of Developmental Psychology," in *Psychology in Social Context*, ed. Allan R. Buss (New York: Irvington, 1979), p. 340.

97. Ibid., p. 340.

Chapter 9

1. See Frances F. Korten, Stuart W. Cook, and John I. Lacey, eds., *Psychology and the Problems of Society* (Washington, D.C.: American Psychological Association, 1970) for a variety of articles on psychology's roles in society.

2. David Bakan, "Clinical Psychology and Logic," *American Psychologist* 11 (December 1956): 655.

3. Carlton W. Berenda, "Is Clinical Psychology a Science?" *American Psychologist* 12 (December 1957): 725.

4. Ibid., p. 725.

5. Starke R. Hathaway, "A Study of Human Behavior: The Clinical Psychologist," *American Psychologist* 13 (June 1958): 263.

6. Marvin W. Kahn and Sebastian Santostefano, "The Case of Clinical Psychology: A Search for Identity," *American Psychologist* 17 (April 1962): 185.

7. Leonard Small, "Toward Professional Clinical Psychology," *American Psychologist* 18 (September 1963): 558.

8. Ibid., p. 558.

9. Harvey Peskin, "Unity of Science Begins at Home: A Study of Regional Factionalism in Clinical Psychology," *American Psychologist* 18 (February 1963): 96.

10. Ibid., p. 96.

11. Ibid., p. 100.

12. David A. Rodgers, "In Favor of Separation of Academic and Professional Training," *American Psychologist* 19 (August 1964): 680.

13. George W. Albee, "The Uncertain Future of Clinical Psychology," *American Psychologist* 25 (December 1970): 1071.

14. Karl Menninger, *The Vital Balance* (New York: Viking, 1963), pp. 419-20.

15. See Menninger (1963) for an appendix listing and discussing classification systems of human problems extending back to the ancient Sumerians and Egyptians (1500 B.C.).

16. Norman D. Sundberg, Leona E. Tyler, and Julian R. Taplin, *Clinical Psychology: Expanding Horizons* (Englewood Cliffs, N.J.: Prentice-Hall, 1973), pp. 35, 40.

17. Ibid., p. 33.

18. Ibid., p. 33.

19. Robert I. Watson, "A Brief History of Clinical Psychology," *Psychological Bulletin* 50 (1953): 332.

20. Sundberg et al., p. 40.

21. Based mostly on Sundberg et al.

22. Watson (1953), p 340.

23. John M. Reisman, *The Development of Clinical Psychology*, (New York: Appleton-Century-Crofts, 1966), p. 271.

24. Ibid., p. 271.

25. Sol L. Garfield, "Psychotherapy: A 40-Year Appraisal," *American Psychologist* 36 (February 1981): 175-6.

26. Ibid., p. 175.

27. Ibid., p. 175.

28. See Appendices A and B for survey results concerning the most important people, influences, and events in post-World War II American psychology.

29. E. Lowell Kelly, "Clinical Psychology: The Post-War Decade," in *Current Trends in Psychological Theory: A Bicentennial Program*, Wayne Dennis et al. (Pittsburgh: University of Pittsburgh Press, 1961). Kelly contends that the chief reason clinical psychology grew during the late 1940s and 1950s was the Veterans Administration's formal position on the functions of clinical psychologists and their insistence that only individuals with appropriate Ph.D. degrees be classified as clinical psychologists. The document of primary importance was V.A. Circular 105 (1946).

30. David Shakow, "Clinical Psychology Seen Some 50 Years Later," *American Psychologist* 33 (February 1978): 148-58.

31. Ibid., p. 153.

32. Victor C. Raimy, *Training in Clinical Psychology* (New York: Prentice Hall, 1950).

33. Maurice Korman, ed., *Levels and Patterns of Professional Training in Psychology: Conference Proceedings, Vail, Colorado, July 25-30, 1973* (Washington, D.C.: American Psychological Association, 1976).

34. Nathan W. Perry, "Why Psychology Does Not Need Alternative Training Models," *American Psychologist* 34 (July 1979): 609.

35. Henryk Misiak and Virginia S. Sexton, *History of Psychology: An Overview* (New York: Grune & Stratton, 1966), p. 184.

36. See chapter 4, "The Freudian Influence," for a discussion of projective techniques.

37. The Minnesota Multiphasic Personality Inventory (MMPI) was published in 1943 by Starke R. Hathaway and J.C. McKinley. The instrument was carefully developed by selecting items that differentiate between people classified as normal and those classified as representing a particular abnormality such as schizophrenia, paranoia, depression, or hysteria. Some items also propose to measure masculinity and femininity tendencies. By the middle 1950s more than 100 MMPI studies were being published annually. See George S. Welsh and Grant W. Dahlstrom, *Basic Readings on the MMPI in Psychology and Medicine* (Minneapolis: University of Minnesota Press, 1956).

38. As described by Cronbach, "Factor analysis is a systematic method for examining the meaning of a test by studying its correlation with other variables. The investigator gives a large collection of tests to the same persons. The analysis tries to determine how many distinct abilities are being measured reliably...." Lee J. Cronbach, *Essentials of Psychological Testing*, 2nd ed. (New York: Harpers &

Brothers, 1949, 1960), p. 247. The procedure is complex and time-consuming, but the availability of high-speed electronic computers following World War II greatly facilitated factor analytic research.

39. Paul E. Meehl, *Clinical Versus Statistical Prediction: A Theoretical Analysis and a Review of the Evidence* (Minneapolis: University of Minnesota Press, 1954).

40. Hans J. Eysenck, "The Effects of Psychotherapy: An Evaluation," *Journal of Consulting Psychology* 16 (1952): 319-24.

41. Carl R. Rogers, in *A History of Psychology in Autobiography*, ed. Edwin G. Boring and Gardner Lindzey (New York: Appleton-Century-Crofts, 1967), 5: 343.

42. Carl R. Rogers, *The Clinical Treatment of the Problem* (Boston: Houghton Mifflin, 1939).

43. Carl R. Rogers, *Client-Centered Therapy: Its Current Practice, Implications, and Theory* (Boston: Houghton Mifflin, 1951).

44. Carl R. Rogers, "A Theory of Therapy, Personality and Interpersonal Relationships as Developed in the Client-Centered Framework," in *Psychology: A Study of a Science*, ed. Sigmund Koch (New York: McGraw-Hill, 1959), 3: 184-256.

45. Carl R. Rogers, in Boring and Gardner, p. 373.

46. Carl R. Rogers, "In Retrospect: Forty-Six Years," *American Psychologist* 29 (February 1974): 116.

47. The Q-sort technique, developed by William Stephenson, involves asking each client to sort a set of self-descriptive statements, each statement printed on a separate card, into a predetermined number of piles "from the items most characteristic of himself to those least characteristic." Carl R. Rogers, *On Becoming a Person* (Boston: Houghton Mifflin, 1961), p. 232.

48. An article based on material presented by Rogers and Skinner entitled "Some Issues Concerning the Control of Human Behavior" was published in *Science* 124 (1956): 1057-66.

49. Rogers, (1974), p. 118.

50. See Appendix A.

51. Albert R. Gilgen and Stevan K. Hultman, "Authorities and Subject Matter Areas Emphasized, in *Annual Review of Psychology, 1950-1974*," *Psychological Reports* 44 (1979), pp. 1255-62.

52. Eysenck was the fourth most referred to psychologist in the *Annual Review of Psychology* during the 1950-1974 period. Gilgen and Hultman (1979).

53. Hans J. Eysenck, "The Effects of Psychotherapy: An Evaluation," *Journal of Consulting Psychology* 16 (1952): 322.

54. In 1949 and 1950 Eysenck published several articles criticizing clinical training in American universities.

55. See Hans H. Strupp, "The Outcome Problem in Psychotherapy Revisited," *Psychotherapy* 1 (1963): 1-13.

56. Paul E. Meehl, *Clinical Versus Statistical Prediction: A Theoretical Analysis and Review of the Evidence* (Minneapolis: University of Minnesota Press, 1954), p. 3.

57. Ibid., p. 4.

58. Ibid., p. 3.

59. The Minnesota Multiphasic Personality Inventory (MMPI), which became the most respected and widely used objective test of personality during the

post-World War II period, was constructed by selecting statements that differentiated "normals" from a variety of "abnormals" regardless of the content of the statements.

60. Julian B. Rotter, "Psychotherapy," in *Annual Review of Psychology* (1960), 11: 381.

61. Donald H. Ford and Hugh B. Urban, "Psychotherapy," in *Annual Review of Psychology* (1967), 18: 367.

62. Eugene T. Gendlin and Joseph F. Rychlak, "Psychotherapeutic Processes," in *Annual Review of Psychology* (1970), 21: 155.

63. Lloyd H. Silverman, "Psychoanalytic Theory: 'The Reports of My Death Are Greatly Exaggerated,'" *American Psychologist* 31 (September 1976): 621-37.

64. Leonard Krasner, "Behavior Therapy," in *Annual Review of Psychology* (1971), 22: 487.

65. As discussed in chapter 6, the terms behavior modification, originally coined by Skinner to refer to techniques for changing behavior based on positive reinforcement, to some degree replaced the concept of behavior therapy. The meanings of both terms are now rather ambiguous.

66. See Gary E. Schwartz, "Biofeedback as Therapy: Some Theoretical and Practical Issues," *American Psychologist* 28 (August 1973): 666-73.

67. (a) William C. Budd, "Free Will Versus Determinism," *American Psychologist* 14 (January 1959): 49-50: (b) William C. Budd, "Is Free Will Really Necessary?" *American Psychologist* 15 (March 1960): 217-18; (c) Gwynn Nettler, "Free Will and Cruelty," *American Psychologist* 16 (August 1961): 529; (d) Wolf Wolfensberger, "The Free Will Controversy," *American Psychologist* 16 (January 1961): 36-7; (e) Ludwig Immergluck, "Determinism-Freedom in Contemporary Psychology: An Ancient Problem Revisited," *American Psychologist* 19 (April 1964): 270-81.

68. Anthony Wilden, "Piaget and the Structure as Law and Order," in *Structure and Transformation; Developmental and Historical Aspects*, Klaus F. Riegel and George C. Rosenwald (New York: Wiley, 1975), p. 90.

69. Rollo May, Ernest Angel, and Henri F. Ellenberger, eds., *Existence; A New Dimension in Psychiatry and Psychology* (New York: Basic Books, 1958).

70. Julian B. Rotter, "Psychotherapy," in *Annual Review of Psychology* (1960), 11: 387.

71. Douglas A. Bernstein and Michael T. Nietzel, *Introduction to Clinical Psychology* (New York: McGraw-Hill, 1980), p. 416.

72. See Irvin D. Yalon, *The Theory and Practice of Group Therapy* (New York: Basic Books, 1975) for a comprehensive treatment of group therapies.

73. Lewin's contributions are discussed in more detail in chapter 3.

74. "Guidelines for Psychologists Conducting Growth Groups," *American Psychologist* 28 (October 1973): 933.

75. See "Nader Group Releases First Consumer Guide to Psychotherapists," *APA Monitor* 6 (December 1975): 11, 16.

76. Paul H. Wender and Donald F. Klein, "The Promise of Biological Psychiatry," *Psychology Today* (February 1981): 25-41.

77. Norman D. Sundberg, "A Note Concerning the History of Testing," *American Psychologist* 9 (April 1954): 150-1.

78. Howard F. Hunt, "Clinical Methods: Psychodiagnostics," in *Annual Review of Psychology* (1950), 1: 207.

79. Julian B. Rotter, "Clinical Methods: Psychodiagnostics," in *Annual Review of Psychology* (1953), 4: 312.

80. Goldine C. Gleser, "Projective Methodologies," in *Annual Review of Psychology* (1963), 14: 415.

81. Seymour Fisher, "Projective Methodologies," in *Annual Review of Psychology* (1967), 18: 165.

82. Ibid., pp. 184-5.

83. H. Barry Molish, "Projective Methodologies," in *Annual Review of Psychology* (1972), 23: 577.

84. Ibid., p. 579.

85. Sol L. Garfield and Richard Kurtz, "Clinical Psychologists in the 1970s," *American Psychologist* 31 (January 1976): 1-9.

86. Leonard D. Eron and Leopold O. Walder, "Test Burning: II," *American Psychologist* 16 (May 1961): 238.

87. Ibid., p. 238.

88. *American Psychologist* 20 (February 1965): 123-46.

89. Launor F. Carter, "Psychological Tests and Public Responsibility," *American Psychologist* 20 (February 1965): 123.

90. Orville G. Brim, Jr., "American Attitudes Toward Intelligence Tests," *American Psychologist* 20 (February 1965): 125.

91. Samuel Messick, "Personality Measurement and the Ethics of Assessment," *American Psychologist* 20 (February 1965): 136.

92. Michael Amrine, "The 1965 Congressional Inquiry Into Testing: A Commentary," *American Psychologist* 20 (November 1965): 859.

93. Ibid., p. 860.

94. William H. Whyte, *The Organization Man* (New York: Simon and Schuster, 1956).

95. Banesh Hoffman, *The Tyranny of Testing*, (New York: Crowell-Collier Press, 1962).

96. Hillel Black, *They Shall Not Pass* (New York: Morrow, 1963).

97. Martin L. Gross, *The Brain Watchers* (New York: Random House, 1962).

98. Congressman Cornelius E. Gallagher, Chairman of the Committee, "Testimony Before House Special Subcommittee on Invasion of Privacy of the Committee on Government Operations," *American Psychologist* 21 (May 1966): 404.

99. See Irving L. Horowitz, "The Life and Death of Project Camelot," *American Psychologist* 21 (May 1966): 445-54. Most of this issue concerns Project Camelot.

100. See Frank L. Schmidt and John E. Hunter, "Racial and Ethnic Bias in Psychological Tests: Divergent Implications of Two Definitions of Test Bias," *American Psychologist* 29 (January 1974): 1-8.

101. APA Task Force on Employment Testing of Minority Groups, "Job Testing and the Disadvantaged," *American Psychologist* 24 (July 1969): 637-50.

102. Ronald P. Carver, "The Two Dimensions of Tests: Psychometric and Edumetric," *American Psychologist* 29 (July 1974): 512. Carver quotes R. Glaser and A.J. Nitko, 1971.

103. Ibid., p. 512.

104. Arthur R. Jensen, "How Much Can We Boost IQ and Scholastic Achievement?" *Harvard Educational Review* 39 (Winter 1969).

105. Jerry Hirsch claims that the "explosion of interest" in the nature-nurture

issue is attributable mostly to physicist and Nobel Prize winner William P. Shockley's stong advocacy of eugenics to cure society's problems. Jerry Hirsch, "To 'Unfrock the Charlatans,'" *SAGE Race Relations Abstracts* 6 (May 1981): 1-65.

106. Arthur R. Jensen, *Bias in Mental Testing* (New York: Free Press, 1980), preface, p. ix.

107. Oakley S. Ray, *Drugs, Society, and Human Behavior* (St. Louis: Mosby, 1972), p. 142.

108. Ibid., p. 143.

109. M. Brewster Smith and Nicholas Hobbs, "The Community and the Community Mental Health Center," *American Psychologist* 21 (June 1966): 499.

110. Ibid., p. 499.

111. David L. Snow and Peter M. Newton, "Task, Social Structure, and Social Process in the Community Mental Health Center Movement," *American Psychologist* 31 (August 1976): 591.

112. Ibid., p. 591.

113. Ibid., p. 592.

114. Ira Iscoe, "Community Psychology and the Competent Community," *American Psychologist* 29 (August 1974): 607.

115. Ibid., p. 607.

116. (*a*) Chester C. Bennett, "Community Psychology: Impressions of the Boston Conference on the Education of Psychologists for Community Mental Health," *American Psychologist* 20 (October 1965): 832-5; (*b*) Leonard D. Goodstein and Irwin Sandler, "Using Psychology to Promote Human Welfare: A Conceptual Analysis of the Role of Community Psychology," *American Psychologist* 33 (October 1978): 882-92.

117. (*a*) Bennett, p. 833; (*b*) Bertram S. Brown and S. Eugene Long, "Psychology and Community Mental Health: The Medical Muddle," *American Psychologist* 23 (May 1968): 335-41.

118. Seymour B. Sarason, "Community Psychology, Networks, and Mr. Everyman," *American Psychologist* 31 (May 1976): 326.

119. Goodstein and Sandler.

120. Thomas S. Szasz, "The Myth of Mental Illness," *American Psychologist* 15 (February 1960): 113-18.

121. Ibid., p. 115.

122. George W. Kisker, *The Disorganized Personality* (New York: McGraw-Hill, 1964).

123. Ibid., p. 3.

124. See Karl Menninger, *The Vital Balance* (New York: Viking Press, 1963).

125. See Edward Zigler and Leslie Phillips, "Psychiatric Diagnosis: A Critique," *Journal of Abnormal and Social Psychology* 3 (1961): 607-18.

126. "Virginia Clinicians Beat Blues on Appeal," *APA Monitor* 11 (August/September 1980): 1.

127. "CAPPS to Sue Blue Cross/Blue Shield; Precedence Sought for Independence," *APA Monitor* 4 (April 1973): 6.

128. Douglas A. Bernstein and Michael T. Nietzel, *Introduction to Clinical Psychology* (New York: McGraw-Hill, 1980), p. 487.

129. Ibid., p. 489.

130. See Appendix B.

BIBLIOGRAPHY

Books

Adorno, Theodor W.; Frenkel-Brunswik, Else; Levinson, Daniel J.; and Sanford, R. Nevitt. *The Authoritarian Personality* (New York: Harper, 1950).

Allport, Floyd. *Theories of Perception and the Concept of Structure* (New York: John Wiley & Sons, 1955).

Allport, Gordon W. *The Nature of Prejudice* (Cambridge, Mass.: Addison-Wesley, 1954).

American Psychological Association. *Biographical Directory of the American Psychological Association* (1975).

Annual Review of Psychology (1950-81) Stanford, Calif,: Annual Reviews), 1-32.

Army Air Forces Aviation Psychology Program Research Reports (Washington, D.C.: Government Printing Office, 1947).

Arnold, Magda B., ed. *Feelings and Emotions: The Loyola Symposium* (New York: Academic Press, 1970).

Attneave, Fred. *Applications of Information Theory to Psychology: A Summary of Basic Concepts, Methods, and Results* (New York: Holt, 1959).

Bakan, David. *Sigmund Freud and the Jewish Mystical Tradition* (Princeton, N.J.: Van Nostrand, 1958).

Baltes, Paul B., and Schaie, Warner K., eds. *Life-Span Developmental Psychology: Personality and Socialization* (New York: Academic Press, 1973).

Berelson, Bernard, and Steiner, Gary A. *Human Behavior: An Inventory of Scientific Findings* (New York: Harcourt, Brace & World, 1964).

Bernstein, Douglas A., and Nietzel, Michael T. *Introduction to Clinical Psychology* (New York: McGraw-Hill, 1980).

Birren, James E., ed. *The Handbooks of Aging* (New York: Van Nostrand Reinhold, 1977).

Black, Hillel, *They Shall Not Pass* (New York: Morrow, 1963).

Blake, Robert R., and Ramsey, Glenn V. *Perception, An Approach to Personality* (New York: Ronald Press, 1951).

Bloom, Lynn Z. *Doctor Spock: Biography of a Conservative Radical* (Indianapolis: Bobbs-Merrill, 1972).

Boring, Edwin G. *A History of Experimental Psychology*. 2nd ed. (New York: Appleton-Century-Crofts, 1957).

Boring, Edwin G.; Langfeld, Herbert S.; Werner, Heinz; and Yerkes, Robert M., eds. *A History of Psychology in Autobiography* (Worcester, Mass.: Clark University Press, 1952), 4.

Boring Edwin G. and Lindzey, Gardner. *A History of Psychology in Autobiography* (New York: Appleton-Century-Crofts, 1967), 5.

Borko, Harold, ed. *Computer Applications in the Behavioral Sciences* (Englewood Cliffs, N.J.: Prentice-Hall, 1962).

Bowlby, John. *Maternal Care and Mental Health* (New York: Schoken Books, 1951).

Bray, Charles W. *Psychology and Military Proficiency* (Princeton: Princeton University Press, 1948).

Brazier, Mary Agnes Burniston, ed. *The Central Nervous System and Behavior* (New York: Josiah Macy, Jr. Foundation, 1960).

Bridgman, Percy W. *The Logic of Modern Physics* (New York: Macmillan, 1927).

Broadbent, Donald E. *Perception and Communication* (New York: Pergamon Press, 1958).

Brome, Vincent. *Freud and His Early Circle: The Struggles of Psychoanalysis* (London: Heinemann, 1967).

Bruner Jerome S., and Krech, David, eds. *Perception and Personality: A Symposium* (New York: Greenwood Press, 1950, 1968).

Burns, B. D. *The Mammalian Cerebral Cortex* (London: Edward Arnold, 1958).

Buss, Allan R., ed. *Psychology in Social Context* (New York: Irvington, 1979).

Cantril, Hadley, ed. *Tensions That Cause Wars* (Urbana: University of Illinois Press, 1950).

Carmichael, Leonard, ed. *Manual of Child Psychology*. 2d ed. (New York: Wiley, 1946, 1954).

Chaplin, James P., and Krawiec, T. S. *Systems and Theories of Psychology*. 2d ed. (New York: Holt, Rinehart, and Winston, 1968).

————. *Systems and Theories of Psychology*. 4th ed. (New York: Holt, Rinehart and Winston, 1979).

Chomsky, Noam. *Syntactic Structures* (The Hague: Mouton, 1957).

Choron, Jacques. *Death and Western Thought* (New York: Colliers Books, 1963.)

Christie, Richard, and Jahoda, Marie, eds. *Studies in the Scope and Method of "The Authoritarian Personality"* (Glencoe, Ill.: Free Press, 1954).

Cohen, David. *Psychologists on Psychology* (New York: Taplinger, 1977).

Coleman, James C. *Abnormal Psychology and Modern Life*. 4th ed. (Glenview, Ill.: Scott Foresman, 1972).

Cooper, Robert G. *Principles of Development* (Westwood, Mass.: The PaperBook Press, 1977).

Cronbach, Lee J. *Essentials of Psychological Testing*. 2d ed. (New York: Harper & Brothers, 1949, 1960).

Daugherty, William E., and Janowitz, Morris. *A Psychological Warfare Casebook* (Baltimore: The Johns Hopkins Press, 1958).

Davie, Maurice, *Refugees in America: Report of the Committee for the Study of Recent Immigration from Europe* (New York: Harper, 1947).

Delgado, José Manuel. *Physical Control of the Mind: Toward a Psychocivilized Society* (New York: Harper and Row, 1969).

Dennis, Wayne et al. *Current Trends in Psychological Theory: A Bicentennial Program* (Pittsburgh: University of Pittsburgh Press, 1961).

Dennis, Wayne, ed. *Historical Readings in Developmental Psychology* (New York: Appleton-Century-Crofts, 1972).

De Risi, William J., and Butz, George. *Writing Behavioral Contracts* (Champaign, Ill.: Research Press, 1975).

Dollard, John, and Miller, Neal E. *Personality and Psychotherapy* (New York: McGraw-Hill, 1950).

Eccles, John C. *The Physiology of Synapses* (New York: Academic Press, 1964).

Eisdorfer, Carl, and Lawton, M. Powell, eds. *The Psychology of Adult Development and Aging* (Washington, D.C.: American Psychological Association, 1973).

Elias, Merrill F., Elias, Penelope K., and Elias, Jeffrey W. *Basic Processes in Adult Developmental Psychology* (St. Louis: Mosby, 1977).

Estes, William K.; Koch, Sigmund; MacCorquodale, Kenneth; Meehl, Paul E.; Mueller, Conrad G. Jr.; Schoenfeld, William N.; and Verplanck, William S. *Modern Learning Theory* (New York: Appleton-Century-Crofts, 1954).

Evans, Richard I. *The Making of Psychology* (New York: Knopf, 1976).

Factors Determining Human Behavior (papers presented at the Harvard Tercentenary Conference of Arts and Sciences, Cambridge, Mass., Harvard University Press, 1937).

Farberow, Norman L., ed. *Taboo Topics* (New York: Atherton Press, 1963).

Feifel, Herman, ed. *The Meaning of Death* (New York: McGraw-Hill, 1959).

Feigenbaum, Edward A., and Feldman, Julian, eds. *Computers and Thought* (New York: McGraw-Hill, 1963).

Fermi, Laura. *Illustrious Immigrants: The Intellectual Migration from Europe, 1930-41* (Chicago: University of Chicago Press, 1968, 1971).

Flanagan, John C.; Sanford, Fillmore H.; Macmillan, John W.; Kennedy, John L.; Melton, Arthur W.; Williams, Frederick W.; Baier, Donald E.; and Finch, Glen. *Current Trends: Psychology in the World Emergency* (Pittsburgh: University of Pittsburgh Press, 1952).

Flavell, John H. *The Developmental Psychology of Jean Piaget* (Princeton, N.J.: Van Nostrand, 1963).

Fleming, Donald, and Bailyn, Bernard, eds. *The Intellectual Migration: Europe and America, 1930-1960* (Cambridge, Mass.: Harvard University Press, 1969).

Frankl, Viktor. *Man's Search for Meaning: An Introduction to Logotherapy* (Boston: Beacon Press, 1962). Paperback edition (New York: Washington Square Press, 1963).

Freedman, A. E. *The Planned Society: An Analysis of Skinner's Proposals* (Kalamazoo, Mich.: Behaviordelia, 1972).

Gaito, J., ed. *Macromolecules and Behavior* (New York: Academic Press, 1966).

Galbraith, John Kenneth. *The Affluent Society* (Boston: Houghton Mifflin, 1958).

Gesell, Arnold L. *Studies in Child Development* (New York: Harpers & Brothers, 1948).

Gibson, James J. *The Perception of the Visual World* (Boston: Houghton Mifflin, 1950).

Gilgen, Albert R., ed. *Contemporary Scientific Psychology* (New York: Academic Press, 1970).

Ginsberg, Herbert, and Opper, Sylvia. *Piaget's Theory of Intellectual Development* (Englewood Cliffs, N.J.: Prentice-Hall, 1979).

Goulet, L. R., and Baltes, Paul B., eds. *Life-Span Developmental Psychology: Research and Theory* (New York: Academic Press, 1970).

Grinder, Robert E. *A History of Genetic Psychology: The First Science of Human Development* (New York: Wiley, 1967).

Gross, Martin L. *The Brain Watchers* (New York: Random House, 1962).

————. *The Psychological Society: A Critical Analysis of Psychiatry, Psychotherapy, Psychoanalysis and the Psychological Revolution* (New York: Random House, 1978).

Guthrie, Edwin R. *The Psychology of Learning* (New York: Harper & Row, 1935).

Hall, Calvin S., and Lindzey, Gardner. *Theories of Personality* (New York: Wiley, 1957).

Harris, Dale B., ed. *The Concept of Development: An Issue in the Study of Human Behavior* (Minneapolis: University of Minnesota Press, 1957).

The Harvard List of Books. 4th ed. (Cambridge: Harvard University Press, 1971).

Hebb, Donald O. *The Organization of Behavior* (New York: Wiley, 1949).

Helson, Harry, and Bevan, William, eds. *Contemporary Approaches to Psychology* (Princeton, N.J.: D. Van Nostrand, 1967).

Hess, Eckhard H. *Imprinting: Early Experience and Developmental Psychobiology of Attachment* (New York: Van Nostrand, 1973).

Hilgard, Ernest R., and Bower, Gordon H. *Theories of Learning*. 3rd ed. (New York: Appleton-Century-Crofts, 1966).

Historical Statistics of the United States, Colonial Times to 1970. Bicentennial Edition. (Washington: Government Printing Office, 1975), 1.

Hoffman, Banesh. *The Tyranny of Testing* (New York: Crowell-Collier Press, 1962).

Holland, James G., and Skinner, B. F. *The Analysis of Behavior* (New York: McGraw-Hill, 1961).

Hull, Clark L. *Principles of Behavior* (New York: Appleton-Century-Crofts, 1943).

————. *Essentials of Behavior* (New Haven: Yale University Press, 1951).

————. *A Behavior System* (New Haven: Yale University Press, 1952)

Hull, Clark L.; Hovland, Carl I.; Ross, Robert T.; Hall, Marshall; Perkins, Donald T.; and Fitch, Frederic B. *Mathematico-Deductive Theory of Rote Learning: a Study in Scientific Methodology* (New Haven: Yale University Press, 1940).

Humphrey, George. *Thinking: An Introduction to its Experimental Psychology* (New York: Wiley, 1963).

Hunt, J. McVicker. *Intelligence and Experience* (New York: Ronald Press, 1961).

Jaynes, Julian. *The Origin of Consciousness in the Breakdown of the Bicameral Mind* (Boston: Houghton Mifflin, 1977).

Jensen, Arthur R. *Bias in Mental Testing* (New York: Free Press, 1980).

Kaufman, Lloyd. *Sight and Mind: An Introduction to Visual Perception* (New York: Oxford University Press, 1974).

Kelly, George A. *A Theory of Personality: The Psychology of Personal Constructs* (New York: W. W. Norton, 1955, 1963).

Kelman, Herbert, ed. *International Behavior: A Social-Psychological Analysis* (New York: Holt, Rinehart and Winston, 1965).

Kendler, Howard H. and Spence, Janet T., eds. *Essays in Neobehaviorism; A Memorial Volume to Kenneth W. Spence.* (New York: Appleton-Century-Crofts, 1971).

Kent, Sherman. *Strategic Intelligence* (Princeton: Princeton University Press, 1949).

Kisker, George W. *The Disorganized Personality* (New York: McGraw-Hill, 1964).

Klinger, Eric, ed. *Imagery: Concepts, Results, and Applications* (New York: Plenum Press, 1981).

Koch, Sigmund, ed. *Psychology: A Study of a Science* (New York: McGraw-Hill, 1959), 3.

Köhler, Wolfgang. *The Mentality of Apes* (New York: Harcourt, Brace, 1925).

———. *Gestalt Psychology* (New York: Liveright, 1929).

Korman, Maurice, ed. *Levels and Patterns of Professional Training in Psychology: Conference Proceedings, Vail, Colorado, July 25-30, 1973* (Washington, D.C.: American Psychological Association, 1976).

Korten, Frances F.; Cook, Stuart W.; and Lacey, John I., eds. *Psychology and the Problems of Society* (Washington, D.C.: American Psychological Association, 1970).

Krech, David; Crutchfield, Richard S.; and Ballachey, Egerton L. *Individual in Society* (New York: McGraw-Hill, 1962).

Kübler-Ross, Elizabeth. *On Death and Dying* (New York: Macmillan, 1969).

Kuhn, Thomas S. *The Structure of Scientific Revolutions* (Chicago: University of Chicago Press, 1962).

Lenneberg, Eric H. *Biological Foundations of Language* (New York: Wiley, 1967).

Lerner, Richard M. *Concepts and Theories of Human Development* (Reading, Mass.: Addison-Wesley, 1976).

Linebarger, Paul M. A. *Psychological Warfare* (Washington, D.C.: Combat Forces Press, 1948, 1952).

Lynn, Richard. *Attention, Arousal, and the Orienting Reaction* (Oxford: Pergamon Press, 1966).

Maccoby, Eleanor E.; Newcomb, Theodore M.; and Hartley, Eugene L., eds. *Readings in Social Psychology.* 3rd ed. (New York: Holt, 1958).

Maier, Henry W. *Three Theories of Child Development: The Contributions of Erik H. Erikson, Jean Piaget, and Robert R. Sears and Their Applications* (New York: Harper and Row, 1965, 1969).

Marrow, Alfred J. *The Practical Theorist: The Life and Work of Kurt Lewin* (New York: Basic Books, 1969).

Marx, Melvin H. *Learning: Theories* (New York: Macmillan, 1970).

Marx, Melvin H., and Hillix, William A. *Systems and Theories in Psychology* (New York: McGraw-Hill, 1963).

May, Rollo; Angel, Ernest; and Ellenberger, Henri F., eds. *Existence; A New Dimension in Psychiatry and Psychology* (New York: Basic Books, 1958).

McClelland, David C., ed. *Studies in Motivation* (New York: Appleton-Century-Crofts, 1955).

McCoy, Vivian R.; Ryan, Colleen; and Lichtenberg, James W. *The Adult Life Cycle: Training Manual and Reader* (Lawrence, Kansas: Adult Life Resource Center, University of Kansas, 1978).

Meehl, Paul E. *Clinical Versus Statistical Prediction: A Theoretical Analysis and a Review of the Evidence* (Minneapolis: University of Minnesota Press, 1954).

Menninger, Karl. *The Vital Balance* (New York: Viking, 1963).

Miller, George A. *Psychology: The Science of Mental Life* (New York: Harper & Row, 1962).

Miller, George A.; Galanter, Eugene; and Pribram, Karl H. *Plans and the Structure of Behavior* (New York: Holt, Rinehart and Winston, 1960).

Miller, James G. *Living Systems* (New York: McGraw-Hill, 1978).

Misiak, Henryk, and Sexton, Virginia Staudt. *History of Psychology: An Overview* (New York: Grune & Stratton, 1966).

Mitford, Jessica. *The American Way of Death* (New York: Simon and Schuster, 1978).

Moray, Neville. *Attention: Selective Processes in Vision and Hearing* (New York: Academic Press, 1970).

Murchison, Carl, ed. *Handbook of Child Psychology* (Worcester, Mass.: Clark University Press, 1931).

Murphy, Gardner. *In the Minds of Men* (New York: Basic Books, 1953).

Murray, Edward J. *Sleep, Dreams, and Arousal* (New York: Appleton-Century-Crofts, 1965).

National Society for the Study of Education. *The Psychology of Learning* (Yearbook, 1942), 91.

Neisser, Ulric. *Cognitive Psychology* (New York: Appleton-Century-Crofts, 1967).

Nelson, Benjamin N., ed. *Freud and the 20th Century* (Cleveland: World Publishing, 1957).

Nesselroade, John R., and Reese, Hayne W., eds. *Life-Span Developmental Psychology: Methodological Issues* (New York: Academic Press, 1973).

Ornstein, Robert E. *The Psychology of Consciousness* (San Francisco: W. H. Freeman, 1972).

――――, ed. *The Nature of Human Consciousness* (San Francisco: W. H. Freeman; New York: Viking Press, 1973).

Osgood, Charles E.; Suci, George J.; and Tannenbaum, Percy H. *The Measurement of Meaning* (Urbana: University of Illinois Press, 1958).

Packard, Vance. *The Hidden Persuaders* (New York: D. McKay, 1957).

Pavlov, Ivan P. *Conditioned Reflexes: An Investigation of the Physiological Activity of the Cerebral Cortex* (New York: Dover, 1960; London: Oxford University Press, 1927).

――――. *Lectures on Conditoned Reflexes*, trans. S. Belsky (Moscow: Foreign Languages Publishing House, 1955).

Penfield, Wilder. *The Excitable Cortex in Conscious Man* (Springfield, Ill.: Thomas, 1958).

Poon, Leonard W., ed. *Aging in the 1980s: Psychological Issues* (Washington, D.C.: American Psychological Association, 1980).

Postman, Leo, ed. *Psychology in the Making: Histories of Selected Research Problems* (New York: Knopf, 1962).

Pribram, Karl H., ed. *Brain and Behavior: I. Mood, States and Mind: Selected Readings* (Harmondsworth: Penguin, 1969).

Raimy, Victor C. *Training in Clinical Psychology* (New York: Prentice-Hall, 1950).

Ray, Oakley S. *Drugs, Society, and Human Behavior* (St. Louis: Mosby, 1972).

Redl, Fritz, and Wineman, David. *Children Who Hate: The Disorganization and Breakdown of Behavior Controls* (Glencoe, Ill.: Free Press, 1951).

Reisman, John M. *The Development of Clinical Psychology* (New York: Appleton-Century-Crofts, 1966).

Riegel, Klaus F., and Rosenwald, George C. *Structure and Transformation; Developmental and Historical Aspects* (New York: Wiley, 1975).

Roback, Abraham, ed. *Present-Day Psychology* (New York: Philosophical Library, 1955).

Robinson, D. B. *The 100 Most Important People in the World Today* (New York: Putman, 1970).

Rogers, Carl R. *The Clinical Treatment of the Problem* (Boston: Houghton Mifflin, 1939).

———. *Client-Centered Therapy: Its Current Practice, Implications, and Theory* (Boston: Houghton Mifflin, 1951).

———. *On Becoming a Person* (Boston: Houghton Mifflin, 1961).

Rokeach, Milton. *The Open and Closed Mind* (New York: Basic Books, 1960).

———. *The Three Christs of Ypsilanti* (New York: Knopf, 1964).

Rowland, G. Thomas. *The Mind of Man: Some Views and a Theory of Cognitive Development* (Englewood Cliffs, N.J.: Prentice-Hall, 1971).

Sachar, Abram L. *A History of the Jews*. 3d ed. (New York: Knopf, 1930, 1940, 1948).

Sansweet, Stephen J. *The Punishment Cure* (New York: Mason/Charter, 1975).

Scheerer, Constance, ed. *Cognition: Theory, Research, Promise* (New York: Harper & Row, 1964).

Scott, Walter D. *The Theory of Advertizing* (Boston: Small, Maynard & Co., 1903).

Selye, Hans. *The Stress of Life* (New York: McGraw-Hill, 1956).

Shannon, Claude E., and Weaver, Warren. *The Mathematical Theory of Communication* (Urbana, Ill.: University of Illinois Press, 1949, 1963).

Sheehy, Gail. *Passages: Predictable Crises of Adult Life* (New York: Dutton, 1976).

Shirer, William L. *The Rise and Fall of the Third Reich; A History of Nazi Germany* (New York: Simon and Schuster, 1960).

Shneidman, Edwin S.; Farberow, Norman L.; and Litman, Robert E. *The Psychology of Suicide* (New York: Science House, 1970).

Skinner, B. F. *The Behavior of Organisms* (New York: Appleton-Century-Crofts, 1938).

———. *Walden Two* (New York: Crowell-Collier-Macmillan, 1948).

———. *Science and Human Behavior* (New York: Macmillan, 1953).

———. *Verbal Behavior* (New York: Appleton-Century-Crofts, 1957).

———. *Cumulative Record* (New York: Appleton-Century-Crofts, 1959).

———. *The Technology of Teaching* (New York: Appleton-Century-Crofts, 1968).

———. *Contingencies of Reinforcement: A Theoretical Analysis* (New York: Appleton-Century-Crofts, 1969).

———. *Beyond Freedom and Dignity* (New York: Knopf, 1971).

———. *About Behaviorism* (New York: Knopf, 1974).

———. *Particulars of My Life* (New York: Knopf, 1976), 1.

———. *Reflections on Behaviorism and Society* (Englewood Cliffs, N.J.: Prentice-Hall, 1978).

———. *The Shaping of a Behaviorist* (New York: Knopf, 1979), 2.

Skinner, B. F., and Ferster, C. B. *Schedules of Reinforcement* (New York: Appleton-Century-Crofts, 1957).

Solomon, Philip; Kubzansky, Philip E.; Leiderman, P. Herbert; Mendelson, Jack H.; Trumbull, Richard; and Wexler, Donald. eds. *Sensory Deprivation* (Cambridge, Mass.: Harvard University Press, 1961).

Spock Benjamin. *The Pocket Book of Baby and Child Care* (New York: Pocket Books, 1946).

Statistical Abstracts of the United States (Bureau of the Census, 1980).

Stolz, Stephanie B. *Ethical Issues in Behavior Modification* (San Francisco: Jossey-Bass, 1978).

Stone, J. Joseph; Smith, Henrietta T.; and Murphy, Lois B., eds. *The Competent Infant: Research and Commentary* (New York: Basic Books, 1973).

Stouffer, Samuel A.; Suchman, Edward A.; DeVinney, Leland, C.; Starr, Shirley A.; and Williams, Robin M. Jr. *The American Soldier: Adjustment During Army Life* (Princeton: Princeton University Press, 1949).

Stouffer, Samuel A.; Lumsdaine, Arthur A.; Lumsdaine, Marion H.; Williams, Robin M.; Smith, M. Brewster; Janis, Irving L.; Star, Shirley A.; and Cottrell, Leonard S., Jr. *The American Soldier: Combat and Its Aftermath* (Princeton: Princeton University Press, 1949).

Stouffer, Samuel A.; Guttman, Louis; Suchman, Edward A.; Lazarsfeld, Paul F.; Star, Shirley A.; and Clausen, John A. *Measurement and Prediction* (Princeton: Princeton University Press, 1950).

Stuitt, Dewey B. *Personnel Research and Test Development in the Bureau of Naval Personnel* (Princeton: Princeton University Press, 1947).

Sundberg, Norman D.; Tyler, Leona E.; and Taplin, Julian R. *Clinical Psychology: Expanding Horizons* (Englewood Cliffs, N.J.: Prentice-Hall, 1973).

Thorndike, Edward L. *Animal Intelligence; Experimental Studies* (New York: Macmillan, 1911).

Tomkins, Silvan S. *Affect, Imagery, Consciousness* (New York: Springer, 1962), 1.

Triandis, Harry C., and Lambert, William W. *Handbook of Cross-Cultural Psychology*. 6 vols. (Boston: Allyn and Bacon, 1980).

Ulrich's International Periodical Directory, 17th ed. (New York: R. R. Bowker, 1977).

U.S. Office of Strategic Services. *Assessment of Men* (New York: Rinehart, Holt & Co., 1948).

Watson, John B. *The Psychological Care of Infant and Child* (New York: Norton, 1928).

Weiner, Irving B., ed. *Clinical Methods in Psychology* (New York: Wiley, 1976).

Welsh, George S., and Dahlstrom, Grant W. *Basic Readings on the MMPI in Psychology and Medicine* (Minneapolis: University of Minnesota Press, 1956).

Wertheimer, Max. *Productive Thinking* (New York: Harper and Row, 1959).

White, Robert W. *The Abnormal Personality* (New York: Ronald Press, 1948, 1956).

Whorf, Benjamin L. *Language, Thought, and Reality* (Cambridge, Mass.: MIT Press 1956).

Whyte, William H. *The Organization Man* (New York: Simon and Schuster, 1956).

Wiener, Norbert. *I Am a Mathematician* (New York: Doubleday, 1956).

Witkin, Herman A.; Lewis, H. B.; Hertzman, M.; Machover, K.; Meissner, P. Bretnall; and Wapner, S. *Personality through Perception, an Experimental and Clinical Study* (New York: Harper, 1954).

Wolfle, Dael., ed. *Human Factors in Military Efficiency: I. Aptitude and Classification. II. Training and Equipment* (Washington, D.C.: Applied Psychology Panel National Defense Research Committee, 1947).

Wolfle, Dael. *America's Resources of Specialized Talent* (New York: Harper, 1954).

Worden, Frederic G.; Swazeg, Judith P.; and Adelman, George, eds. *The Neuro-sciences, Paths of Discovery* (Cambridge, Mass.: MIT Press, 1975).

Yalom, Irvin D. *The Theory and Practice of Group Therapy* (New York: Basic Books, 1975).

Articles

Albee, George W. "The Uncertain Future of Clinical Psychology." *American Psychologist* 25 (December 1970):1071-80.

Albee, George W. and Dickey, Marguerite. "Manpower Trends in Three Mental Health Professions." *American Psychologist* 12 (February 1957):57-70.

Alpert, Harry. "Social Science, Social Psychology, and the National Science Foundation." *American Psychologist* 12 (February 1957):95-8.

Amrine, Michael. "The 1965 Congressional Inquiry Into Testing:A Commentary." *American Psychologist* 20 (November 1965):859-70.

APA Task Force on Employment Testing of Minority Groups. "Job Testing and the Disadvantaged." *American Psychologist* 24 (July 1969):637-50.

Bakan, David. "Clinical Psychology and Logic." *American Psychologist* 11 (December 1956):655-62.

Bayley, Nancy. "Behavioral Correlates of Mental Growth: Birth to Thirty-Six Years." *American Psychologist* 23 (January 1968):1-17.

Bennett, Chester C. "Community Psychology: Impressions of the Boston Conference on the Education of Psychologists for Community Mental Health." *American Psychologist* 20 (October 1965):832-5.

Berenda, Carlton W. "Is Clinical Psychology a Science?" *American Psychologist* 12 (December 1957):725-9.

Berg, Irwin A. "The Use of Human Subjects in Psychological Research." *American Psychologist* 9 (March 1954):108-11.

Bettelheim, Bruno. "Individual and Mass Behavior in Extreme Situations." *Journal of Abnormal and Social Psychology* 38 (1943):417-52.

Blough, Donald S. "A Method for Obtaining Psychophysical Thresholds From the Pigeon." *Journal of the Experimental Analysis of Behavior* 1 (1958):31-48.

Bower, T.G.R. "The Visual World of Infants." *Scientific American* 215 (1966): 80-92.

Brim, Orville G., Jr. "American Attitudes toward Intelligence Tests." *American Psychologist* 20 (February 1965):125-30.

Britt, Steuart Henderson, and Morgan, Jane D. "Military Psychologists in World War II." *American Psychologist* 1 (1946):423-37.

Brown, Bertram S., and Long, S. Eugene. "Psychology and Community Mental Health: The Medical Muddle." *American Psychologist* 23 (May 1968):335-41.

Bruner, Jerome S., and Goodman, C. C. "Value and Need as Organizing Factors in Perception." *Journal of Abnormal and Social Psychology* 42 (1947):33-44.

Budd, William C. "Free Will Versus Determinism." *American Psychologist* 14 (January, 1959):49-50.

———. "Is Free Will Really Necessary?" *American Psychologist* 15 (March 1960): 217-18.

Camfield, Thomas M. "The Professionalization of American Psychology, 1870-1917." *Journal of the History of the Behavioral Sciences* 9 (January 1973):66-75.

Carter, Launor F. "Psychological Tests and Public Responsibility." *American Psychologist* 20 (February 1965):123-4.

Carver, Ronald P. "The Two Dimensions of Tests: Psychometric and Edumetric." *American Psychologist* 29 (July 1974):512-18.

Cavanaugh, John C. "Early Developmental Theories; A Brief Review of Attempts to Organize Developmental Data Prior to 1925." *Journal of the History of the Behavioral Sciences* 17 (1981):38.

Chomsky, Noam. Review of B. F. Skinner's *Verbal Behavior. Language* 35 (1959): 26-58.

————. "The Case Against B. F. Skinner." *The New York Review of Books* (December 1971):18-24.

Cronbach, Lee J. "The Two Disciplines of Scientific Psychology." *American Psychologist* 12 (November 1957):671-84.

Cronbach, Lee J.; Farnsworth, Paul R.; and Bouthilet, Lorraine. "The APA Publications Program: Status and Prospects, 1955." *American Psychologist* 10 (March 1955):110-20

Dailey, John T. "A Plan for Integrated Programs of Personnel Research and Development." *American Psychologist* 9 (October 1954):629-31.

Darley, John G. "Psychology and the Office of Naval Research: A Decade of Development." *American Psychologist* 12 (June 1957):305-23.

Duncker, Karl. "On Problem Solving." *Psychological Monograph* 58 (1945), No. 270.

Elkind, David. "Piaget." *Human Behavior* (August 1975):115-21.

Ellis, Albert, and Conrad, Herbert S. "The Validity of Personality Inventories in Military Practice." *Psychological Bulletin* 45 (1948):385-426.

Endler, Norman S., Rushton, J. Philippe, and Roediger, Henry L. III. "Productivity and Scholarly Impact (Citations) of British, Canadian, and U.S. Departments of Psychology (1975)." *American Psychologist* 33 (December 1978):1064-82

Eron, Leonard D., and Walder, Leopold O. "Test Burning: II." *American Psychologist* 16 (May 1961):237-44.

Eysenck, Han J. "The Effects of Psychotherapy: An Evaluation." *Journal of Consulting Psychology* 16 (1952):319-24.

Fantz, Robert L. "Pattern Vision in Young Infants." *Psychological Record* 8 (1958): 43-47.

————. "The Origin of Form Perception." *Scientific American* 204 (1961):66-72.

Fiske, Donald W. "Must Psychologists be Experimental Isolationists?" *American Psychologist* 2 (January 1947):23, 28.

Fromm-Reichmann, Frieda. "Psychotherapy of Schizophrenia." *American Journal of Psychiatry* 111 (December 1954):410-19.

Garfield, Eugene. The 100 Most-Cited Social Sciences Citation Index Authors. 2. A Catalog of their Awards and Academy Memberships." *Current Contents* 45 (1978): 5-15.

Garfield, Sol L. "Psychotherapy: A 40-Year Appraisal." *American Psychologist* 36 (February 1981):174-83.

Garfield, Sol L., and Kurtz, Richard. "Clinical Psychologists in the 1970s." *American Psychologist* 31 (January 1976):1-9.

Gibson, Eleanor J. and Walk, Richard D. "The Visual Cliff." *Scientific American* 202 (1960):64-71.

Gibson, James J. "The Concept of the Stimulus in Psychology." *American Psychologist* 15 (1960):694-703.

Gibson, James J., and Gibson, Eleanor J. "Perceptual Learning: Differentiation or Enrichment?" *Psychological Review* 62 (1955):32-41

Gilgen, Albert R. "The Exchange Model: Missing Link between Physiobehavioral Psychology and Phenomenological Inquiry?" *Irish Journal of Psychology* 2 (1971):75-86.

———. "Converging Trends in Psychology." Paper presented at the Meeting of the American Psychological Association, New Orleans, 1974.

———. "Important Events and Influences in Post-World War II American Psychology: A Survey Study." *JSAS Catalog of Selected Documents in Psychology* 10 (November 1980), Ms. 2144.

———. "Major Recipients of National Institute of Mental Health Funds: The Million Dollar Club." *JSAS Catalog of Selected Documents in Psychology* 11 (February 1981), Ms. 2170.

———. "Important People in Post-World War II American Psychology: A Survey Study." *JSAS Catalog of Selected Documents in Psychology* 11 (February 1981), Ms. 2171.

Gilgen, Albert R., and Hultman, Stevan K. "Authorities and Subject Matter Areas Emphasized, in *Annual Review of Psychology, 1950-1974.*" *Psychological Reports* 44 (1979):1255-62.

Gilgen, Albert R., and Tolvstad, Kristin. "Major Recipients of National Science Foundation Funds for Psychological Research." *JSAS Catalog of Selected Documents in Psychology* 11 (August 1981), Ms. 2278.

Goodstein, Leonard D., and Sandler, Irwin. "Using Psychology to Promote Human Welfare: A Conceptual Analysis of the Role of Community Psychology." *American Psychologist* 33 (October 1978):882-92.

"Guidelines for Psychologists Conducting Growth Groups." *American Psychologist* 28 (October 1973):933.

Guilford, J. P. "Some Lessons from Aviation Psychology." *American Psychologist* 3 (January 1948):3-11.

Guttman, Norman. "On Skinner and Hull: A Reminiscence and Projection." *American Psychologist* 32 (May 1977):321-28.

Harlow, Harry F. "The Nature of Love." *American Psychologist* 13 (December 1958):673-85.

Harrington, Gordon M. "Responses to the Skinner Stimulus." *The North American Review* 257 (Summer 1972):59-62.

Hathaway, Starke R. "A Study of Human Behavior: The Clinical Psychologist." *American Psychologist* 13 (June 1958):257-65.

Helson, Harry. "Adaptation-Level as a Basis for a Quantitative Theory of Frames of Reference." *Psychological Review* 55 (1948):297-313.

Hess, Eckhard H. "'Imprinting' in Animals." *Scientific American* 198 (1958):81-90.

Hirsch, Jerry. "To 'Unfrock the Charlatans'." *SAGE Race Relations Abstracts* 6 (May 1981):1-65.

Horowitz, Irving L. "The Life and Death of Project Camelot." *American Psychologist* 21 (May 1966):445-54.

Hunt, William A., and Stevenson, I. "Psychological Testing in Military Clinical Psychology: I. Intelligence Testing (pp. 25-35); II. Personality Testing (pp. 107-15)." *Psychological Review* 53 (1946).

Immergluck, Ludwig. "Determinism-Freedom in Contemporary Psychology: An Ancient Problem Revisited." *American Psychologist* 19 (August 1964):270-81.

Iscoe, Ira. "Community Psychology and the Competent Community." *American Psychologist* 29 (August 1974):607-13.

James, Richard D. "Group Therapy's Help in Coping with Stress is Minor, Studies Show." *The Wall Street Journal* (April 16, 1979), pp. 1, 22.

Jarvik, Lissy F. "Thoughts on the Psychobiology of Aging." *American Psychologist* 30 (May 1975):576-83.

Jensen, Arthur R. "How Much Can We Boost IQ and Scholastic Achievement?" *Harvard Educational Review* 39 (Winter 1969).

Kahn, Marvin W., and Santostefano, Sebastian. "The Case of Clinical Psychology: A Search for Identity." *American Psychologist* 17 (April 1962):185-89.

Kalish, Richard A. "Death and Bereavement: An Annotated Social Science Bibliography (with Supplement)." Xeroxed by author (1965).

Kelman, Herbert. "Reducing Conflict to a Science." *APA Monitor* 12 (January 1981):5, 55.

Klopfer, W. G. "The Short History of Projective Techniques." *Journal of the History of the Behavioral Sciences* 9 (1973):60-65.

Kluckhohn, Clyde. "An Anthropologist Looks at Psychology." *American Psychologist* 3 (October 1948):439-42.

Kronk, Philip C. "Role of Women Psychologists During the Second World War." *Psychological Reports* 45 (1979):111-16.

Lamb, Michael E. "Paternal Influences and the Father's Role: A Personal Perspective." *American Psychologist* 34 (October 1979):938-43.

Lashley, Karl S.; Chow, K. L.; and Semmes, Josephine. "An Examination of the Electrical Field Theory of Cerebral Integration." *Psychological Review* 58 (1951):123-36.

Leuba, Clarence, and Federighi, Henry. "A Course in the Life Sciences." *American Psychologist* 3 (January 1948):30-34.

Levine, Seymour. "Stimulation in Infancy." *Scientific American* (May 1960):80-98.

Levinson, Daniel J. "A Note on the Similarities and Differences between Projective Tests and Ability Tests." *Psychological Review* 53 (1946):189-94.

Marquis, Donald G. "Research Planning at the Frontiers of Science." *American Psychologist* 3 (October 1948):430-38.

McClelland, David. "Freud and Hull: Pioneers in Scientific Psychology." *American Scientist* 45 (1957):101-13.

McLean, Dorothy. "Child Development: A Generation of Research." *Child Development* 25 (1954):3-8.

McNemar, Quinn. "Opinion-Attitude Methodology." *Psychological Bulletin* 43 (1946):289-374.

Messick, Samuel. "Personality Measurement and the Ethics of Assessment." *American Psychologist* 20 (February 1965):136-42.

Miller, James G. "Toward a General Theory for the Behavioral Sciences." *American Psychologist* 10 (September 1955):513-31.

Moruzzi G., and Magoun, H. W. "Brain Stem Reticular Formation and Activation of the EEG." *Electroencephalography and Clinical Neurophysiology* 1 (1949): 455-73.

Murphy, Lois. "Coping Devices and Defense Mechanisms in Relation to Autonomous Ego Functions." *Bulletin of the Menninger Clinic* 24 (1960):144-53.

Myers, C. Roger. "Journal Citations and Scientific Eminence in Contemporary Psychology." *American Psychologist* 25 (November 1970):1041-48.

"Nader Group Releases First Consumer Guide to Psychotherapists." *APA Monitor* 6 (December 1975):11, 16.

Nettler, Gwynn. "Free Will and Cruelty." *American Psychologist* 16 (August 1961): 529.

Olds, James. "Pleasure Centers in the Brain." *Scientific American* (October 1956): 105-16.

Otten, Alan L. "Ethical Quandaries." *The Wall Street Journal* (September 18, 1975), p. 22.

Perry, James M., and Hunt, Albert R. "After Cleaning House, Carter Will Attempt to Deal with Crisis of Confidence by Stressing Leadership." *The Wall Street Journal* (August 23, 1979), p. 3.

Perry, Nathan W. "Why Psychology Does Not Need Alternative Training Models." *American Psychologist* 34 (July 1979):603-11.

Peskin, Harvey. "Unity of Science Begins at Home: A Study of Regional Factionalism in Clinical Psychology." *American Psychologist* 18 (February 1963): 96-100.

Rodgers, David A. "In Favor of Separation of Academic and Professional Training." *American Psychologist* 19 (August 1964):675-80.

Rogers, Carl R. "Some Issues Concerning the Control of Human Behavior." *Science* 124 (November 30, 1956):1057-65. [Rogers-Skinner debate].

———. "In Retrospect: Forty-Six Years." *American Psychologist* 29 (February 1974): 115-23.

Sarason, Seymour B. "Community Psychology, Networks, and Mr. Everyman." *American Psychologist* 31 (May 1976):317-28.

Schachter, Stanley, and Singer, Jerome. "Cognitive, Social, and Physiological Determinants of Emotional State." *Psychological Review* 69 (1962):379-99.

Schaie, K. Warner. "A General Model for the Study of Developmental Problems." *Psychological Bulletin* 64 (1965):92-107.

Schmidt, Frank L., and Hunter, John E. "Racial and Ethnic Bias in Psychological Tests: Divergent Implications of Two Definitions of Test Bias." *American Psychologist* 29 (January 1974):1-8.

Schwartz, Gary E. "Biofeedback as Therapy: Some Theoretical and Practical Issues." *American Psychologist* 28 (August 1973):666-73.

Shakow, David. "Clinical Psychology Seen Some 50 years later." *American Psychologist* 33 (February 1978):148-58.

Shakow, David, and Rapaport, David. "The Influence of Freud on American Psychology." *Psychological Issues* 13 (1964).

Silverman, Lloyd H. "Psychoanalytic Theory: 'The Reports of My Death Are Greatly Exaggerated.'" *American Psychologist* 31 (September 1976):621-37.

Skinner, B. F. "Two Types of Conditioned Reflex: A Reply to Konorski and Miller." *Journal of General Psychology* 16 (1937):272-79.

————. "Some Issues Concerning the Control of Human Behavior." *Science* 124 (November 30, 1956):1057-65. [Rogers-Skinner debate].

————. "Pigeons in a Pelican." *American Psychologist* 15 (January 1960):28-37.

Small, Leonard. "Toward Professional Clinical Psychology." *American Psychologist* 18 (September 1963):558-62.

Smith, M. Brewster, and Hobbs, Nicholas. "The Community and the Community Mental Health Center." *American Psychologist* 21 (June 1966):499-509.

Snow, David L., and Newton, Peter M. "Task, Social Structure, and Social Process in the Community Mental Health Center Movement." *American Psychologist* 31 (August 1976):582-94.

Sperry, R. W. "Hemisphere Deconnection and Unity in Conscious Awareness." *American Psychologist* 23 (1968):723-33.

Stellar, Eliot. "The Physiology of Motivation." *Psychological Review* 61 (1954): 5-22.

Strupp, Hans H. "The Outcome Problem in Psychotherapy Revisited." *Psychotherapy* 1 (1963):1-13.

Sulman, A. Michael. "The Humanization of the American Child: Benjamin Spock as a Popularizer of Psychoanalytic Thought." *Journal of the History of the Behavioral Sciences* 9 (1973):258-65.

Sundberg, Norman D. "A Note Concerning the History of Testing." *American Psychologist* 9 (April 1954):150-51.

————. "The Practice of Psychological Testing in Clinical Services in the United States." *American Psychologist* 16 (February 1961):79-83.

Szasz, Thomas S. "The Myth of Mental Illness." *American Psychologist* 15 (February 1960):113-18.

Tanner, W. D., and Swets, J. A. "A Decision Making Theory of Visual Detection." *Psychological Review* 61 (1954):401-9.

Taylor, Franklin V. "Psychology and the Design of Machines." *American Psychologist* 12 (May 1957):249-58.

"Torture as Policy: the Network of Evil." *Time* (August 16, 1976), pp. 31-4.

Tryon, Robert C. "Psychology in Flux: The Academic-Professional Bipolarity." *American Psychologist* 18 (March 1963):134-43.

Watson, John B. "Psychology as the Behaviorist Views it." *Psychological Review* 20 (1913):158-77.

Watson, Robert I. "A Brief History of Clinical Psychology." *Psychological Bulletin* 50 (1953):321-46.

Wender, Paul H., and Klein, Donald F. "The Promise of Biological Psychiatry. *Psychology Today* (February 1981):25-41.

"What Makes a Researcher "Good Copy?" *APA Monitor* (August 1975): pp. 1, 8.

White, Sheldon H. "Children in Perspective." *American Psychologist* 34 (October 1979):812-14.

Wiesel, T. N., and Hubel, D. H. "Comparison of the Effects of Unilateral and Bilateral Eye Closure on Cortical Unit Responses in Kittens." *Journal of Neurophysiology* 28 (1965):1029-40.

Williams, Richard N. "Structuralism and the Cognitive Revolution." *Philosophical Psychologist* 12 (1978):18-29.

Wohlwill, Joachim F. "Developmental Studies of Perception." *Psychological Bulletin* 57 (1960):249-88.

Wolf, Theta H. "Gesell-Senn 'Controversy.'" *American Psychologist* 12 (October 1957):648-50.

Wolfensberger, Wolf. "The Free Will Controversy." *American Psychologist* 16 (January 1961):36-7.

———. "Ethical Issues in Research with Human Subjects." *Science* 155 (January 6, 1967):47-51.

Wolfle, Dael. "Comparisons Between Psychologists and Other Professional Groups." *American Psychologist* 10 (June 1955):231-37.

———. "Diversity of Talent." *American Psychologist* 15 (August 1960):535-45.

Zeigarnik, Bluma. "Das Behalten Erledigter und Unerledigter Handlungen, III." [The Memory of Completed and Uncompleted Actions.] *Psychologische Forschung* 9 (1927):1-85.

Zigler, Edward, and Phillips, Leslie. "Psychiatric Diagnosis: A Critique." *Journal of Abnormal and Social Psychology* 3 (1961):607-18.

NAME INDEX

SUBJECT INDEX

About the Author

ALBERT R. GILGEN is Professor and Head of the Psychology Department at the University of Northern Iowa at Cedar Falls. His earlier works include an edited volume, *Contemporary Scientific Psychology*, as well as numerous scholarly articles. He was a Fulbright-Hays exchange lecturer at University College, Galway, Ireland in 1971-72.